SEWING
SCHOOL BASICS

SEWING
SCHOOL BASICS

A step-by-step course for first-time stitchers

Includes 9 full-size pull-out patterns

JANE BOLSOVER

CICO BOOKS
LONDON NEW YORK

For Barbara, my guardian angel

Published in 2014 by CICO Books
an imprint of Ryland Peters & Small
519 Broadway, 5th Floor, New York NY 10012
20–21 Jockey's Fields, London WC1R 4BW

www.rylandpeters.com

10 9 8 7 6 5 4 3 2 1

A CIP catalog record for this book is available from the
Library of Congress and the British Library.

ISBN: 978 1 78249 089 0

Printed in China

Project editor: Gillian Haslam
Copy editor: Alison Wormleighton
Design: Alison Fenton
Technical illustrations: Stephen Dew
Decorative illustrations: Hannah George
Equipment photography: Martin Norris
Project photography: Caroline Arber and Penny Wincer
Stylists: Nell Haynes and Catherine Woram

**All instructions in this book contain both standard
(imperial) and metric measurements. Please use only one
set of measurements when cutting out and sewing as they
are not interchangeable.**

Some illustrations for basic techniques have appeared in
Jane Bolsover's companion book, *Sewing Machine Basics*.

Contents

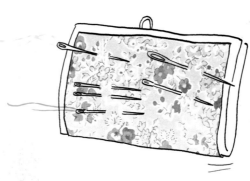

Introduction

After the success of my last sewing book, *Sewing Machine Basics*, I was delighted to be asked to write a second introductory book to sewing, but this time also incorporating hand sewing in the form of appliqué, embroidery, patchwork, quilting, and smocking, as well as many more sewing techniques such as making ruffles and more types of collars, sleeves, and fastenings.

Ever since I was a small child I have loved making things, and as soon as my grandmother had shown me how to use my mother's electric sewing machine, there was just no stopping me. What I really love about sewing is the fact that you can sit down with a piece of fabric and some thread, and in a very short time produce wonderful things for yourself and your home. Many times I have been asked whether I knit as well, but knitting has always been too slow for me. Armed with my needle and thread, I can create something in a couple of hours—anything from beautiful new pillows and cushions to a simple dress ready to wear the same evening.

At one time, sewing was an accomplishment that every woman learned as a matter of course, but over the past few decades the pace of life has taken its toll. Many people have told me that they used to sew but no longer have time, while others have said that they have never been shown, and so gradually the skills begin to fall by the wayside. But sewing is not difficult to learn—it just needs a little patience and practice, to gradually build up your confidence. Once you have the hang of it, you'll soon discover the magic that I have always known.

The instructions and clear illustrations in this book will take you step by step through all the techniques you need to create gorgeous and unique things for yourself. At the end of each workshop, you will find a project, which uses the skills you have just learned, as well as some from the previous workshops. I have enjoyed putting together this collection of new projects, many with a hint of retro, which I feel you will be keen to make and adapt for yourself. I wish you good fun in learning how to sew and many happy days of stitching ahead.

Jane Bolsover

How to use this book

This book has been written for people who wish to learn how to sew or those who are returning to it after a long break and need a refresher. It can be used either on its own or alongside my previous book, *Sewing Machine Basics*. Because many people will not have both, we have included some essential basic techniques that are also in that book, but there is also a great deal of information that is only in this new book, and, of course, all of the projects are totally new.

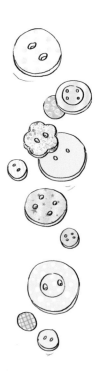

Section 1: Let's get started

This first section introduces you to the basic equipment that you will need to start sewing. So many books have pages of equipment, much of which I feel is unnecessary and can add up to quite a high cost. I have therefore pared everything down to the bare minimum to get you started, and have then mentioned a few pieces that you may wish to add as you become more proficient.

In this section I also introduce you to the exciting process of choosing fabrics and I show you how to measure yourself correctly to enable you to buy the best-fitting patterns for your figure. In case alterations are needed to create a better fit, there is a guide on how to make simple pattern adjustments that are not too scary for the beginner. Once armed with your pattern and your fabric, you learn how to prepare them for sewing and how to cut out your garment pieces.

Take time to read through this section, as it contains the foundations for creating successful projects, ensuring that you have selected the right type of fabric and the best-fitting pattern, and also that the pieces are cut out as accurately as possible, before you begin sewing.

Section 2: Workshops and projects

In this section you will find twelve workshops, which start with the very basics and then build in complexity as your confidence grows, including both machine and hand stitching, plus simple embroidery stitches. It is therefore important to work your way through this book workshop by workshop, and not be tempted to jump ahead to a project that takes your fancy before you are completely ready to tackle what is involved.

At the end of the workshops, you will find an exciting selection of projects, designed to incorporate the techniques that you have just learned and also build on what has been covered in previous workshops. They range from stylish projects for the home to flattering garments that you will wear over and over again.

Finally, bound into the back of this book, are two pattern sheets containing full-sized patterns for all of the projects included in this book, ready for you to trace.

All the information is presented in an accessible way, with easy-to-follow step-by-step instructions and illustrations explaining every stage. The clear explanations of all the techniques and terminology, as well as a helpful quick-reference glossary of common sewing terms, will make this book an essential reference source for you. I also hope that you find it enjoyable to work through, inspiring you and giving you the confidence to take your sewing skills further, to even more exciting projects of your own.

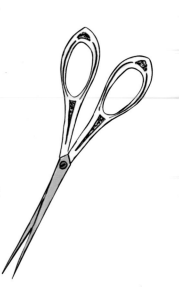

Tools for the job

You're going to need some basic pieces of equipment before you rush out and buy your fabric, but don't worry—you don't need to spend a fortune to make your sewing more successful and enjoyable. This chapter takes you through all the tools you will need, from sewing machine to pins, needles and iron.

Your sewing machine

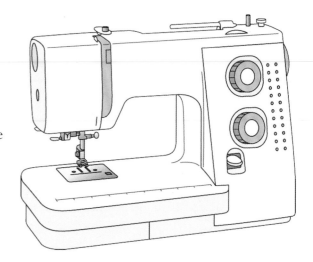

There are many different brands of sewing machines to choose from, each offering a wide range of stitch options. For basic dressmaking, the stitches you will use the most are straight stitch (for sewing seams) and zigzag (for finishing edges and also for working buttonholes). However, if you have access to a more sophisticated model, then you will be able to make use of decorative stitches as well. If purchasing from new, look for a machine that sits firmly on a table—you'll find portable versions useful and easier to set up and put away.

Special feet

Special feet are provided with a new sewing machine or can be bought separately. They are nearly all worth the trouble of learning to use them, as they are designed to make the stitching of certain processes so much easier. The most useful feet are the zigzag foot, zipper foot, buttonhole foot, blind-hem foot, overcast foot, and rolled-hem foot. See page 53 for more about machine feet, and refer to your instruction manual for further details.

Machine needles

Pick the right type for your machine, and remember, the lower the number, the thinner and finer the needle. A size 10 (70) needle, for example, is suitable for lightweight fabrics, while size 16 (100) is good for thick, heavy fabrics. Size 12 (80) and 14 (90) needles are best for medium-weight fabrics.

Needles also have different points, each designed for a certain type of fabric: sharp-point for woven fabrics, ballpoint for knitted fabrics, extra-fine point for denim and canvas, and wedge point for leather. Universal needles are also available, which are between sharp-point and ballpoint in sharpness and are designed for use on both woven and knitted fabrics. There are also many specialty needles, such as those for machine embroidery, quilting, and metallic threads. See page 21 for a needle and thread selection chart.

TIPS
Get to know your sewing machine properly by reading the instruction manual carefully. If you are purchasing a new machine, check whether the manufacturer offers free tuition in using it at their retailers' stores.

If the needle is not inserted into your machine in the correct way, you won't be able to sew, so do check your instruction manual when inserting the needle.

If your bobbin goes into your machine from the side, then the flat part of the needle faces the right-hand side of the machine. If your bobbin goes into the front of your machine, the flat part of the needle faces away from you.

Basic sewing equipment and aids

Apart from your machine, nearly all the only other tools you need will fit neatly inside your sewing box. Some of these items you may already have around your home, so you may only need to add a few more. However, if you are starting from scratch, then buy, beg, or borrow what you need to get you started.

Tape measure

This is essential for most measuring jobs, from taking body measurements to lining up all your pattern pieces on the fabric or measuring hems and buttonholes. Buy one in a flexible, non-fraying material that has metal ends and is numbered on both sides. Remember, a cheap tape measure may not be accurate!

Dressmaker's shears

Dressmaker's shears have handles that will take the thumb on one side and three fingers on the other. They are more heavily made than scissors and have bent handles that allow the fabric to lie flat on the table while you are cutting out your pattern pieces (see page 30). Go for the best quality you can afford, with blades that are at least 7–8in (18–20cm) long. Treat your shears well and never use them for cutting anything other than fabric. Cutting paper with them will blunt them very quickly, and dropping them can easily put them out of alignment and damage the points.

Small, pointed scissors

A sharp pair of pointed scissors, with blades that are no more than 3in (7.5cm) long, is useful for trimming and clipping seams and cutting thread ends after stitching.

Pins

Pins come in a range of lengths and sizes to suit different fabric types. For general sewing, glass- or plastic-headed pins are the easiest to handle. Make sure that you buy plenty of them and store them in a pincushion to keep them safe and accessible.

Hand-sewing needles

Hand-sewing needles should be fine enough to slip through the fabric, yet strong enough not to break. The needles known as sharps are the most commonly used for hand sewing. They are available in a variety of sizes and points, numbered 1 to 12—unlike with machine needles, the larger number, the shorter and finer the needle. Size 9 is the most useful basic size for hand sewing. When choosing a needle size for your stitching, consider the type of fabric you will be sewing; normally, the lighter the fabric, the thinner the needle. See page 71 for information on embroidery needles.

Needle threader

A needle threader makes it easy to thread hand needles and also machine needles. Its wire loop is inserted into the eye of the needle and the thread is fed through the loop. The wire loop is then pulled out of the needle, bringing the thread with it and so threading the needle.

Bodkin

This thick, blunt, needle-shaped tool is useful for threading cord, elastic, etc. Types of bodkin vary—some have an eye through which the cord or elastic is threaded, and others have a tweezer or safety pin closure.

Quick unpick or seam ripper

This tool can be used to unpick incorrect stitches and seams quickly. It can also be used to cut the slits in buttonholes once they are stitched. You might find one of these included in your sewing machine accessories, but it will probably be small and difficult to hold, so buy one with a large handle. Remember, seam rippers can be dangerous so keep the top on and keep them away from children.

Thimble

You may not think a thimble is essential, but by the time you have stitched on a few buttons, installed a zipper, or sewn through some thick fabric by hand, you will very much want to use one! A thimble prevents your middle finger from being punctured when you are hand sewing. Find one that fits you comfortably and is made of metal, as plastic ones are liable to split.

TIPS

If you are left-handed you will find it hard to cut out with normal scissors, so look on the Internet for versions that are designed especially for left-handed people, where the blades are reversed to give you a cleaner cut.

For general sewing choose stainless steel pins as they don't rust and can be picked up easily with a magnet if they get spilled on the floor.

To test for the correct needle size, pass a few needles of different sizes through the fabric in an inconspicuous place and see which one passes through the fabric most easily and leaves the smallest hole.

If you don't have a bodkin, then a small or medium-size safety pin can work quite well as a substitute.

The cutting surface

You will need a large, flat, firm surface, such as a dining table or a clean area of the floor, on which you can fold and cut out your fabric. Pins and shears can leave scratch marks and will present a danger to children, so make sure that the surface is protected or is one that you are not worried about, and that children cannot get near it.

Chalk markers

Chalk is ideal for marking around your pattern pieces onto fabric. It can be bought in wedge form, known as tailor's chalk, which is very economical; the edges can be sharpened with a knife. Alternatively, go for a chalk pencil, which is perfect for marking pocket positions, buttonholes, and the points of darts. Some chalk pencils have a brush attached, although marks are easily removed. Avoid wax, as it often leaves a greasy mark on your fabric, especially when melted with an iron, which you might find hard to remove.

Tracing wheel

This is a simple tool with multiple teeth on a wheel, attached to a handle; the teeth can be either serrated or smooth. It is used with dressmaker's carbon paper for transferring pattern markings, such as pleats, darts, and appliqué lines, onto the wrong side of fabric. Always place a piece of thick cardboard underneath the fabric to protect your work surface.

Dressmaker's carbon paper

This comes in packs containing several colors and is used with a tracing wheel. Test it on a scrap of fabric before using on your garment, to ensure that it doesn't show on the right side of the fabric.

Yardstick (meter stick)

This 36in- (1m-) long ruler is handy for both dressmaking and for measuring up and making home furnishings.

Steam iron and ironing board

Whether you are ironing out fabric creases or pressing seams, the combination of steam and heat is indispensable, so invest in a high-quality model that weighs at least 1lb (500g), because a lightweight portable one won't be good enough for pressing in pleats or properly applying fusible interfacings. Choose an ironing board that's easy to adjust to the right height. For techniques that require a lot of pressure, you might find that lowering the board so that you can lean on the iron will make the process easier. See Pressing Points below for more tips on pressing success.

Pressing points

To ensure that your hand-sewn garments look like custom couture and not hapless homemade, learn how to use your iron and other pressing tools to their full potential.

■ Don't make the common mistake of confusing ironing with pressing with an iron. They are not the same. Ironing is a back-and-forth motion designed to remove wrinkles. Pressing is a lift-up-and-set-back-down motion that builds smoothness and shape into your garment.

■ "Press as you go" is a motto to sew by. It means that you never cross one seam with another until the first seam is pressed. If you stick to this basic principle on every project you undertake, from a simple hem to a carefully tailored garment, it will look better and last longer.

■ Get into the habit of using a pressing cloth, especially when pressing on the right side of the fabric. Pressing cloths prevent scorch marks and shine. You can purchase specially treated cloths or use a piece of cotton muslin, a man's handkerchief, or self-fabric.

■ Slipping strips of brown paper bags or recycled envelopes under seam allowances, darts, and facings before pressing prevents ridges forming on the outside of the garment.

■ Avoid tedious back-and-forth trips to the ironing board by organizing your sewing so that you can "batch press." Stitch up several sections, then take the whole group to the ironing board. It also makes life a lot easier if you arrange your sewing space so that the ironing board is close to your sewing machine.

■ Not all fabrics can be pressed, so check the recommended pressing instructions for your fabric, and as a safeguard test a sample piece of your fabric first.

■ Always keep the base of your iron clean so that you don't spoil your project while pressing. Specialist iron soleplate cleaner can be purchased from hardware shops, or over the Internet, to remove marks and adhesive from the base of the iron without scratching the surface.

Choosing paper patterns and fabrics

With the vast array of patterns available today, it is possible to sew the latest fashions straight from the catwalks, but whether you prefer something that is high fashion or more classic, it is the fabric that will make or break your garment. In this chapter we help you to understand fabrics, so that you make the best choice. We also show you how to take body measurements to enable you to select the right size of pattern and how to make simple alterations.

Measuring up

Before you buy a paper pattern, you need to know your own measurements. Don't rely on your dress size, as this can vary from brand to brand, so you will need to measure yourself accurately before you head to the shops. On page 12 you will find a chart that you can use for recording these measurements. For information on taking children's measurements, see pages 112–13.

Your body measurements

It's not easy to take your own body measurements, so ask a friend to help you. For best results strip down to your underwear and take off your shoes. Tie a piece of tape or string around your waist and wiggle around; it will settle at your natural waistline and give you a helpful guide for taking vertical measurements.

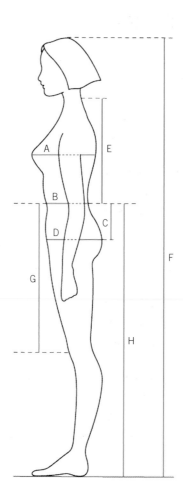

A—Bust: Measure around the fullest part; do not allow the tape measure to slip down at the back.

B—Waist: Take this measurement around the waist where the string has settled; hold the tape firmly, but make sure it is comfortable.

C—Waist to hips: This is the distance from your waist straight down to the widest part of your hips, approximately 7–8in (18–21cm) from your waistline.

D—Hips: Take the tape measure around the widest part of your hips.

E—Back neck (nape) to waist: Measure from the bone at the base of your neck, down the center back to the string tied around your waist.

F—Height: Remove your shoes and stand with your back against a wall. Place a ruler on top of your head, mark the wall lightly with a pencil, and measure from the mark to the floor.

G—Finished length (skirt): Measure from the string at your waist down to the required hem depth.

H—Finished length (pants/trousers): Measure from the waist to the floor at the side of your body.

Measurement chart

Photocopy this chart and fill in your measurements as a handy reminder to take with you when you go to choose a pattern. You can also refer to it later if you need to make any simple pattern alterations. In the first column, write your measurements; in the second column, record the pattern's body measurements (you will find these printed on the pattern envelope, see opposite); and in the third column, write the difference between the two measurements. A difference of $^1\!/_4$ in (6mm) in length and $^3\!/_8$ in (1cm) in width means that you should adjust the pattern slightly (see pages 24–6). It is advisable to recheck your measurements every six months to make sure that you have not changed in size.

Area to measure	Your measurements	Pattern measurements	Difference
Bust			
Waist			
Waist to hip			
Hips			
Back neck to waist			
Height			
Pattern size			

Selecting a pattern

Most fabric stores stock patterns, which are available for you to select from pattern catalogs. These are arranged into different sections, such as dresses, blouses, easy-to-make garments, and designer garments or evening wear. Printed alongside the illustration or photograph for each style are details of the various design options, or "views," available within the pattern, plus fabric suggestions, the notions required (see opposite), and fabric quantities. However, in addition to commercial patterns, there are also free sources of patterns published in magazines and books. All these patterns work in much the same way, but there are a few differences in how they look.

Figure types

Commercial patterns are produced for specific figure types, the details of which are printed at the back of the pattern catalog. You will need to compare your measurements, especially the vertical ones—height, back neck to waist, and waist to hip—to assess what figure type you most closely resemble. Women's figures vary greatly in shape from one person to another, so this is an attempt by the pattern companies to try to avoid as many fitting problems as possible for you. Although figure types are not supposed to relate to age groups, an age range may be suggested by the styles available in that group. It is best, however, to stay within your figure type if possible, to ensure that the pattern will be a good fit.

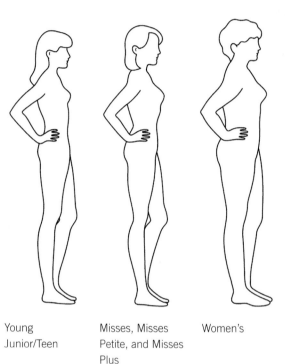

Young
Junior/Teen

Misses, Misses
Petite, and Misses
Plus

Women's

Young Junior/Teen: This group is for the young, developing miss—about 5ft 2in (157cm) to 5ft 5in (165cm) without shoes—with a small bust, waist larger in proportion to hips, and hips measured at 7in (18 cm) below the waist.

Misses, Misses Petite, and Misses Plus: The "Misses" figure is considered to be the average figure type—height 5ft 5in (165cm) to 5ft 6in (167.5cm) without shoes—with a well-developed and proportioned body. The hips are measured at 8in (20.5cm) below the waist, and the back neck to waist is longer than the other figure types. The "Misses Petite" figure is 1in (2.5cm) shorter overall than "Misses," with the hip measured at 7in (18cm) below the waist, but the proportions are similar. "Misses Plus" is for the well-proportioned and developed figure.

Women's: For the larger, more fully mature figure—average height 5ft 5in (157cm) to 5ft 6in (167cm) without shoes—with the hip measured at 8in (23cm) below the waist.

What are notions?

Also known as haberdashery, notions are all the trimmings, fastenings, and any other items that you will need, in addition to the fabric, to complete your garment. For more information on inserting zippers, turn to page 53, and for attaching various fastenings, from buttons to hooks and eyes, see pages 44–6 and 135–9.

Commercial patterns

These are made up of three main parts: the envelope, the instruction sheet, and the pattern pieces on tissue paper. Some patterns are multi-sized, so check the key to see which line you need to cut along for your size.

Front envelope information

The front shows the finished garment, with photographs or illustrations, plus the various views. It will also show the ease of the pattern's construction; always choose a style rated as "easy" for your first attempt.

Back envelope information

A wealth of information is printed on the back of the envelope, including a detailed size-and-yardages chart, the finished garment measurements, recommended fabrics for the style, the notions (see above right) required, and outline drawings of the garment with details such as darts or zippers.

Inside the envelope

An instruction sheet or sheets provide the following information:
- Outline drawings of all the views
- A diagram of each pattern piece and its number
- Cutting layouts
- Information on how to use your pattern
- Step-by-step sewing instructions for each view
- The folded pattern tissue with each pattern piece printed individually, ready for you to cut out

Buying the right pattern size

Armed with your measurement chart from page 12, compare your measurements with the chart in the pattern catalog and decide which figure type is most like your own. Few people have a standard figure, so there are likely to be differences between the chart measurements and your own; depending on the pattern you choose, it is best to select a size that corresponds to the most important area of fit. Be guided by the description on the pattern—for example, a blouse may be described as "fitted," "loose-fitting," or "very loose-fitting," so if you don't want a loose fit, say, then choose a smaller size or another style.

Dresses, blouses, and jackets: Choose a pattern nearest to your bust size and adjust the other measurements to fit.

Skirts and pants (trousers): Choose a pattern nearest to your hip size and adjust the waistline to fit.

Multi-patterns: If your pattern includes several different garments, such as a blouse, skirt, and pants, select the size that corresponds to your bust size and adjust the other areas if necessary. If there is a large difference, or you are worried about adjusting the fit, buy two sizes of the same pattern and use the appropriate pattern pieces from each. However, many styles come with multiple sizes in one pattern envelope, which can be a great help if your bust is one size and your hips another.

Complimentary patterns

Patterns provided in books like this one or in magazines are a great way to introduce yourself to dressmaking, as you do not have to spend a fortune on patterns to start with. The fact that they are free does not mean they are not as good—some fit a lot better than commercial patterns! Although these patterns are not supplied in envelopes, the same information is usually supplied, though in a different format. For instructions on using the patterns at the back of this book, see page 192.

The style

The garment and its variations are usually illustrated with photographs, which are printed along with the step-by-step sewing instructions in the main book or magazine.

Types of complimentary patterns

Full size: The best type of complimentary pattern is printed full size on separate large pieces of paper, normally inserted at the center or the back of the publication. You will need to trace each pattern piece before you start (see page 24), as there are often a multitude of different patterns and sizes printed on both sides of a sheet. Some simple joining and extending of pattern pieces may also be necessary, as they may be too large to fit on the sheet in one piece.

Scaled down: The other type of complimentary pattern is scaled down and printed onto a graph for you to redraw at full size. This type of pattern is fine for simple basic shapes, such as tunics, pillows, and children's dressing-up costumes, but is not recommended for more complex, fitted styles. Not only is scaling up by hand time-consuming, but it leaves room for error. Also, your pattern pieces may not piece together accurately, and therefore your final garment could be spoiled.

Size and fabric information

The chart giving yardages (meterages) for each size is normally printed with the pattern sheet, but instead it may be with the step-by-step instructions in the main book or magazine. You will need to compare your measurements to find the correct size to trace and the right amount of fabric to buy. The recommended fabrics, notions, and outline drawings will also be supplied. These, too, may be printed either with the step-by-step instructions or on the separate pattern sheet.

Looking at fabrics

Today's fabrics are in tune with fashion, and when you are faced with such an exciting array, the choice can be bewildering. It's essential to read the fabric suggestions on the pattern, setting out which are suitable to make the style as the designer intended.

All fabrics are made from yarn, created by spinning together fibers that either come from natural sources, such as wool or cotton, or are man-made, like polyester. Different fibers are often spun together to improve the appearance, performance, and care of a fabric. It is the fiber or blend of fibers that gives a fabric its own unique properties and determines its end use and care.

Fabrics are categorized as woven, knitted, or nonwoven. In woven fabrics, lengthwise yarns (the "warp") and crosswise yarns (the "weft") are interwoven on a loom. Every woven fabric has two firm, finished edges—the selvages—along the length. Rearranging the weave pattern creates different weave structures, such as plain, twill, satin, or pile weave. Knitted fabrics, which are made using needles to interweave yarn into connected loops, can be flat or tubular. Nonwoven fabrics include felt, bonded fabrics, laminated fabrics, and netting.

Natural fibers

Fiber type	Characteristics	Examples of materials	Laundry guide
Cotton	Named after the plant it comes from. Fiber length greatly affects quality (eg, the long fiber from Egypt is fine and lustrous, while the short fiber from India is the roughest). Strong—and even stronger when wet—and also absorbent and cool to wear, but creases and shrinks unless treated.	Calico, chambray, chintz, corduroy, cotton flannel, cotton voile, drill, denim, gingham, moleskin, muslin, organdy, poplin, seersucker, terrycloth.	Easy to wash and can take high temperatures. Can be bleached if color instructions permit. Can be ironed with a hot iron and does not scorch easily.
Linen	Comes from the flax plant and is one of oldest textiles in the world. Very strong, absorbent, and cool to wear, but has no stretch or elasticity. Creases badly and shrinks unless treated.	Lightweight linen and handkerchief linen for blouses; medium-weight for dresses; and medium-weight to heavy for suits and coats.	Some washable, others dry-clean-only—check label. Washable linens are easy to wash and become softer with use. Use hot steam iron to remove creases from dry fabric, but iron while still damp after washing.
Silk	Created by the silkworm (primarily from China or India) as it spins its cocoon. The only natural fiber that is a filament (continuous thread), the fiber can be hundreds of meters long, which produces silk's wonderful sheen. It dyes well and is strong, absorbent, warm, and crease resistant, but sunlight and perspiration will weaken it.	Silk brocade, chiffon, crepe de chine, damask, georgette, organza, satin, and taffeta; plus dupion, habotai, noil, pongee, sandwashed, shantung, shot, thai, and wild silk.	Dry-cleaning generally preferable, as detergent and dyes from other clothes may adversely affect silk. For washable silk, carefully hand wash with mild suds and lukewarm water. Iron on a low setting when damp; do not use steam, as it can create watermarks.
Wool	Spun from the fleece of sheep or other hairy animals, so quality varies with breed. Finest wools come from shorter fibers; longer fibers produce coarser yarns. Most luxurious and expensive are cashmere and mohair from goats, angora from rabbits, and alpaca from alpacas. Wool repels liquids, absorbs moisture, but is not very strong (and loses strength when wet); attracts moths. Crease resistant but can shrink when washed, unless treated.	Astrakhan, baratica wool, cashmere, houndstooth, serge, tartan, and tweed; plus wool bouclé, challis, crepe, flannel, jersey.	Usually dry-cleaned, but nowadays some can be washed by hand or machine, using gentle soap. If wool gets wet, dry garment at room temperature away from heat and use steam iron on low setting, pressing on reverse side.

Man-made fibers

Fiber type	Characteristics	Examples of materials	Laundry guide
Acetate	Made from cotton waste fibers and wood pulp. Relatively weak, tends to crease, and can melt at high temperatures, but will not shrink or stretch; drapes well, has luster, and dyes well.	Fabrics and linings that resemble silk or satin and that drape well.	Usually dry-cleaned; but if laundering is indicated, hand wash in warm water with mild suds; do not twist or wring out, or soak colored items. Iron on synthetics setting while damp.
Acrylic	Made from a synthetic combination of coal and gas; has a unique wool-like feel. Soft, bulky, and light, yet strong and crease resistant. It is non-absorbent and dyes well but tends to collect static and to pill. Often blended with other fibers.	Fake fur, polar fleece, ponte roma, single knits.	Can be machine washed and tumble dried on a warm setting. Iron at low temperature—it melts on a high setting.
Elastane	Lycra™ and Spandex™ are common brand names for elastane, which can stretch up to 500 percent without breaking and will recover immediately. Strong, lightweight, and non-absorbent, it is mixed with other fibers to add elasticity to them.	Knitted fabrics for sportswear, leisurewear, and lingerie, plus woven fashion fabrics for body-hugging garments.	Hand or machine wash in lukewarm water. Do not use chlorine bleach on any fabric containing elastane. Rinse thoroughly and drip dry. If ironing is required, iron quickly at a cool setting.
Metallic	Usually produced from aluminum, but not very strong; adds glitter to evening fabrics and trims, but can tarnish unless coated with protective film.	Lamé, Lurex™, and Liquid Gold. Often mixed with other fibers and made into glittery fabrics.	Follow care instructions provided. Many have to be dry-cleaned, but some may be washed at low temperature. If permitted, iron on a low setting, but is sensitive to heat and will discolor if steam is used.
Nylon	First fabric to be made entirely from chemicals. Is very strong and crease resistant, has low absorbency, won't shrink or stretch, but tends to pill and collect static electricity. Can be molded and permanently pleated or embossed with heat.	Used in knitted fabrics for sportswear, leisurewear, lingerie, linings, ciré, fake fur.	Most items made from nylon can be machine washed and tumble dried at low temperatures. To minimize static electricity, use a dryer sheet when tumble drying. Iron only with a warm iron.
Polyester	Strong, crease resistant, with low absorbency and many end uses. Warm, but can collect static electricity. Can be permanently pleated, pressed, and embossed. Often blended with natural fibers to improve their quality and reduce cost.	Polyester crepe, double knit, lining, organza, polar fleece, satin, shirting, twill.	Can usually be machine washed and tumble dried on a low setting. Dries very quickly and needs minimal ironing; if needed, use a moderately warm iron. Most can also be dry-cleaned.
Rayon (viscose)	Created from wood pulp; has similar properties to silk, is soft and absorbent, and drapes well. Retains body heat and dyes well, but is not strong. Tends to crease, stretch, and shrink. Often blended with other fibers.	Crepe, jersey, linings.	Most should be dry-cleaned, but some can be hand or machine washed, using mild lukewarm or cool suds. Do not wring or twist. While still damp, press on wrong side with iron at moderate setting.

Choosing a fabric

Choosing fabric is both exciting and enjoyable, and you will soon become familiar with the qualities of the various types. However, if you are uncertain at this stage, it is much better to ask for advice than to make an expensive mistake. To achieve a good result, always follow the list of suggested fabrics that comes with the pattern. Do not pick an expensive fabric for your first attempt at sewing, and try to gain a little experience with woven fabrics before you tackle knitted or specialty fabrics that require more expertise. Avoid large checks and prints for the same reason; you want your first experience to be enjoyable and not a disappointment.

Unroll a length of the fabric and drape it over yourself, preferably in front of a mirror, to see how it falls and whether it suits you. Squeeze a corner to see if it creases or goes back to normal. Read the label to see what fibers it is made from, whether it can be laundered, and how easy it is to sew. If no information is provided, then ask the sales assistant.

Fabric with a nap

If you are thinking of buying a fabric that has a "nap"—ie, a fabric in which the pile lies in one direction (and looks different when viewed from the other direction), or a one-way design in which the design motifs are not facing the same way in both directions—then all the pattern pieces will need to be laid in one direction. This means that you will probably need to buy extra fabric. Commercial patterns usually give fabric quantities for napped fabrics if they recommend them in their fabric guide (see page 13). If you are not sure how much extra fabric you will need, ask the sales assistant.

Fabric-buying checklist

Before your fabric is cut from the roll, have a good look for defects that indicate poor quality and remember to double-check with the assistant as to its suitability for your project.

Basic checks to make
- Make sure that the weight and drape of the fabric suit the item you are planning to make.
- The width should correspond to the fabric details given with the pattern or should be wide enough to cut out any large pieces you need.
- A lining fabric may be required if you want to avoid stretch and ensure comfort and longer wear, or if you are using a fine or sheer fabric (see page 19).
- Fabric care is a big consideration. Check whether it can be laundered, as dry-cleaning costs can soon add up.

The weave
- It should be firm—if you can move the threads with your fingernails, they can separate with wear and develop weak areas or holes around the stitching, called slippage. Some fabrics are designed to have an open weave, which is fine so long as the threads do not shift.

- It should be uniform in texture, to ensure even wear. Check for thick or thin areas by holding it up to the light.
- The weft yarns (see page 15) running across the width of the fabric should meet the selvages at a right angle, otherwise the fabric is off-grain (see page 27).
- If the fabric frays easily, it will be more difficult to work with. You will need to finish the edges of the cut pieces before sewing them together.

The dye color
- Check that the fabric is evenly dyed. Avoid fabrics where the color has faded on a central crease line, or where the color can be rubbed off the fabric surface onto a white tissue.
- Make sure you buy enough fabric, as rolls can vary in color if they come from different dye batches.

The print design
- Symmetrical and geometric prints should meet the selvages at right angles; otherwise it is very difficult to match corresponding seams or edges.
- Remember that one-way designs or pile fabrics may mean you have to buy extra fabric.
- Print colors should be even, with no white spots on areas that should be colored.

The overall finish
- Rub the fabric between your fingers. If fine powder appears, then there is too much sizing, which is added as a finish to bulk up a cloth and disguise poor quality.
- Crush the fabric to see if it sheds its creases. If it doesn't, it will always look crumpled.

Underlying fabrics

In the fabric quantities chart section of your pattern, you may also see quantities for lining and interfacing. These fabrics are the hidden parts of a garment that help it retain its shape and help it wear longer. There are four main types of underlying fabrics: interfacing, lining, interlining, and underlining. Each has a specific function that influences the garment's appearance, but the most commonly used are interfacing and lining.

Underlying fabric	Purpose	Where used	Types	Points for buying
Underlining	Always stitched as one layer with main fabric. Used to provide support; to reinforce seams and other construction details on delicate fabrics such as lace; to give opacity to sheer fabrics and hide their inner construction from outside; to prevent stretching in areas of stress; and to act as a layer on which to attach hems, facings, and interfacings.	Whole garments or sections of garments.	For lightweight fabrics, use batiste and habotai silk. For medium-weight fabrics, use taffeta, muslin, and organdy. For lace, use crepe de chine and satin. Special underlining fabrics are also available in a wide range of weights and colors.	Should not hold back natural drape of garment. Should be relatively stable and lightweight, with care instructions similar to garment's, and in color and finish (eg, soft or crisp) appropriate to garment.
Interfacing	Adds strength and stability to edges and garment details; prevents stretching.	Entire garment pieces such as collars, cuffs, flaps, belts, and garment areas such as opening edges, buttonholes, hemlines, neck edges, armholes.	Woven or nonwoven; fusible or sew-in; lightweight, medium-weight, or heavy. Comes in neutral colors such as white, charcoal, black. Woven canvas interfacings are available for tailoring.	Should be lighter than the fabric and should give support and body without overpowering main fabric. Care instructions should be compatible with garment. For general use, nonwoven fusible interfacings are ideal; save sew-in types for sheer or fine fabrics where fusible adhesive might show through.
Interlining	Makes a garment or curtain thicker and warmer.	Bodies of jackets and coats; sometimes sleeves; bespoke handmade curtains and bed quilts.	Lightweight, fluffy fabrics, such as brushed cotton or flannelette, make good interlinings, as they trap air and increase insulation. Special insulating fabrics are also available, such as polyester and cotton battings, and bump, domette, and sarille (see pages 82 and 169).	Needs to be lightweight and not too bulky. Should provide warmth, and care instructions need to match rest of garment or project.
Lining	Gives a luxurious finish and covers up internal construction details; allows garment to slide on and off easily; supports loosely woven fabrics and prevents them from stretching around seat of pants (trousers) and skirts.	Entire jackets, coats, vests (waistcoats), dresses, skirts, and pants, or parts of these.	Acetate, polyester taffeta, and blouse fabrics are most suitable for everyday garments. For luxury and woolen garments, use silk.	Color is important, especially if garment opens to reveal lining. Its weight and care instructions should be compatible with garment. It should be smooth, opaque, and durable, preferably with an anti-static finish.

Interfacing

Interfacing is a special type of fabric applied to the inside of a garment to strengthen and stiffen specific parts, such as collars, facings, and buttonholes. It comes in several weights and degrees of stiffness to suit different purposes—the heavier your fabric, the heavier the interfacing you will need. There are nonwoven and woven types, fusible or sew-in, but fusible are the easiest to use. If you are unsure which is best for your fabric, ask the sales assistant to recommend one to you.

Applying fusible interfacing

Fusible interfacings, also known as iron-on interfacings, are the easiest to use. They have a heat-activated adhesive on one side and are attached to the wrong side of garment pieces using heat and pressure from a hand iron; they are recommended for the novice sewer. You will generally find laundry care symbols printed on a label at the end of the roll, plus they are often also printed down the side edges of the interfacing itself, along with the iron setting, pressing times, and whether or not you need a damp cloth. There are two methods of application: the dry-heat method and the damp-cloth method.

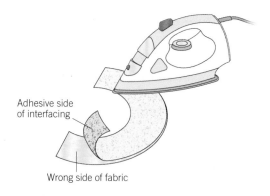

Adhesive side of interfacing

Wrong side of fabric

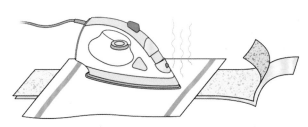

Dry-heat method: Lay the cut-out interfacing piece, adhesive side down, on the reverse side of the fabric piece. Set your iron to the correct temperature (do not use steam) and glide the iron over the interfacing for the stated amount of time, pressing down firmly as you iron. After ironing, lay the fused parts flat and allow them to cool for 20–30 minutes before sewing, to ensure the pieces have bonded securely.

Damp-cloth method: Apply as for the dry-heat method shown on the left, but lay a damp pressing cloth over the top of the interfacing and fabric, and press down firmly without using a gliding action. Remove the cloth and cool as for the dry-heat method.

Lining

A lining gives your garment a smooth, luxurious feeling, adding comfort as well as a quality finish. It is assembled separately, as though it were a second garment. It can be cut from the same pattern as your garment, or it may have separate pieces included in the pattern. The lining is placed inside a garment, wrong side to wrong side, and can be either fully stitched in place, such as in a yoke, or attached along the top edges to hang free.

Fabrics used for lining may or may not be specially made for the purpose. There is a wide choice of special fabrics in the lining sections of fabric stores but, on the other hand, there are many dress fabrics such as silk crepe, taffeta, satin, and tricot that also make beautiful linings, as in the Organdy Evening Skirt project on page 140. To be suitable, a fabric should be smooth to the touch, soft, pliable, and light enough in weight not to interfere in any way with how the main garment hangs.

If you want to add a lining to a garment but it isn't included with the pattern, choose the pattern pieces which you would like to line, and use these pieces to work out the yardage by laying them into the width of lining fabric.

TIPS

If all four types of underlying fabrics were being used, the order of application would be underlining first, interfacing second, then interlining, and finally lining.

Always try fusible interfacing on a scrap of fabric before you iron it on, to make sure you have the right heat and pressure to set it in place. Once it is cooled completely, you should not be able to peel it off very easily.

To avoid "seating" on pants and skirts, add a half lining to the back part of the garment, finishing halfway down the top leg or skirt.

TIP

When you are buying thread, unwind the thread end from the spool and lay it over your fabric; the color will look slightly different from how it looks on the spool.

Thread

The last thing you will need to purchase before you start sewing is the thread. Thread for constructing garments needs to be strong, durable, and stretchy. Like fabrics, there is a wide range available, in various thicknesses, finishes, and fiber contents, all created for different purposes. However, for all types of stitching, a good-quality thread is a lot easier to use, and yields better results, than so-called "bargain" thread. A good thread is strong, smooth (not fuzzy), colorfast, and, most importantly, consistent in thickness.

Choosing thread

The type of thread you select is mainly influenced by your fabric choice. The fiber content need not be the same as your fabric, but heavy fabrics will require a heavier thread and lightweight fabrics a finer one. Using the correct size of thread may reduce puckering, a problem frequently encountered when sewing lightweight fabrics—see the chart opposite for recommendations.

Spun polyester thread is a good all-purpose choice, as it is strong, it has stretch, it won't fray, snap, shrink, or rot, and it usually has the best color choice. Finding a thread that matches the color of your fabric exactly is not always possible, in which case choose one that is a shade darker or, on a printed or plaid fabric, one that matches the main color. If in doubt, ask the sales assistant for help.

Specialty threads

A variety of specialty threads, from metallic to "invisible," is available for specific purposes, such as buttonholes or embroidery.

Topstitching thread

This is a strong, heavy polyester thread with a high luster, ideal for bold decorative sewing, buttonholing, and button sewing. Best results are achieved with topstitching thread in the needle and sew-all thread in the bobbin.

Mercerized cotton thread

Mercerization is a treatment for cotton thread that gives it a lustrous, smooth appearance and strengthens it. Mercerized cotton thread is especially suitable for machine embroidery. It comes in different sizes: size 30 is medium-fine and size 60 is very fine.

Stranded embroidery floss

Also called stranded cotton, stranded embroidery floss is a loosely twisted, slightly glossy, six-stranded thread (in which each strand is made up of two twisted plies), usually made from cotton but also available in silk or linen, that is used for hand embroidery. Stranded floss is the standard thread used for basic embroidery, as you can vary your results depending on the number of strands you use together (see page 71).

Perle cotton

Also known as pearl cotton or coton perlé, this is a tightly twisted, two-ply hand-embroidery thread with a high sheen. Sold in skeins, it is available in five sizes (No. 3, 5, 8, 12, and 16, in which 3 is the heaviest and 16 the finest).

Metallic thread

This is a shiny, metalized thread with a polyester core, used for machine and decorative hand stitching. It is available in a variety of colors.

Monofilament nylon thread

A clear, transparent, or "invisible" thread, this is available in two shades—natural for light fabrics and smoke for dark ones. The higher the number, the thicker and stronger the thread; for example, 80s is like a cobweb while 520s is like fishing line. It needs to be used under a dome or net on a sewing machine to control the inherent slipperiness.

Spool sizes

The largest range of colors for home sewers comes in 100yd (100m) spools, although white, black, and a few selected colors are available in larger, 200yd (200m), 400yd (400m), 500yd (500m), and 1,000yd (1,000m) spools, which are useful when you are making larger projects such as curtains and patchwork quilts. Specialty threads come in various sizes, from 8.7yd (8m) skeins of embroidery threads to 33yd (30m) spools of topstitching threads.

Needle, thread, and stitch-length selection

This chart is a quick-reference guide to the recommended thread, needle, and stitch length combinations for most basic home-sewing jobs.

Fabric	Machine needle	Thread	Stitch lengths in mm (newer machines)	Stitches per inch (2.5cm) (older machines)
Woven fabrics in man-made or natural fibers, such as linen, cotton, wool, velvet, and chiffon	Regular sharp-point needle, size 12 (80)	Polyester thread	2.5	10–11
Woven fabrics in natural fibers only, such as cotton, linen, wool, and velvet	Regular sharp-point needle, size 12 (80)	Cotton or poly-cotton thread	2.5	10–11
Finely woven fabrics in natural fibers only, such as silk, silk velvet, chiffon, and wool	Regular sharp-point needle, size 10 (70)	Silk or polyester thread	2.0	12
Fine knitted fabrics, made from man-made, silk, cotton, or wool fibers	Fine ballpoint needle, size 10 (70)	Polyester thread	2.5	10–11
Heavy knitted fabrics, made from man-made or natural fibers, such as jersey or fleece	Medium ballpoint needle, size 12–14 (80–90)	Polyester thread	3.0	9–10
Dense fabrics such as twill, denim, heavy linen, and canvas	Extra fine-point needle, size 12–14 (80–90)	Heavy-duty polyester thread or linen twist	4.0	6–7
Leather, suede, imitation leather and suede, and plastic	Wedge-point (leather) needle, size 14–16 (90–100)	Heavy-duty polyester thread or linen twist	4.5	6

Preparing paper patterns and cutting out

You've bought your fabric and got your pattern, but don't know where to start? Faced with a jargon-loaded pattern, it might seem easier to go on buying readymade items, but don't give up. With a little patience you can create beautiful and original clothes and soft furnishings for your home. In this section you will learn how to get to grips with the pattern, make basic pattern alterations, and cut out all the pattern pieces from fabric, ready for sewing.

Preparing the pattern

First, read through all the pattern instructions carefully. They may not make sense yet, but once you start to follow them step by step, the information will all fall into place. Choose which version—known as a view—you are going to make, and select the correct pattern pieces. Make sure that the size of the finished garment will match your vital statistics (these tend to be given on commercial patterns only) and, if not, adjust the appropriate pattern pieces (see pages 24–6).

How to select the right pattern pieces

The pattern piece diagram enables you to easily identify the pattern pieces you need. If your pattern doesn't have one of these, then it will probably have a list of the pieces. As a last resort, look at the cutting layouts (see page 29), which can help you to identify them. The pattern pieces themselves are each clearly labeled by name, number, and view(s).

1 Front
2 Side front
3 Back
4 Collar
5 Sleeve A
6 Sleeve binding A
7 Sleeve band A
8 Sleeve B
9 Sleeve band B
10 Buttonhole guide
11 Pocket
12 Ruffle

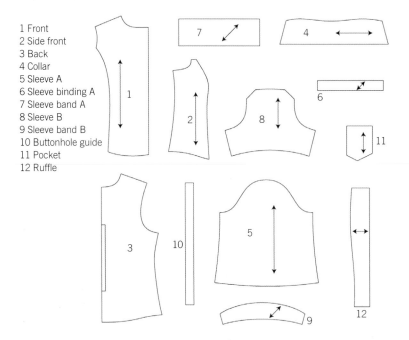

Typical pattern piece diagram
The example of a pattern piece diagram illustrated here shows how all the pattern pieces included in a pattern may look. It will show the pieces needed for all the views, and also whether any pieces need to be extended. There is often an accompanying key identifying which pieces are needed for each view. In the example shown here, view A will need pattern pieces 1, 2, 3, 4, 5, 6, 7, 10, 11, and 12; view B will need 1, 2, 3, 4, 8, 9, 10, 11, and 12.

Understanding pattern markings

All pattern pieces, whether commercial or complimentary, have pattern markings or symbols. These provide you with information essential for every step of the process, from identifying the pattern pieces to cutting out and constructing the garment. They are fairly standard on all patterns, but it helps to understand the functions they perform. They can basically be split into two main groups: markings for preparation and cutting out, and construction markings. The most common are shown here.

Markings for preparation and cutting out

These markings are to help you cut out the pattern pieces, make pattern alterations, and lay out the pattern pieces correctly on your fabric.

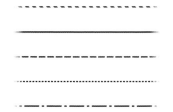

Cutting lines: Multi-sized patterns have different cutting lines for each size. See the key for the correct line for your size and follow it around each pattern piece carefully.

Alteration lines: These parallel double lines act as alteration lines to show you where to lengthen or shorten a pattern piece (see pages 24–5).

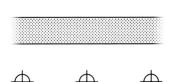

Joining marks: These marks are used when two pieces of a pattern have to be joined together to make one complete pattern piece. The symbols, which can vary with the pattern brand, may be a shaded area or a row of crossed circles at the edges to be joined. Overlap the matched symbols to join the pieces together and form a whole piece.

Straight grain or grainline: A straight line with arrowheads denotes that this line needs to be placed on the straight grain of the fabric (see page 27), an even distance from the selvage.

Foldline: Your pattern pieces often represent half a garment, so this symbol indicates that you should place your pattern piece exactly on the folded edge of the fabric to create a whole piece. Make sure that it is carefully lined up with the fold, as it is easy to increase or decrease the size of your garment piece inadvertently.

Construction markings

The following marks are either to help you sew your cut-out pieces together correctly or to show the positions of fastenings and garment features.

Notches: Marked as triangles or diamonds, notches are used for accurately matching pattern pieces when sewing. You will find single, double, or triple notches, which correspond with those on adjoining garment pieces.

Dots and circles: Showing the position of pockets, buttons, and zippers, for example, dots also mark points to sew up to or cut into. Small circles or squares can be used as extra matching aids for joining pieces, such as a sleeve to a shoulder seam, or a collar to a neckline.

Buttonholes and buttons: A buttonhole  is normally shown as a line, denoting its position and length, and the button position may be marked with a short crossed line or a dot.

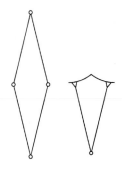

Darts: These are marked on patterns with the aid of notches and dots, linked together with solid or broken stitching lines that meet at a point (see pages 118–19).

Tracing a complimentary pattern

Patterns like the ones inserted in the back of this book generally offer a multitude of different patterns and sizes printed on both sides of a pattern sheet, often overlapping and printed in different colors for each pattern piece. You will therefore need to trace the pattern pieces you need before you can start. To use full-size patterns like the ones inserted in this book, simply follow these four easy steps.

1 Make a note of the pattern pieces you need and check the key to find out which line you should follow for your size.

2 Carefully trace around the appropriate lines onto tracing paper (or baking parchment) and cut out each pattern piece following the lines you have traced.

3 Lay the pieces back on the pattern sheet to double-check that you have traced along the correct lines, then transfer all information appropriate to your size, including the words and pattern markings, to each pattern piece.

4 Add extra length to pieces if required, and join relevant pattern pieces if requested.

Handling commercial patterns

Tissue paper patterns tear easily, so don't be in too much of a rush. Take your time to unfold all the sheets and prepare the pieces properly, and follow these four simple steps.

1 Open out your pattern tissues and, using the pattern piece diagram, identify the pieces you need for the view and size you are making. Put the remaining pieces back in the envelope to avoid any confusion.

2 Smooth out the sheets and press out the creases with a warm dry iron if necessary, then cut out each piece, cutting well outside the actual cutting lines; the excess tissue is useful if you have to make pattern alterations.

3 If your measurements do not match those of the chart size exactly, you may need to adjust the fit and/or length. Make any necessary pattern alterations (see below) before you trim the pattern to your size.

4 When you are satisfied that the fit and length are correct, trim the pattern pieces along the cutting lines for your measurements.

Basic pattern alterations

Before you purchased your pattern, you made a note of your body measurements using the chart on page 12, which was to help you select your pattern size, with the aim of getting the best fit. However, you may still need to make some basic alterations, the most common being the length. It is best to make length adjustments first, followed by any waist alterations.

Bodice

Some patterns will indicate the best place to do this alteration, but if it is not shown, draw a straight line through the pattern 2in (5cm) above the waist, at right angles to the straight grain marked on the pattern piece.

It is important to keep the alteration exactly at right angles to the grainline, or to the center front or center back when the pattern piece will be placed on a fold (see page 23), to ensure that the pattern is kept true to the straight grain of the fabric.

Too long: Make a pleat measuring half the depth of the required amount along the alteration line, keeping it even all along the fold. Tape it in place. To ensure that the original shape is retained, redraw a new side seam on the pattern, tapering it smoothly and gradually into the original line. Don't forget to alter the corresponding pattern pieces to match.

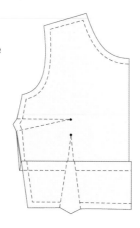

Too short: Cut along the alteration line and place a piece of paper underneath the cut. Carefully spread out the pattern pieces to the alteration amount, measuring along the line to ensure that the gap is even, and then tape the extra paper in place. Don't forget to alter all the corresponding pattern pieces by the same amount. Redraw the side seams to keep the line as close as possible to the original shape.

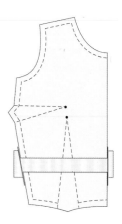

Sleeves

For a non-fitted sleeve you can make the alteration in one step at the elbow position. If you're using a fitted sleeve pattern, you will need to adjust the length equally above and below the elbow. Draw your alteration lines right across the sleeve exactly at right angles to the straight grain.

Too long: For a non-fitted sleeve, fold along the alteration line and make a tuck equal to half the required amount, keeping it even all along the line. Pin or tape in place, then redraw the sleeve side seams, keeping in line with the original shape, as shown in the diagram. For a fitted sleeve, divide the alteration amount into two equal parts above and below the elbow.

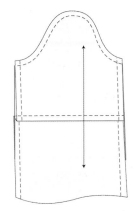

Too short: Cut along the alteration line, then place a piece of paper underneath the cut. Open out the cut edges, spreading them out by the required amount for your alteration. Measure along the line to ensure that the gap is even and the grainlines are lined up. Tape in place. If you have a fitted sleeve, divide the alteration measurement in two and add half the amount above the elbow and half below it, as shown in the diagram. Redraw the sleeve side seams linking the cut edges, keeping in line with the original shape.

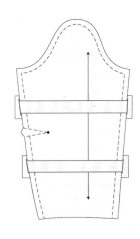

TIP
Don't meddle with the size and shape of your armhole or sleeve top until you are very skilled. Complicated alterations like this are best left alone until you gain experience with less difficult adjustments.

Skirts and pants

How you lengthen or shorten pants (trousers) and skirts depends on whether or not they are straight. If they are, the alteration is done at the hem, but if they are tapered or flared by a large amount, it is done by drawing an alteration line at right angles to the grainline.

Too long: Shortening a slim skirt or straight pant legs is very easy—just trim away the desired amount from the hem edge. If they are tapered or flared, draw an alteration line, then make an even pleat as shown in the illustrations for a too long bodice or too long sleeves.

Too short: To lengthen straight pant legs or a slim skirt, simply stick a piece of paper under the hemline and add the extra length to the hem edge, as shown in the diagram, then alter the corresponding pattern pieces to match. If they are tapered or flared, draw an alteration line, cut along the line, and spread the pattern as for a too short bodice or too short sleeves.

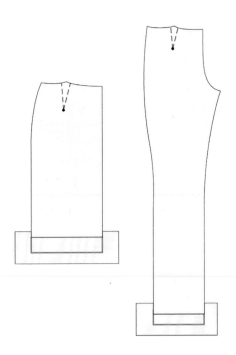

TIP

As a larger-than-average waist may include a distended stomach, it may be advisable also to shorten the darts a little at the front.

Altering the waist

You can make quick adjustments to increase or decrease the waist on skirts or pants by altering either the darts or the side seams. However, do not reduce or increase the waist by more than 1in (2.5cm) in total using these methods, or you may affect the style of the garment.

Too loose: If you want to make the waist smaller and you have a small waist and large hips, take in the darts. Or if you have a small waist and average-size hips, take in the side seams.

Too tight: If you want to make the waist larger and you have a thick waistline and a straight-up-and-down figure, let out the darts. Or if you have a thick waistline and larger hips, let out the side seams.

Adjusting the waistband (or facing): If you have made any of the waist adjustments detailed on this page, you'll need to adjust the waistband (or facing) to correspond.

■ If you have taken in or let out the darts, you will need to add or subtract the same amounts at the dart positions on the waistband (or facing)—these are usually marked with notches on the pattern.

■ If you have taken in or let out the side seams, you will need to add or subtract the same amounts at the side seams of the waistband (or facing).

■ To do this, either cut and spread the pattern out evenly by the amounts you need to add and tape a piece of paper underneath, or deduct them by pleating out the required amounts. Tape in place.

Taking in darts: Decide on the amount by which you need to take in the waist. Divide this amount by the number of darts around the waistline; for example, if you are taking the waist in by 1in (2.5cm) and if there are four darts, that equals 1/4 in (6mm) per dart. Divide this new measurement in half and make a mark each side of each dart at the waistline by this amount on both the front and the back; in the example, that

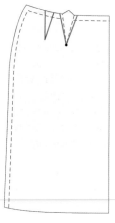

would be 1/8 in (3mm) each side of each dart. Taper down from the marks to the original point. Never make darts too wide or you will find it difficult to taper them and will end up with unsightly points just above the hips. In that case, it might be better to add additional small darts instead, positioning them symmetrically.

Letting out darts: Decide on the amount by which you need to let out the waist. Divide this amount by the number of darts around the waistline and then divide that figure in half to find how much narrower to make the dart on each side. Mark the decrease just inside each dart at the waist edge on both the front and the back, tapering down to the original point.

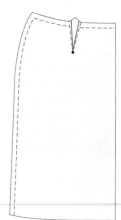

Taking in side seams: Decide on the amount by which you need to take in the waist. Deduct a quarter of that amount from the waist at each front and back side seam, tapering the new line back to the original hipline. Where there are more seams at the waistline, such as in a paneled skirt, divide the amount to alter the waist evenly among all the seams.

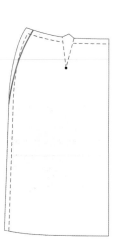

Letting out side seams: Decide on the amount by which you need to let out the waist. Add a quarter of that amount to the waist at each front and back side seam, then taper the new line back to the original hipline. Where there are more seams at the waistline, such as in a paneled skirt, divide the amount to alter the waist evenly between all seams.

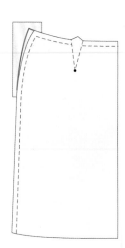

Get set for cutting

Cutting out often seems a daunting process for first-time sewers, but it will not be a problem if you take your time and prepare your fabric properly.

Basic fabric terms

Before you start to cut out or even lay out the fabric ready for cutting, it is a good idea to familiarize yourself with some basic fabric terms.

Straight grain: Most fabric preparation relates to the grain of the fabric. The grain describes the direction of the threads in a woven fabric. Pattern pieces are usually cut out on the straight grain, also called the lengthwise grain, following the warp yarns (see page 15). The straight grain runs parallel to the selvage (see diagram).

Selvage

Straight grain

Crosswise grain

True bias

Selvage

Crosswise grain: This follows the weft yarns (see page 15), which run from one selvage to the other, and it has more give, or stretch, than the straight grain. If the weft yarn does not meet the selvage at a right angle, the fabric is off-grain. As a rule, the crosswise grain is only used vertically for certain design features, such as placing a border print around a hemline.

Bias grain: The bias grain is an imaginary line that intersects the other two grainlines diagonally and has the most stretch. The "true bias," which lies at a 45-degree angle to the straight grain and the crosswise grain, has the greatest give of all. A bias-cut garment will drape softly but will also have an unstable hemline. Binding is cut on the bias grain if it has to curve around a finished edge such as a neckline (see page 147).

Nap: This term is used loosely in dressmaking to refer not only to fabrics that have a pile finish, such as velvet, but also to those with a printed one-way design, such as flowers pointing in one direction (see page 17). Dressmaking patterns often have "with nap" cutting layouts (see page 29) to show you how to place the pattern pieces on this type of fabric.

Fabric widths: Dress fabrics generally come in three widths: approximately 36in (90cm), 45in (112cm), and 60in (150cm). Decorator (soft furnishing) fabrics are usually about 54in (137cm) wide. The fabric quantities chart printed on the back of a pattern envelope or with your complimentary pattern will indicate how much fabric to buy for the specific project in the different fabric widths (see pages 13 and 14).

Straightening fabric ends

Proper fabric preparation is essential to make cutting out as easy and accurate as possible. After pressing your fabric to remove any wrinkles and creases, you will need to straighten the ends; this must be done with every fabric to ensure that it can be folded evenly with the grains aligned.

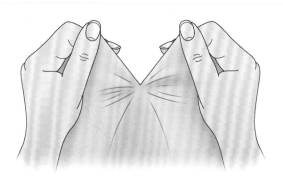

Tearing woven fabric

If the fabric can be torn, snip into the selvage and grasp each side of the snip, then simply tear across. If the strip runs off to nothing partway across, snip further down and tear again.

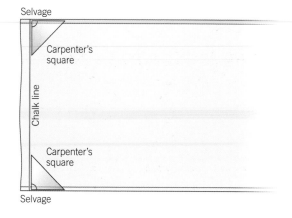

Trimming method

If your fabric won't tear, then use this method. Mark a line at a right angle to both selvages, using a carpenter's square (set square) or right-angled object such as a book, plus a yardstick and tailor's chalk (see page 10), then cut along it.

Identifying the right side

Before you can start to lay out your fabric, you will need to make sure that you know which is the right and which is the wrong side of the fabric. Usually it is obvious, but sometimes it's not! Here are a few clues to help you, but if you still are not sure, pick the side you like best and mark it with chalk, so that you will remember.

■ Smooth fabrics are shinier on the right side.
■ Pre-folded cottons and linens are right side out and wools wrong side out.
■ Textures and prints look clearer on the right side.
■ Noticeable nubs and yarn ends are more visible on the wrong side.
■ The selvage is smoother on the right side.

Laying out fabrics ready for cutting

Do not attempt to lay out your pattern pieces on the fabric piecemeal. If you have no large table, then use the floor. Lay out the fabric, or as much of it as you can, folding it as suggested on your cutting layout (see opposite). The fabric layers must lie smooth and flat, with the selvages straight and the trimmed end at right angles to it.

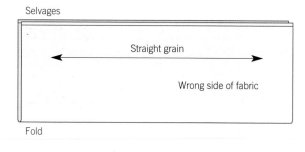

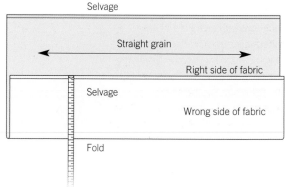

Standard lengthwise fold

This is made along the straight (lengthwise) grain, with the selvages matching exactly along one edge. Pin the selvages together at regular intervals if the fabric is slippery and moves around easily.

Partial or double lengthwise fold

When a partial or double lengthwise fold is made, use a tape measure, at regular intervals, to measure the distance from the fold to the selvage to ensure it remains uniform along the length of the fabric.

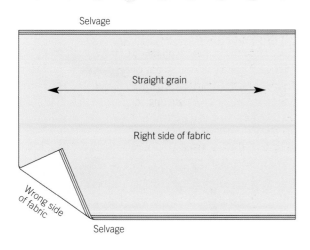

Selvage

Straight grain

Right side of fabric

Wrong side of fabric

Selvage

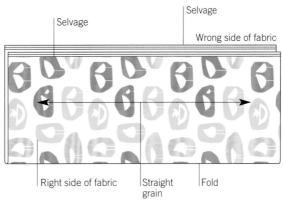

Selvage

Selvage

Wrong side of fabric

Right side of fabric | Straight grain | Fold

No fold required
Lay the fabric right side up when no fold is required.

Napped fabrics
Fold the fabric with the wrong sides together if you are cutting one with a pile, a design that needs matching, or a design with large motifs.

Cutting out

Now that your pattern pieces are ready, and you understand how to prepare your fabric for cutting out, it's time to study your cutting layouts.

Using the cutting layouts

Cutting layouts show how your fabric should be laid out (see below), and where the various pattern pieces should be placed if you are to achieve the most economical fabric usage given in the fabric quantities chart—the amount you followed to purchase your material. Always read the key that comes with the layouts, as it provides the information you need to cut out your pieces correctly.

Understand cutting layouts
Each layout gives the numbers of the pattern pieces required for that view, so you can check that you have not missed any out. It also shows whether any pattern pieces have to be extended or lengthened and whether they need to be cut from lining and/or interfacing (see pages 18 and 19) as well as from fabric. Find the layout(s) for your view, size, and fabric width. With the layout diagram beside you, place all the pattern pieces on the fabric, as shown in the diagram.

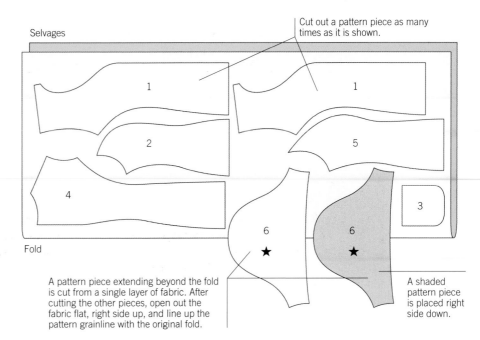

Selvages

Cut out a pattern piece as many times as it is shown.

Fold

A pattern piece extending beyond the fold is cut from a single layer of fabric. After cutting the other pieces, open out the fabric flat, right side up, and line up the pattern grainline with the original fold.

A shaded pattern piece is placed right side down.

TIP

To get used to using dressmaker's shears and cutting in a smooth way, buy yourself a piece of striped fabric and practice cutting along the stripes. This can be a little bit boring, but it will certainly help you to cut out more smoothly and accurately, which will ensure that your projects will fit together more easily.

Almost ready to cut

With the pattern pieces in position, it's time to think about cutting out. Accuracy is vital—not only will the fit of the garment be better, but cutting inside or outside the cutting lines can make a difference to the size. This guide is pretty much a guarantee against making mistakes, so use it as a checklist:

■ Make sure the straight grain/grainline on each pattern piece runs parallel to the selvage by measuring from each end of the straight grain arrow to the selvage and moving the pattern pieces until the distances are equal.
■ Check that foldlines on pattern pieces are placed exactly on the fold of the fabric.
■ If you are using a tissue pattern, pin the trimmed pattern pieces (see page 24) to the fabric, spacing the pins about 8in (20cm) apart and pinning through both fabric layers on a double thickness, or weight them down.

■ If you are using a traced pattern on thicker paper, weight down your pattern pieces and mark carefully around each piece with tailor's chalk (see page 10), then remove the weights and pattern pieces. Carefully pin inside each cutting line, pinning through both fabric layers on a double thickness.
■ Before cutting out, double-check the pattern pieces against the cutting layout to make sure that they are all there and are positioned correctly.

Let's cut!

After you have straightened the ends of the fabric, laid it out correctly, and pinned or drawn your pattern pieces in place, you are ready to start cutting. The scissors should slide along the fabric, making long cuts on the straight pieces and shorter cuts on the curves. Take time and care to cut smoothly, to avoid making jagged edges. Good, sharp dressmaker's shears (see page 9) are best for the job; never use blunt ones, which would make the fabric edges fray.

How to cut accurately

■ If you pinned your trimmed pattern pieces (see above) onto the fabric, carefully cut around the edges of the pattern along the cutting lines. Do not cut inside or outside the cutting line.
■ If you have chalked around your pattern pieces instead (see above), then cut along the chalk lines.
■ Do not cut through any foldlines.

How to use dressmaker's shears correctly: Place your left hand lightly on the pattern piece or layers of fabric to be cut and hold the shears in your right hand (if you are left-handed, reverse the instructions—see tip on page 9). Open the blades and slide the lower blade under the fabric, making sure that the shears rest on the table and that the fabric is only slightly raised. Make one long, smooth cut using the full length of the blades. To continue, reopen the blades, slide them under the fabric again, and move your left hand along, next to the blades, to stabilize the fabric. Carry on in this manner until your piece is cut out. Don't be tempted to lift up the shears or the fabric while you are cutting, as this would move the fabric around and distort the piece you are cutting out.

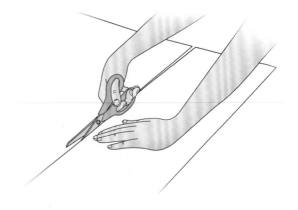

Almost ready to sew

Before removing the pattern pieces from the fabric, you need to transfer all your construction markings; you will then be ready to start sewing. If you are a complete beginner and are not used to a sewing machine, then follow our guide here, to help you get familiar with your machine. Once you feel fairly confident, then you are ready to move on to exciting things! The workshops that follow in Section 2 of this book are designed to develop your skills, so work through them consecutively. Take your time—and, most importantly, have fun!

Transferring pattern markings

If using a tissue pattern, transfer all the construction markings to the fabric before unpinning the pattern pieces. If using a traced pattern, place the pattern pieces back on top of the corresponding cut pieces, ready to transfer the pattern markings.

Marking notches

Notches can be marked by cutting around the extending outer edges of the diamonds or by making a snip 1/8 in (2–3mm) deep into the seam allowances at the triangles.

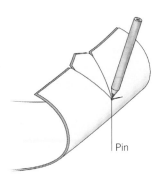

Pin

Marking dots, circles, and darts

For dots, circles, and darts, make a small hole in the pattern and mark the position with a chalk pencil (see page 10) on the top layer of fabric. At the dot position, push a pin straight down through the fabric layers and mark the dot on the other layer of fabric with a chalk pencil. If you wish, you can also draw in the dart lines with a chalk pencil and ruler to help you with your stitching (see page 118), or make rows of uneven basting stitches (see page 33).

Using a sewing machine

There is no magical fast track to getting used to your sewing machine—you just need to sit down and start sewing with it, then practice, practice, and practice. Here are a few pointers, however, to get you started.

Placing the fabric in the machine

Find a piece of firm cloth and sit down at your machine. Turn on the power, then place the fabric under the presser foot (you can start anywhere on the fabric, but it might be easier near an edge). Lower the presser foot onto the fabric. Grasp hold of the thread ends from your bobbin and from the needle with your left hand—doing this each time you start to sew is an important habit to get into, as it will stop the thread ends being dragged down into the bobbin case or the needle becoming unthreaded.

Mastering the foot pedal

Carefully press down the foot pedal, slowly at first to see how the machine feels. When you are happy, speed up a bit; stitch across the fabric as many times as you like. Remember to raise your needle to its highest point and lift the presser foot in order to reposition the fabric each time ready for stitching again. It doesn't matter at this stage if the stitching goes wonky—this is all about getting used to how much pressure you need on the pedal to control the machine. It's a bit like using the gas pedal on a car!

Sewing straight lines

Once you get the hang of the speed control, you can start sewing straight lines. One of the best ways to do this is to buy yourself some woven striped fabric and simply try to follow the lines with your stitching. This is all about "steering." Place your hands flat on the bed of the machine, with one at each side of the presser foot (not too close though, as you don't want to catch your fingers on the needle), then, using both hands to steer the fabric under the foot, try to follow the lines. You might find this difficult at first, but keep trying, as you will need to be able to sew in a straight line for seams, and practice helps. Now it's time to move on to the first workshop and start creating beautiful things for yourself, your home, and your family and friends.

Before you start to sew
■ Familiarize yourself with all the controls on your machine.
■ Place your sewing machine on a firm table and make sure that you have a comfortable chair that is the correct height for you to operate the machine controls and reach the foot pedal without straining. The pedal should sit flat on the floor, facing you.
■ Make sure that the power cord (lead) can reach an electric outlet (socket) safely, without being pulled too taut or being in a position that someone could trip over it. Always use an extension cord if you are not sure.

Workshop 1

Plain sewing

Plain sewing is a term applied to stitches, seams, and finishes that are used for sewing garments and home furnishings, as distinct from decorative embroidery stitches, which are featured in Workshop 4. This workshop guides you step by step through everything you need to know to start sewing and complete your first project—a basic pillow (cushion), embellished with simple running stitches.

Pinning fabric layers

Pinning the fabric layers will anchor them together and stop them from slipping out of position while you sew.

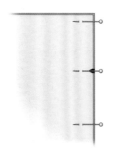

Place the fabric pieces with right sides together (unless instructed otherwise), raw edges even, and any corresponding pattern markings (see page 23) matching. Check your pattern to find out the width of the seam allowance—the distance between the seamline and the edge of the fabric—and then insert pins into the seam allowances. You can place your pins running either along the seamline or parallel to it; however, inserting them at right angles, with the pin heads close to the raw edge and the tips extending just beyond the seamline, will make them easier to remove when you are sewing.

Hand sewing

TIPS

Cut the thread at an angle, using sharp scissors. Don't break or bite the thread, as it will make the end fray so it is impossible to pass through the eye of the needle. If you still have difficulty, use a wire needle-threader (see page 9), available from notions (haberdashery) departments.

Hand sewing can be either temporary—when it is known as basting and is used to hold sections together while you are constructing seams—or permanent, used when the garment pieces need to be sewn together invisibly.

Securing your thread

Whether your hand sewing is temporary or permanent, you will need to secure the end of the thread when you start stitching. This can be done with a knot tied in the end of the thread or by making a couple of backstitches. The end of your hand sewing is usually secured with two backstitches.

Knotting a thread end

1 Thread your needle. To knot the thread, hold the end of the thread between your thumb and index finger and, with your other hand, wind the remaining thread over and around your finger. Hold the remaining thread taut and slide your index finger firmly back along your thumb, so that the thread twists to form a loop.

2 Slide the loop off the top of your fingernail, but hold it firmly in place between your finger and thumb. Pull the remaining thread to tighten the loop and form the knot.

Securing with backstitch

Bring the needle and thread to the upper side of the fabric at A. Insert the needle through all the fabric layers at B, one stitch length behind A, and bring it back up again at A. Repeat to form another backstitch in the same place. Trim the thread end.

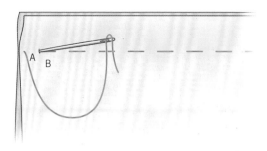

Basting

There are various types of basting stitches, but all are used to hold two or more pieces of fabric together temporarily as you work. The most common ones are even basting stitch, which gives a good control of the fabric; uneven basting stitch, for general use; and slip basting, which allows you to match stripes, checks, and large prints exactly at seamlines.

Note: These instructions are for a right-handed person; reverse the instructions if you are left-handed.

Even basting

This is best used on smooth, slippery fabrics that can slide or move against each other and also for seams that need to be carefully controlled, such as curved seams, seams with multiple fabric layers, and seams with ease stitching or gathers (see pages 43 and 104).

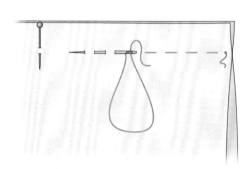

Working from right to left, take evenly spaced stitches about ¼ in (6mm) long through the fabric layers, sewing close to the seamline but within the seam allowance. Take several stitches onto your needle at one time, before drawing the thread through the fabric.

Uneven basting

Uneven basting is a good stitch for edges where less control is required during machine stitching. It is also used to mark position lines such as stitching lines for pleats or large darts.

Working from right to left, take stitches about ¼ in (6mm) long and 1in (2.5 cm) apart through the fabric layers, sewing close to the seamline but within the seam allowance. You can use longer and more widely spaced stitches to mark a stitching line.

Slip basting

This stitch is very useful when you need to match two pieces of patterned fabric, whether it is a large print, a check, or a stripe, because it is worked on the right side of both pieces of fabric.

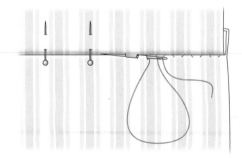

Press one edge of one fabric piece to the wrong side along the seamline. With the right sides up, place this folded edge along the seamline of the corresponding piece, so that the pattern matches exactly, and pin it in place as shown. Working from right to left and keeping your stitches evenly spaced, take a ¼ in (6mm) stitch through the lower piece on the seamline next to the fold, then take the next stitch through the fold of the upper piece. Continue alternating the stitches in this way, removing the pins as you go.

TIPS

If your thread starts to twist, hold both ends of the thread and let the needle dangle down, so that the thread starts to untwist itself while you carefully slide your fingers down the thread with your other hand.

As you gain more expertise, you will find that you can dispense with basting on many simple seams. Just pin the layers together as shown, then machine stitch the seam, stitching slowly and carefully over the pins to avoid breaking the needle; alternatively, remove the pins as you stitch.

Permanent stitches

None of the following hand stitches is difficult to master, but they all require a little patience to keep them neat and evenly sized. **Note:** These instructions are for a right-handed person; reverse the instructions if you are left-handed.

Backstitch

This is a very strong stitch that looks like machine stitching on one side of the fabric and like overlapping stitches on the other. As well as securing hand sewing (see page 33), it can be used to repair seams.

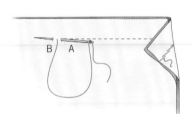

Thread your needle and secure the thread. Working from right to left, bring the needle and thread through to the front of the fabric. Insert the needle at A, $1/16-1/8$ in (2–3mm) to the right of the point where it emerged, and bring it up at B, the same distance to the left of the point where it originally emerged. Draw the thread through and repeat, inserting the needle again the same distance to the right of where it has just emerged, and continue in this way along the line.

Blanket stitch

This stitch was originally used to hem the edges of blankets, hence its name. Today it is mainly used as a decorative embroidery stitch. See page 72 for how to work this stitch.

Blind hemming

This is a stitch used to fasten hems in place invisibly. For how to do this hand hemming stitch, see page 64.

Herringbone stitch

This decorative stitch can also be used as a strong functional stitch to secure hems. See page 72 for how to do it.

Overcast stitch

This stitch is the most effective way of finishing a raw edge by hand, as the thread snakes smoothly along, enclosing the fabric's raw edges.

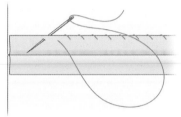

Thread your needle and secure the thread. Working from right to left, take tiny diagonal stitches over the edge of each seam allowance, about $1/8$ in (3mm) deep and $1/4$ in (6mm) apart.

Running stitch

This is worked just like even basting stitch (see page 33), except that the stitches are smaller. Running stitch is mainly used for hand gathering (see page 106), though it can also be used as a decorative stitch.

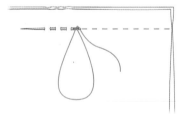

Thread your needle and secure the thread. Working from right to left, weave the needle in and out of the fabric, taking several stitches onto the needle before drawing the thread through.

Slip hemming

For how to work this invisible hemming stitch, see page 64.

Slipstitch

Slipstitch is nearly invisible and is used to sew up a seam, or a gap in a seam, quickly and easily from the right side of the fabric.

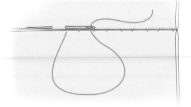

Thread the needle and secure the thread. Working from right to left, bring the needle through one folded edge, slip the needle through the fold of the opposite edge for about $1/4$ in (6mm), and draw the needle and thread through. Continue in this way to join both edges.

Whipstitch

Whipstitch is generally used to stitch two finished edges together, but it can also hold a raw edge or a finished edge securely against a flat surface.

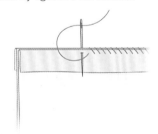

Thread the needle and secure the thread. Working from right to left, insert the needle at right angles through the edges, picking up one or two threads from the back and then from the front edge; draw the thread through. Insert the needle in the back edge to the left of the first stitch and bring it out through the front edge. Continue in this way until the two edges are joined. Slanted stitches will be produced, which can be short or long, depending on how close together your stitches are.

Preparing to stitch a seam

A seam is created when you machine stitch two or more pieces of fabric together with a seam allowance. It's important to stitch exactly on the seamline, and the use of seam guides and basting will make this easier.

Seam guides

Before you start to stitch any type of seam, you will need to double-check what width of seam allowance has been included on your pattern. This is $^5/_8$ in (1.5cm) on most commercial patterns, but on smaller projects and enclosed areas, such as collars and cuffs, it could be reduced to $^3/_8$ in (1cm). A seam guide is a huge help for keeping your stitching straight. Guidelines can often be found stamped into your machine's needle plate (the silver plate that sits under the machine foot), but if your machine does not have these markings, then masking tape or a magnetic seam guide is a good alternative. Practice using seam guides on scrap pieces of fabric, to give yourself confidence before you start your first project.

Needle plate guidelines
Most sewing machines have a needle plate that is etched with measured guidelines. The guidelines can be positioned to the right, left, and front of the needle and are usually marked in eighths of an inch and millimeters, so you can select the correct guideline for any given seam allowance or row of stitching. Line up the edges of your fabric against the guidelines and keep them aligned as you sew. Some bobbin covers are also marked with horizontal crosslines, which can be used as a pivoting guide for stitching corners.

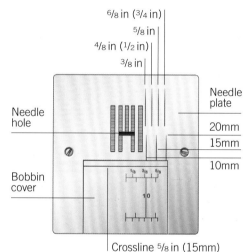

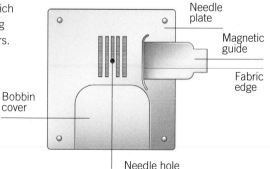

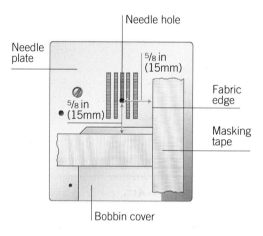

Masking tape
Stick a strip of masking tape $^5/_8$ in (1.5cm), or the width of your seam allowance, to the right and front of the needle hole to use as a guide. Align the fabric edge with the left-hand edge of the tape when you stitch.

Magnetic seam guides
Magnetic seam guides are available from good notions (haberdashery) stores. They are great for using with mechanical machines, but the magnets can interfere with electronic models. They obviously also need a metal surface to adhere to.

Machine basting

As already discussed, it is best to pin (see page 32) and then baste all seams together before machine stitching, for accuracy. Basting is usually done by hand (see page 33), but in some cases it is more desirable to do it by machine, such as when applying a zipper (see page 54) or when checking a garment for fit. To do this, set your machine at the longest possible stitch length—around 5 stitches per inch (5.0mm stitch length)—for easy unpicking, and then stitch along the seamline as explained overleaf but without securing the thread.

Stitching plain seams

Most seams are sewn with a straight stitch on your machine. The most popular is the plain seam, in which the seam allowances are pressed open, but in some cases a self-enclosed seam is more appropriate (see page 40).

Securing threads and basic straight seaming

To stop a seam from splitting open, you will need to secure the ends of the stitching at the start and finish of each seam, either by reverse stitching, which is the stronger method, or by tying the thread ends together, which gives a neater, flatter finish. Here is how to stitch a simple seam using each of these methods.

TIPS

Don't reverse stitch beyond the cut edge, as the fabric may then be pulled down into the machine through the hole in the needle plate.

Before you start to sew your seam, test your stitching on a folded scrap of fabric, using the appropriate needle and matching thread, to double-check that your stitch length, tension, and foot pressure are adjusted correctly for the fabric you are using. If they are not, refer to your machine manual for more details.

Simple seam secured with reverse stitching

Pin and then baste the fabric pieces together as explained on pages 32 and 33, then place them under the machine foot, lining up the raw edges with the correct seam guideline. Position the needle on the seamline about 1/2 in (1.2cm) from the top edge, and lower the presser foot. Set your machine to reverse, and then stitch backward, almost to the top edge. Change the setting to stitch forward, and stitch along the seamline to the lower edge, keeping the raw edges on the guideline. Set the machine to reverse once again and stitch backward for 1/2 in (1.2cm) up the seamline. Cut the threads close to the stitching.

Note: In these diagrams we show the reverse stitching alongside the forward stitching, but this is only to make it visible in the diagram. Reverse stitching is actually done on top of the first stitching.

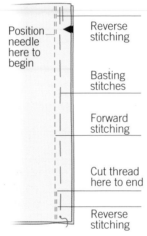

Position needle here to begin

Reverse stitching

Basting stitches

Forward stitching

Cut thread here to end

Reverse stitching

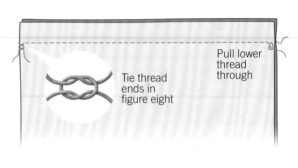

Tie thread ends in figure eight

Pull lower thread through

Simple seam secured with tied ends

Pin and baste the fabric pieces together as explained on pages 32 and 33, then place them under the machine foot, lining up the raw edges with the correct seam guideline. Leaving long thread ends at the top edge, stitch along the seamline from top to bottom. Cut the threads, leaving long ends. At one end, pull on the upper thread to bring a loop of the lower thread to the top of the fabric; use a pin to pull the lower thread through completely, and then tie the ends together in a square (reef) knot. Repeat at the other end of the seamline and cut off the excess thread.

Pressing seams

Pressing at every stage of sewing is essential for a professional finish. Pressing as you go (see page 10) will not only make seams smoother, so that it is easier to piece garments together, but it will also make everything more accessible. If you leave pressing to the very end, you will find it is difficult to get access inside to press properly.

Unpick the basting stitches. Using an iron, press over the seam in the direction in which it was stitched, to embed the stitches. Finally, press the seam open so that the seam allowances lie flat, using your fingers to open out the seam edges as you press.

Stitching shaped seams

When making up a garment or other project, you will come across shaped seams, which either follow a curve, bend around corners, or form acute angles. Here are a few techniques to help you get to grips with these situations.

Stitching a curved seam

A curved seam is stitched in the same way as a plain straight seam, but you need to take care when guiding the fabric under the machine needle, to ensure that the correct seam allowance is kept around the entire edge. To maintain control, use one of the seam guides as described on page 35, a shorter stitch length—around 12 stitches per inch (2.0mm stitch length)—and a slower machine speed.

Stitching an outward-cornered seam

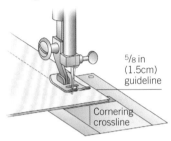

5/8 in (1.5cm) guideline

Cornering crossline

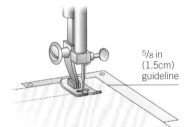

5/8 in (1.5cm) guideline

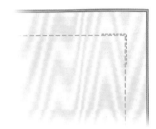

1 If there is no cornering crossline on your bobbin cover, stick a piece of masking tape the same distance in front of the needle hole as the depth of the seam allowance (see page 35). Reverse stitching to start, stitch a 5/8 in (1.5cm) seam toward the corner, stopping with the needle down in the fabric when the bottom edge of the fabric reaches the cornering crossline or edge of your tape. Raise the machine foot.

2 Pivot the fabric on the needle through 90 degrees, bringing the bottom edge of the fabric in line with the 5/8 in (1.5cm) guideline on the needle plate. Lower the foot and continue stitching to the end of the seam, reverse stitching to finish.

3 Strengthen the corner by reinforcing it with a row of small stitches, about 12 stitches per inch (2.0mm stitch length), extending 3/4 in (2cm) either side of the corner, stitching and pivoting accurately on top of the existing stitching line.

Stitching an inward-cornered seam

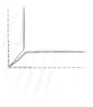

1 Using a tape measure and chalk pencil (see page 10), measure and mark the corner point of the seamline on the wrong side of the upper fabric. Reverse stitch to start, then stitch the seam to the marked corner point, stopping with the needle down in the fabric. Raise the machine foot and pivot the fabric on the needle through 90 degrees. Lower the foot so that it sits parallel to the raw edge and continue stitching to the end of the seam, reverse stitching to finish.

2 Strengthen the corner by reinforcing it with a row of small stitches, about 1/16 in (2mm) long, extending 3/4 in (2cm) either side of the corner, stitching and pivoting accurately on top of the existing stitching line. Using a sharp pair of small, pointed scissors (see page 9), clip into the corner at an angle, close to the stitching, taking care not to cut through the stitches.

Stitching an acute corner

When you are stitching a corner that has a more acute angle, such as on a collar point, the best way to create a neat, well-formed point is to "blunt" the corner by taking one stitch across it on a fine fabric, two on a medium one, or three on a heavy or bulky fabric, rather than pivot the work straight through 90 degrees.

Reducing bulk in plain seams

Stitching the seams neatly and accurately is the first stage of constructing your project, but to get a crisp, professional finish and less of a "homemade" look, you will also need to trim away excess fabric from the seam allowances, so that there won't be unsightly lumps and ridges. This is particularly important on seams that are enclosed, such as collars, cuffs, and waistbands, or where several layers of fabric have been sewn together.

Trimming a right-angled outward corner

To create a sharp, neat angle, cut across the corner of the seam allowances, as shown, close to the stitching, but making sure that you do not cut through the actual stitching. When turning your seam to the right side, use a pair of small, pointed scissors or a knitting needle to carefully push out the point, making sure you do not push too hard and form a hole.

Trimming an acute corner

This type of corner needs a little more fabric trimmed away. Cut across the corner of the seam allowances close to the stitching, as for the right-angled outward corner, then trim away another sliver of fabric from each side, as shown. The aim is to reduce the fabric in the seam allowances so that when the corner is turned right side out, the seam allowances will have room to lie flat.

Trimming seam allowances

When several layers of fabric have been stitched together (for example, when you are applying a waistband or a collar) or when seams are matched (at the crotch or underarm, for example), you can end up with as many as four layers of fabric, making the seam very thick and bulky. Trimming the seam allowances as shown below reduces this thickness.

Grading seams

Also known as layering seams, grading involves trimming the seam allowances to graduated widths so that the narrowest seam allowance is $3/16$ in (5mm) wide and the widest lies next to the most visible seam edge, such as the top collar. If you are using a fabric that frays, don't trim too closely.

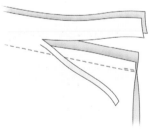

Trimming matched seams

Trim away the fabric corners within the seam allowance after you have stitched the seam, as shown.

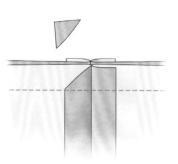

Notching or clipping curved seams

Notches are small wedges of fabric cut from the seam allowances of outward curves, as shown here, to allow them to lie smooth and flat. On inward curves you only need to clip (make snips) into the seam allowances to permit the edges to spread out and lie flat. Use a sharp pair of small, pointed scissors to notch or clip the curve at regular intervals, taking care to cut close to, but not through, the stitches. If the curved seams are to be visible on your project, then you will need to finish the seam allowances (see opposite) prior to notching or clipping.

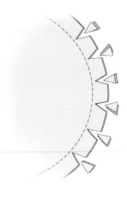

Finishing seam allowances

On woven fabrics in particular, if you don't finish the raw edges they will start to fray, weakening the seams. Finishing, also known as neatening, the seam allowances also gives your projects a cleaner, more professional touch. Here are a few methods of finishing edges with your sewing machine.

Zigzag stitch

This machine stitch can be used on most woven fabrics. It is the fastest way to finish a raw edge, leaving it neat and flat. As well as seam allowances, it is suitable for other raw edges, such as hem or facing edges. Use an overcasting foot if your machine has one, to achieve the smoothest zigzag stitch; this foot has a special pin over which the stitches are formed, stopping them from pulling up tight and creating a lumpy edge.

TIP
If your machine does not do zigzag stitch, straight stitch along the edges using a short machine stitch, ¼ in (6mm) in from the edge of each seam allowance, then trim the edges with pinking shears; alternatively, overcast the edges by hand (see page 34).

Plain zigzag using an overcasting foot
This stitch is best suited to firm, natural fabrics and to heavy or bulky ones.

First trim the edges to remove any fraying, then refer to your instruction manual for the correct stitch settings. Place the edge of your fabric under the overcasting foot, with the pin on the foot along the edge of the fabric, and stitch along the raw edge.

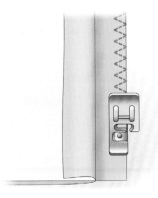

3-step zigzag stitch
Many machines come with a 3-step zigzag or a multi-step zigzag. Rather than stitching one stitch from point to point, the 3-step zigzag has three stitches from point to point. This stops the fabric from puckering and so is used to finish seam allowances on man-made fabrics and other fabrics that tend to pucker.

First trim the edges to remove any fraying, then refer to your instruction manual for the correct stitch settings. Place the edge of your fabric under the overcasting foot, with the pin on the foot along the edge of the fabric, and stitch along the raw edge.

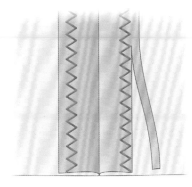

Zigzag without an overcasting foot
Using the normal zigzag foot, stitch on a scrap of your fabric before you begin, to double-check the stitch tension and make sure that it doesn't roll up the fabric edges.

Set your stitch for a medium-width and short-length zigzag, then stitch ⅛ in (3mm) from the edge of the seam allowance. Trim away the outer edge of the fabric, close to the zigzag stitching.

Self-enclosed seams

Self-enclosed or self-finishing seams are very hard-wearing. In this type of seam, the seam allowance is contained within the finished seam, so there are no raw edges to be finished separately. There are four basic types of self-enclosed seams—flat-fell seams, self-bound seams, French seams, and mock French seams. To achieve a neat, professional finish, it is vital to stitch, trim, and press them accurately. The following instructions are given for the standard ⅝ in (1.5cm) seam allowances, but if your seam allowances are wider, it is advisable to trim them down carefully and accurately to ⅝ in (1.5cm), unless your pattern indicates otherwise.

Flat-fell seam

A flat-fell seam is a decorative, double-topstitched seam that is worked on the right side of the fabric, so care must be taken to keep the stitching and pressing even. Flat-fell seams are suitable for jeans, reversible clothes, sportswear, and menswear, or where added strength is needed, but do not use them on very thick fabrics, as they will be much too bulky.

TIP

If you are using a flat-fell seam to join pant (trouser) legs or shoulders, make sure that you press both seams to lie in the same direction.

1 With the wrong sides of the fabric together, machine stitch a ⅝ in (1.5cm) plain straight seam (see page 36). Press the seam allowances open, then press them both to one side. Trim the lower seam allowance to ¼ in (6mm).

2 Carefully fold over the edge of the top seam allowance by ¼ in (6mm), and press flat. Pin at right angles to the seam, enclosing all raw edges, then baste. Machine stitch in place close to the pressed edge, stitching through all layers of fabric and reverse stitching at each end to secure. Remove basting.

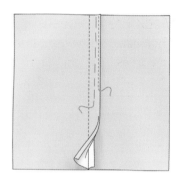

Self-bound seam

Although it is a little fiddly, this seam creates a neat, flat finish for visible seams. It works best with lightweight fabrics that do not fray too easily.

1 With the right sides of the fabric together, machine stitch a ⅝ in (1.5cm) plain straight seam (see page 36). Do not press open, but carefully trim the upper seam allowance to ⅛ in (3mm). Fold over the edge of the lower seam allowance by ⅛ in (3mm) and press flat.

2 Fold the pressed edge over to meet the seamline, so that it just covers the stitching and encloses the raw seam allowances. Pin, baste, and press in place. Machine stitch close to the first pressed edge, stitching through all layers of fabric and reverse stitching at each end to secure. Remove basting and press the seam to one side.

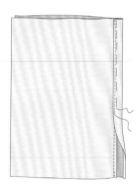

French seam

The French seam is only suitable for joining straight edges on lightweight fabrics. It is stitched twice, first from the right side and then from the wrong side, and is often used on sheer or semi-sheer curtains, duvet covers, and pillowcases, and on some semi-sheer or unlined garments, providing the seams are not curved.

1 With the wrong sides of the fabric together, pin and baste the two edges together. Machine stitch ¼ in (5mm) from the raw edges, reverse stitching at each end to secure.

2 Press the seam open, then refold the fabric, with the right sides together and the stitched line placed exactly on the folded edge. Press the folded edge flat, then pin and baste the pressed edge in place. Machine stitch again, working ⅜ in (1cm) from the seamed edge, enclosing the raw edges, and reverse stitching at each end to secure. Remove basting and press the seam to one side.

Mock French seam

This seam can be used in place of a French seam, especially on curves or when you need to match a pattern.

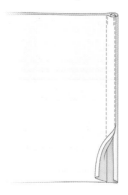

With right sides together, machine stitch a ⅝ in (1.5cm) plain straight seam (see page 36). Trim the seam allowances to ½ in (1.2cm). Turn ¼ in (6mm) to the wrong side on the edges of both seam allowances, and press in place, matching the folded edges. Stitch the folded edges together and press the seam to one side.

Lapped seams

Interlining and batting (wadding) are bulky fabrics and so are best joined with a lapped seam to give a completely flat finish. The raw edges are left unfinished as they are normally enclosed inside the outer fabrics.

With both pieces of fabric right side up, lap one of the raw edges directly over the other by approximately ¾ in (2cm). Pin, baste, and machine stitch the two layers together with a zigzag stitch, or with two rows of straight stitches ¼ in (6mm) apart. Trim the raw edges close to the stitching.

Topstitching

Topstitching consists of rows of machine stitching done from the right side of the fabric, after the seam has been sewn. It can be functional as well as decorative—for example, to hold seam allowances flat, or to attach a pocket.

Topstitching a seam

When topstitching a seam, it may be impossible to see the seam guidelines stamped onto your sewing machine needle plate, so to keep your stitching nice and straight use the width of your machine foot as a guide for $1/4$ in (6mm) stitching. For wider-width topstitching, you can use a row of basting stitches or even a strip of masking tape placed next to the topstitching position as a guide to follow. The thread you use can be normal sewing thread, which works best with fine fabrics, or for thicker fabrics use a heavier specialist topstitching thread (see page 20).

Single topstitching a seam

Single topstitching consists of one row of stitching, usually worked parallel to a seam or an edge.

Finish the seam allowances on a plain seam (see page 39), and press them both to the side you are going to topstitch. Working from the right side, stitch down the side of the seamline, using the presser foot or an alternative method to keep the stitching the same distance from the seamline, and sewing through both seam allowances at the same time.

Double topstitching a seam

Double topstitching consists of two rows of stitching, one on each side of a seamline, placed at equal distances from it.

Finish the seam allowances on a plain seam (see page 39), and press them open. Working from the right side and using the width of your presser foot or an alternative method to keep the stitching an even distance from the seamline, topstitch down both sides of the seam, always stitching in the same direction and stitching through the seam allowances at the same time.

Topstitching around a finished edge

Topstitching is often done around a finished edge, such as a collar, cuffs, or a pocket flap. In these instances the topstitching, which is parallel to the edge, has a double purpose—as well as being decorative, it prevents the underside of the edge from rolling to the outside.

Working from the right side, line up your finished seam edge on the chosen guideline and begin stitching at a raw edge, turning any corners by lifting the presser foot and pivoting your fabric around the needle (see page 37). Trim your threads ends even with the raw edges.

Edge stitching

This is similar to topstitching but the row of machine stitching is worked very close to the edge or the seamline, around $1/16$ in (2mm) from it. Edge stitching can be used as a decorative feature along with topstitching to give a double-topstitching effect to finished edges. It can also be applied along the edges of pleats to help maintain the fold and to give a sharper crease (see page 132). If edge stitching finishes partway down a garment and not at a raw edge, as in pleats, then bring the thread ends through to the underside and tie them (see page 36).

Specialist stitching

This section covers some special stitching techniques, which, though purely functional, are very important in creating a professional-looking garment. These techniques include understitching, staystitching, ease stitching, and sink stitching.

Understitching

Understitching, like topstitching, is done from the right side of the fabric. It is stitched close to the seamline and its purpose is to keep facings and seams lying flat and in a particular direction.

Grade the seam allowances (see page 38), with the narrowest seam next to the facing. With the right side of the facing on top, topstitch close to the seamline, stitching through the facing and the seam allowances at the same time.

Ease stitching

On some garments you may be required to do ease stitching, which provides a bare amount of fullness, called ease, at a place where it is needed. It is worked in the same way as machine gathering (see page 104), but the stitch length is set to about 9 stitches per inch (3.0mm stitch length), and the stitches are drawn up just enough to pull in the fibers of the fabric to fit a smaller area, without forming any puckers or gathers. It creates a rounded curve in an area such as the top of a sleeve (the "cap" or "head") so that it can accommodate the curve at the top of the arm, or at the elbow to allow for bending.

Staystitching

This is a row of machine stitching that is worked on the cut garment pieces before you start to sew them together. It is used on curved and bias seams such as necklines and waist edges, to stop them from stretching while you are sewing the garment.

Sink stitching

Sink stitching, also known as stitch-in-the-ditch, is basically a topstitching method for securing layers of fabric together, with minimal stitching visible, even though it is done from the right side. It is commonly used in patchwork and quilting (see page 84) and for attaching waistbands and linings.

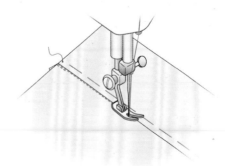

Machine stitch a row of medium-length straight stitches just inside the seam allowance of your cut piece. Lay the cut piece back on your pattern to double-check that it is still the same size and shape. Continue sewing the garment.

Stitch a plain seam and then press the seam allowances to one side. Pin and baste in place the piece that you need to secure to the seam. Working from the right side of your garment, using a straight stitch on your machine and either matching or invisible thread, stitch as close to the seam as you can get without stitching over it, catching the layers of fabric as you sew. When you have finished, the stitches should be barely visible, hidden by the ridge of the seam.

Buttons

Buttons are by far the most popular type of fastening for blouses, coats, and jackets. However, choosing them needs careful consideration. Always stick to the size given on your commercial pattern (as the designer will have chosen the size to suit the garment design), the weight and type of fabric suggested, and the button spacing provided. The buttonhole size (see page 46) will depend entirely on the size and type of button selected.

Button types

Although there is a myriad of button types, from tiny, delicate, pearl ones to huge, bright, bold buttons, there are basically only two types: sew-through buttons and shank buttons.

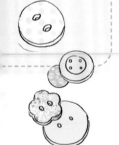

Sew-through buttons
These have either two or four central holes. For decoration, sew-through buttons can be sewn on flat, but for a closure you will need to make a thread shank so that the button will lie flat on top of the buttonhole without pulling on the fabric below; the fabric thickness at the buttonhole indicates the length of shank you need. Sew-through buttons are best for lightweight fabrics and can be sewn on by hand, or by machine if your machine has a button foot and is capable of doing a zigzag stitch.

Shank buttons
A shank button has a small stub or loop called a shank on the back, through which the button is attached. This allows for the thickness of the fabric so that the decorative part of the button sits on top of the buttonhole. Shank buttons are therefore not the best choice for purely decorative use, as they will flop over without having a buttonhole to keep them upright. This type of button is best suited to medium-weight and heavy fabrics.

Jeans buttons
A type of no-sew shank button, the jeans button is really strong and is great for casual pants and jackets. It consists of two separate parts— a lower pin section and a button top—which are positioned on each side of the fabric and then hammered together. This type of button comes in a pack with a special tool for attaching, plus instructions.

Attaching buttons

Buttons usually come under a lot of strain during wear, especially at waistlines and across the bust; if you are not careful, the fabric can even tear. Therefore it is very important to reinforce the layers of fabric with a piece of interfacing (see pages 18 and 19) or at least to make sure that they are stitched onto your garment through a minimum of two layers of fabric. Buttons are best sewn on with a strong topstitching thread, available from notions (haberdashery) stores, but if you are unable to obtain this, then use a double length of regular sewing thread.

Attaching a sew-through button by hand
If you are attaching a button for a closure, rather than as a decorative feature, then you will need to create a thread shank to lift the button away from the fabric surface, allowing for the second layer of fabric (with the buttonhole) to sit comfortably underneath the button without straining the fabric below. The same method is used whether it is a two-hole or a four-hole button.

1 Mark the position of the button with a chalk pencil (see page 10) and secure the thread on the right side of the fabric at the button mark with a backstitch (see page 33). Bring the needle and thread up through one hole in the button and start to pass it down through the second hole.

2 Lay a matchstick across the top of the button and pull the needle through to the wrong side so that the thread holds the matchstick in place. Bring the needle up through the third hole (or the first one again, if the button has only two holes), take it over the matchstick, and pass it down through the fourth hole (or the second again, if the button has only two holes). Take about six stitches through each pair of holes, then carefully slide out the matchstick.

3 Lift the button away from the fabric so that the stitches are taut, and pass the needle back down through the button only. Wind the thread tightly around the stitches to form a thread shank. Secure the thread on the underside with a couple of backstitches.

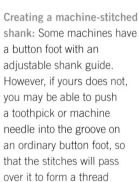

Attaching a sew-through button by machine

If your machine can work a zigzag stitch, then you should be able to attach sew-through buttons by machine. A special foot is usually required for doing this, so check your manual to see whether your machine comes with one as standard, and exactly how to sew buttons in place.

Machine-stitching a button on flat: Drop the feed dog (see your manual for more details), attach the correct foot, and set your machine to zigzag stitch. Mark the button position with a chalk pencil and place the button on top, positioning it under the machine foot with the holes in the button inside the slot in the foot. Lower the foot onto the button. Set the stitch width to the distance between the holes in your button. Slowly sew about ten stitches, then pull the fabric out toward the back of the machine. Cut the threads, pass the upper thread through a hand-sewing needle, and take it through to the underside of the fabric. Knot the ends together and trim off any excess thread.

Creating a machine-stitched shank: Some machines have a button foot with an adjustable shank guide. However, if yours does not, you may be able to push a toothpick or machine needle into the groove on an ordinary button foot, so that the stitches will pass over it to form a thread shank. When you have stitched on the button, wind the upper thread around the shank several times, as shown for step 3 of Attaching a Sew-Through Button by Hand (see above), before passing the upper thread through a hand-sewing needle to take it through to the underside of the fabric. Knot the ends together and trim off any excess thread.

(see above)

TIP
If you are not feeling confident, don't use the machine foot pedal; instead, simply turn the hand wheel manually several times until the button is stitched on.

Attaching a shank button by hand

Manufacturers use special commercial machines to attach shank buttons, but for the homemaker, sewing them on by hand is the only option, as the shank underneath the button is inaccessible to the machine needle.

Mark the position of your button on the right side of the fabric with a chalk pencil (see page 10). Secure your thread on the right side at the mark, using a backstitch (see page 33). Position the button shank on the mark, with the shank hole parallel to the buttonhole. Bring the needle and thread through the shank hole, take the needle down through the fabric layers, and then bring it up on the other side of the shank. Repeat, taking about six stitches through the shank. Secure the thread on the underside with a couple of backstitches.

Reinforcement buttons

A reinforcement button is required at points of great strain and also on heavy fabrics, or where there are many layers of fabric. You can buy clear plastic buttons, made specifically for this purpose, but small shirt buttons will work just as well. However, you will need to make sure that they have the same number of holes as your main buttons. Reinforcement buttons are sewn onto the main garment at the same time as you attach your main button.

Follow the instructions for Attaching a Sew-Through Button by Hand (see page 44), but place the reinforcement button on the inside of your

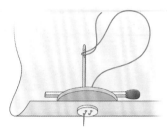

garment, directly under the main button, and sew through both sets of holes on both buttons. On the last stitch, bring the needle and thread through the hole of the main button only, remove the matchstick, and complete the shank.

Buttonholes

In this book we are looking at machine-worked "square" buttonholes, which are the most popular type. You may come across bound buttonholes, especially on tailored garments such as jackets and coats, but it's best not to attempt these till you are more experienced at sewing.

The standard buttonhole is basically a slit made through the fabric, with a bar tack at each end (see opposite), and the edges finished with a machine zigzag stitch. In the past, buttonholes were finished by hand using buttonhole stitch, a special type of blanket stitch with a knot on the raw edge to strengthen it.

Most modern sewing machines offer several buttonhole variations, such as a rounded end for shirts and blouses, and a keyhole shape for thicker fabrics. Check your manual to see what your machine is capable of doing. The buttonhole is stitched through all layers of fabric, and as with attaching buttons, it is advisable to use interfacing to reinforce the area. The buttonhole is not cut until after the stitching has been completed.

Calculating the length

Working out the correct length for a buttonhole is crucial, as it must be large enough to allow the button to pass through easily, but not so large that it won't hold the item securely fastened. Buttonhole sizes are normally marked on sewing patterns, and slider or sensor buttonhole feet (see page 48) set the size of the buttonhole automatically when the button is placed in the rear of the foot, but it is still a good idea to know how to calculate the length for yourself.

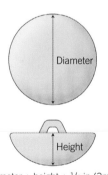

Diameter + height + 1/8 in (3mm) = buttonhole length

The length of the buttonhole for either a sew-through button or a shank button is determined by the diameter and height of the button. Add them together, then add an extra 1/8 in (3mm), which allows for the bar tacks at each end.

Marking buttonholes

Vertical buttonholes normally sit along the center front line of a blouse or jacket, and are marked on a commercial pattern. When the garment edges are overlapped and fastened, the center lines should match. On a vertical buttonhole the button is positioned $1/8$ in (3mm) down from the top. On a horizontal buttonhole the button sits at the end of the buttonhole, so it must be positioned $1/8$ in (3mm) beyond the center front line, so that when the garment is fastened the buttons lie directly along the center.

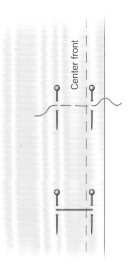

Center front

Place your pattern piece on top of your garment, matching the center front line. Mark the buttonhole positions at each end, with pins placed at right angles to the buttonhole. Remove the pattern piece, but leave the pins in position. Mark a line between the pins with either a chalk pencil or a line of basting stitches.

Stitching buttonholes

Most modern machines have built-in mechanisms that stitch buttonholes either semi-automatically or fully automatically, so there is no need for you to change the needle position or to pivot your fabric manually. However, older sewing machines may ask you to hand-guide the buttonhole, so please check your manual.

Working a semi-automatic buttonhole

A semi-automatic or sliding buttonhole foot has a gauge down the left-hand side to measure the buttonhole length. Before stitching you will need to mark your buttonhole position and move the slide so that the lower mark on the slider is even with the start of the buttonhole marking on your garment. Draw both threads to the left under the foot.

1 Set your machine to the first stage of the buttonhole; you may have to turn your stitch selector or press a memory button on your machine to stitch each part of the buttonhole, so check your manual. Start the stitching—the machine will make the first bar tack. Stitch backward up the left-hand side of the buttonhole, stopping at the top mark.

2 Press the memory button or move your dial to stitch the next bar tack.

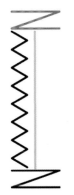

3 Finally, stitch down the remaining side of the buttonhole.

4 Place a pin at each end of the buttonhole just before the bar tacks, to protect them. Using a seam ripper, carefully slit down the center of the buttonhole between the pins.

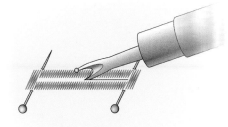

TIPS

If you have mislaid your sewing machine manual, the Internet is a good place to look for advice on sewing machine processes, such as working a buttonhole.

Practice making and slitting buttonholes on scrap fabric before you attempt to work them on your actual garment, to ensure you have the correct size and your stitches are well balanced.

On thicker fabrics, if you find that your stitching is not dense enough, stitch around the buttonhole a second time, directly over the first stitching. This will also give it extra strength.

Working an automatic buttonhole

On a fully automatic buttonhole foot, you can set the buttonhole length by placing a button in the button holder, which cuts out the process of measuring beforehand. Double-check your manual for the correct method for your machine.

Attach the buttonhole foot to your machine and set the machine to a square buttonhole. Put the button in the holder, then pull the button holder to the back and adjust it so that the button is held tightly in place. Pull the buttonhole lever down as far as it will go. Draw both threads to the left under the foot, then place the foot over the buttonhole position, with the needle hole on the foot even with the front end of the buttonhole marking. The machine will complete the whole buttonhole to the correct length, usually all in one operation. Slit the center of the buttonhole, as shown for the semi-automatic buttonhole (see page 47).

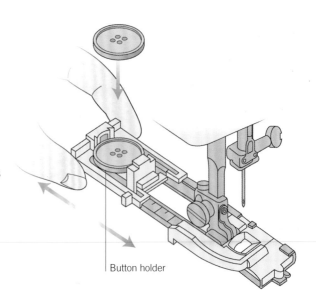

Button holder

Pillow (cushion) types

Although pillows (cushions) appear to come in a great variety of shapes and sizes, they do actually fall into just two categories: knife-edge (as shown in the project on the following pages) and box-edge. A knife-edge pillow is made of two pieces of fabric stitched around the edge. It is thicker in the center and tapers off to the side seams. A box-edge pillow is the same depth across the whole pillow and needs a separate strip of fabric, sometimes called a boxing strip or a gusset, stitched between the top and bottom pieces of fabric. A bolster is actually a box-edge pillow, where the top and bottom pieces are small and the side strip very deep.

   Both knife-edge and box-edge pillows can be used as throw pillows, but the box-edge variety can also be used for seat cushions. Knife-edge pillows are generally soft and filled with feathers or polyester fiber. Box-edge pillows can also have this type of filling, but when used as seat cushions they will be filled with high-density foam, wrapped with polyester batting to make it softer and more rounded.

Making a pillow pattern

If you want to re-cover an existing pillow, or make a different size to the one suggested in the following project, it is best to make yourself a paper pattern to work out how much fabric you will need to buy. To do this you will need to measure your pillow form (cushion pad). The patterns explained opposite allow for zipper closures.

Knife-edge pillow pattern

1 If your pillow form is square or rectangular, measure the length and width; if it is round, measure the diameter. Draw up a pattern piece to these measurements for the front cover, adding a ⅝in (1.5cm) seam allowance to all edges.

2 For the back pattern piece, fold the front pattern in half and trace around the shape onto a second piece of paper, adding a ⅝in (1.5cm) seam allowance to what was the folded edge; this will become your center back seam. This pattern piece will be used to cut out two fabric back pieces.

3 To calculate the zipper length, measure your pattern piece along the center back seam, and allow for a zipper approximately 5in (12.5cm) shorter than this measurement.

Rectangular or square box-edge pillow pattern

1 Measure the length, width, and depth of the pillow form. For the top and bottom pieces, draw up one pattern piece to the measurements for the length and width, adding ⅝in (1.5cm) seam allowance to all edges. This pattern piece will be used to cut out one fabric top and one fabric bottom.

2 A zipper is usually installed into a seam running lengthwise down the center of the side strip, placed at the back of the pillow, to enable the foam pillow form to be inserted into the cover. Therefore, draw up one pattern piece for the back strip, as long as the width measurement and as wide as half the depth measurement, adding a ⅝in (1.5cm) seam allowance to all edges.

3 For the rest of the side strip, draw up a pattern piece as long as twice the pillow length measurement, plus the pillow width measurement, and as wide as the depth of the pillow side, adding a ⅝in (1.5cm) seam allowance to all edges.

4 To calculate the zipper length, allow for a zipper approximately 2in (5cm) shorter than the length of the back strip pattern piece.

Bolster pattern

1 Measure the diameter of the ends, the length of the bolster, and the circumference. Draw up one pattern piece for the main part of the bolster, using the length and circumference measurements. Using the diameter, draw up a second pattern piece, which will be used for both ends. Remember to add a ⅝in (1.5cm) seam allowance to all edges.

2 To calculate your zipper length, measure your main pattern piece along the length measurement, and allow for a zipper approximately 5in (12.5 cm) shorter.

TIP When estimating your fabric quantities and cutting out, always make sure that the edges of the pattern pieces where the zipper is to be applied are placed along the straight grain, parallel to the selvages (see page 27).

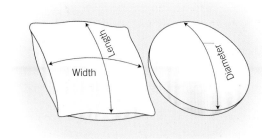
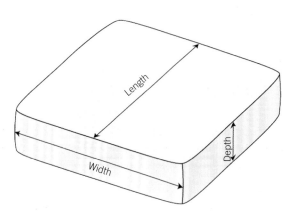
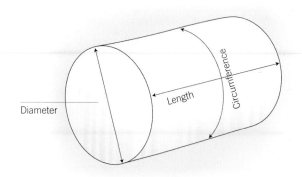

Embellished envelope pillow

An envelope pillow, which has an overlapping opening at the back rather than a zipper, is one of the easiest projects to begin with and a perfect way to put into practice some of the techniques you've just learned in the Plain Sewing workshop. This one uses simple running stitch to embellish the front cover with contemporary circular designs, and is fastened at the back with a button and buttonhole.

Cutting out your fabric

Draw out your pattern pieces on paper—for the front, draw a 17¼ in (44cm) square, and for the backs, draw a 10¼ x 17¼ in (26 x 44cm) rectangle and a 13 x 17¼ in (33 x 44cm) rectangle. Cut out one fabric piece from each of these pattern pieces, making sure that the long edges of the patterns are parallel to the selvages.

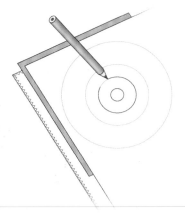

2 Using one color at a time, thread the crewel needle with all six strands of the embroidery floss, with it doubled to create 12 strands, as this will make big, bold stitches. Using the photograph as a guide, and working from the wrong side of the fabric, hand sew parallel rows of running stitches (see page 34) across one of the large circles (2), keeping the stitches about ⅜ in (1cm) in length and as even as possible.

1 Finish all four edges of the front piece (see page 39). Using dressmaker's carbon paper and a pencil, trace the five circular designs from the templates onto the wrong side of the front piece.

You will need

Five circular design templates traced off from the pattern sheets at the back of this book (see page 192)

⅔ yd (50cm) of 54in- (137cm-) wide linen, silk, or velvet fabric

⅛ yd (10cm) of 36- (90cm-) wide lightweight fusible interfacing

Matching thread

16 x 16in (41 x 41cm) pillow form

Stranded embroidery floss in contrasting colors

Crewel needle

Dressmaker's carbon paper

One ⅞ in (22mm) button

One ⅜ in (10mm) reinforcing button

Note

⅝ in (1.5cm) seam allowances are included unless otherwise stated.

Stitch seams with right sides together and notches matching, unless otherwise stated.

3 On the other large circle (5), using a different color of floss, start at the center and sew the running stitches in the spiral pattern, again making the stitches even in length, until you reach the outer edge of the circle. On the medium-size circle (4), stitch bands of longer individual stitches radiating out from the center, changing the color of the floss with each band of stitches. Finally, sew individual straight stitches across the two small circles (1 and 3), scattering them in any direction, until the circles are filled.

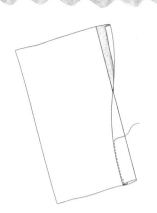

4 From the interfacing (see pages 18 and 19), cut two 1⅝ x 17¼ in (4 x 44cm) rectangles. Iron the interfacing to the wrong side of each back piece along one long edge. Along each interfaced edge, fold and press ⅜ in (1cm) and then a further 1¼ in (3cm) to the wrong side, enclosing the interfacing and raw edge. Pin and machine stitch in place, close to the inner pressed edge of each, and then finish the remaining raw edges of each back piece.

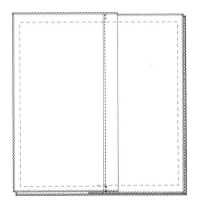

5 Lay the front piece right side up on a flat surface, and then place the smaller back piece right side down on top, with finished edges even. Place the remaining back piece on top of that, right side down, keeping the finished edges even and overlapping the hemmed edges. Pin and baste the pieces together around the four finished edges. Machine stitch the pieces together, pivoting the fabric at the corners (see page 37). Remove the basting, trim the corners (see page 38), and turn the cover right side out through the back opening; press.

6 Using pins, mark the position of the buttonhole (see page 47) on the top back piece, halfway down the opening, equidistant from the edge of the hem and the stitching line, and parallel to them. Keeping the lower back out of the way, machine stitch a buttonhole at the position marked (see pages 47–8). Hand sew the larger button to the underneath back piece to correspond, using the reinforcing button to secure (see page 46). Insert your pillow form through the back opening and fasten with the button.

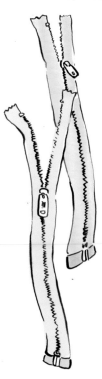

Workshop 2

Zippers

Several different types of zippers are available and this workshop covers the main types and how to apply them, from the basic, centered zipper to the invisible zipper and the more challenging fly front. Once you have mastered these techniques you will be able to make many different projects, including the fabulous bean bag at the end of this workshop.

Types of zippers

Zippers come in various types, weights, and lengths, but there are three basic types: conventional, invisible, and open-ended.

Conventional zippers

A conventional zipper has either plastic or metal teeth attached to a woven tape. The "stops" mean that the zipper is permanently closed at the base and it locks at the top. Available in a wide range of colors, this type of zipper is sewn into an opening in a seam and is suitable for dresses, skirts, and tops. The plastic-toothed varieties are usually lighter and more pliable and so are ideal for lightweight cottons, viscose, silk, and polyester crepe de chine. Use metal zippers for thicker fabrics or where the opening requires a much stronger fastening, such as on jeans.

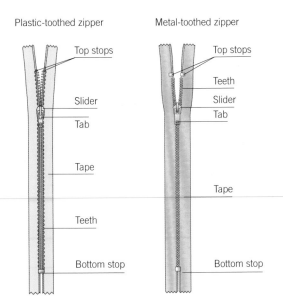

Plastic-toothed zipper — Top stops, Slider, Tab, Tape, Teeth, Bottom stop

Metal-toothed zipper — Top stops, Teeth, Slider, Tab, Tape, Bottom stop

Invisible zippers

An invisible zipper, also known as a concealed zipper, is different from a conventional zipper in both appearance and installation. When the invisible zipper is closed, it is hidden in the seam with no teeth showing on the right side—only the tab at the top can be seen. It has to be applied using an invisible-zipper foot attached to your machine and is stitched in place from the wrong side.

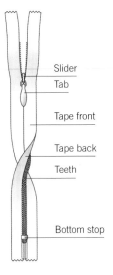

Slider, Tab, Tape front, Tape back, Teeth, Bottom stop

Open-ended zippers

An open-ended, or two-way, zipper is open at both ends and is sewn into a seam that is required to open and close completely. It is available with either plastic or metal teeth, although color choice is usually more restricted than in the other two zipper types. Used in jackets and leisurewear, this type of zipper is applied in much the same way as a conventional zipper, but it can also be sewn with the teeth exposed, as a design feature.

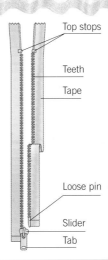

Top stops
Teeth
Tape
Loose pin
Slider
Tab

Zipper application methods

The main methods of installing zippers are centered application, lapped application, and fly front, all of which can be used with conventional zippers—see overleaf. A different method, using a special machine foot, is used to apply an invisible zipper (see page 58), while a double-ended zipper is applied in a variation of either centered or lapped application. All of these methods involve installing the zipper into a seam, but if a zipper is to be applied where there is no seam, exposed application is used (see page 59).

Zipper machine feet

These feet are designed to help you with your zipper application, by guiding your stitching to lie as close to the teeth as possible, ensuring your zipper sits correctly in your garment. You should find a conventional-zipper foot in your sewing machine accessories, but you may have to purchase an invisible-zipper foot separately.

Conventional-zipper feet

Clip-on conventional-zipper foot—top

Clip-on conventional-zipper foot—underside

Screw-on conventional-zipper foot

Invisible-zipper feet

Clip-on invisible-zipper foot

A conventional-zipper foot is used to stitch any seam with more bulk on one side than the other, not only when applying a zipper but also when covering cord (see page 162). It is used in centered, lapped, fly-front, and exposed-zipper application methods. Various types of clip-on conventional-zipper feet are available—they differ quite a lot, but they all do the same job, which is to help you stitch right on the outside edge of the foot, ensuring you are pressed snugly up against the zipper teeth. However, for stitching on heavy-duty zippers and thicker piping cord you will find a screw-on conventional foot works better, as it will allow for more depth and thickness; it usually also has a slider that allows you to move the foot across to the exact position required, making it more accurate. When using a zipper foot, remember to adjust the needle position so that you stitch in the exact spot required.

An invisible-zipper foot usually clips on, but screw-on versions are also available, depending on your machine. Using an invisible-zipper foot makes applying invisible zippers very simple. The teeth of the zipper tuck up inside the tunnels in the foot during stitching so that the stitching line is right under the teeth on the seamline.

Applying a conventional zipper

The two main ways of applying a conventional zipper are centered application, in which the zipper sits along the center of the opening, with the stitching that holds the zipper in place machined on both sides at an equal distance from the seamline, and lapped application, in which one edge of the opening is stitched close to the zipper teeth and the open edge is lapped over the zipper teeth, covering the first row of stitching. A conventional zipper can also be used for a fly front (see pages 56–7).

Centered application

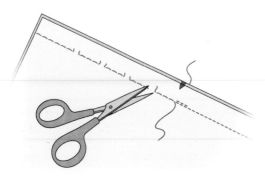

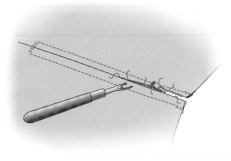

1 Stitch the garment seam up to the zipper notch; reverse stitch to secure. Adjust your machine stitch length to the largest size and machine baste the zipper opening edges together without reverse stitching at the ends. Using a sharp pair of small scissors, snip the stitches on the bobbin thread at 3/8 in (12mm) intervals along the zipper opening, to allow for easy removal later on. Finish the seam allowances (see page 39) and press the seam open.

2 Place the zipper face down on the seam allowances, so that the zipper teeth run down the center of the seam and the bottom stop is just below the notch. Pin and hand baste the zipper in place.

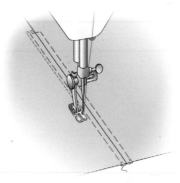

3 Working from the right side of the garment, with a regular stitch length on your machine, stitch the zipper in place. To do this, have your zipper foot to the left of the needle; starting just below the zipper stop at the seamline, stitch three or four stitches across the bottom, pivot your work (see page 37), and stitch up to the top of the zipper, keeping your stitching parallel to the seamline. Reverse stitch at each end of the stitching to secure.

4 Reposition the zipper foot to the right of the needle. Starting again at the base of the zipper, stitch the other side in place, as before. Remove the basting stitches and unpick the seam covering the zipper teeth.

Lapped application

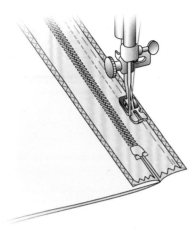

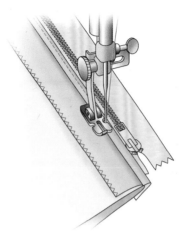

1 Follow step 1 of Centered Application (see opposite). To position the zipper, open out the right-hand seam allowance and place the zipper face down on top, so that the zipper teeth run down the center of the seamline and the bottom stop is just below the notch; pin and baste the zipper in place. Position your zipper foot to the right of the needle and machine stitch in place about ¼ in (6mm) away from the teeth.

2 Turn the zipper face up, forming a fold in the seam allowance. Bring the fold close to the zipper teeth, but not over them, and pin in place. Reposition your zipper foot to the left of the needle and stitch along the edge of the fold through all thicknesses.

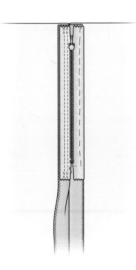

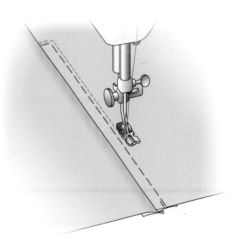

3 Lay your garment out flat, wrong side up. Pin and baste the loose zipper tape in position, through all layers of fabric.

4 Working from the right side of the garment, with a regular stitch length on your machine, stitch the zipper in place. To do this, have your zipper foot to the right of the needle; starting just below the zipper stop at the seamline, work four or five stitches across the bottom, pivot your work (see page 37), and stitch up to the top of the zipper, keeping your stitching parallel to the seamline. Reverse stitch at each end of the stitching to secure. Remove the basting stitches and unpick the seam covering the zipper teeth.

Fly-front application

A fly-front zipper is the traditional method used for men's pants (trousers), and often for women's pants and skirts, as it creates a neat and durable closure. A metal pants (trouser) zipper is recommended as it is stronger, but if the color range is limited a lightweight skirt zipper can be used.

With the advent of unisex clothing, especially jeans, there is often confusion as to which way the zipper should lap. Traditionally for women's clothing it should lap right over left, and for men it is left over right. The following application instructions show the women's direction.

Fly facings

Your pattern will supply all the necessary pattern pieces for applying a fly zipper, but they may differ slightly.

Grown-on facing

Your pattern may have the zipper facings "grown on," rather like ears, as in the left-hand diagram. If this is the case, once you have cut out all your fabric pieces you will need to trim away the facing from the left front to leave a ⅝ in (1.5cm) seam allowance, as shown in the right-hand diagram. Continue to construct the opening as shown in Fly-Front Application, omitting step 2.

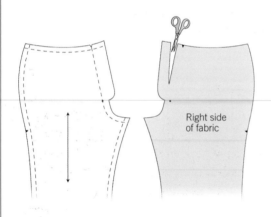

Right side of fabric

Separate facing

In this instance your front pant legs or skirt front will simply have a ⅝ in (1.5cm) seam allowance down the front crotch or center front seam, to which you will need to attach a separate facing to the right front crotch or center front seam. There is no trimming away to be done on the left-hand side. The instructions given here are written for this method.

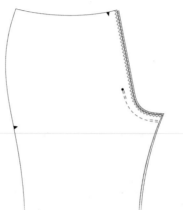

1 Finish the center front crotch edges (if trousers) or center front seam edges (if a skirt)—see page 39. With right sides together and matching the crotch dots, stitch the front legs together from the matched dots to the inside leg edges (on trousers), or from the matched dots to the hem edges (on a skirt), using a ⅝ in (1.5cm) seam and reverse stitching at the ends to secure.

2 Press interfacing to the wrong side of the zipper facing, if your pattern requires you to do so, and finish the long curved edge. Fold the left front of the garment down to expose the right front. With right sides together and matching the waist edges, stitch the long straight raw edge of the facing to the right front opening edge with a ⅝ in (1.5cm) seam, stitching from the waist edges to the matched dots. Press the seam allowances toward the facing, and understitch them to the facing (see page 43). Press the facing to the wrong side.

3 Press under ⅜ in (1cm) on the left front opening edge. Working on the right side of the garment, place the zipper right side up under the pressed edge, with the top of the zipper tapes to the waist edge, or zipper position, as your pattern requires. Baste the zipper in place. With a zipper foot on your machine, stitch the zipper in place along the pressed edge close to the zipper teeth. Snip into the left front crotch seam allowances at the base of the zipper and press toward the right front, or press open if your pattern instructs.

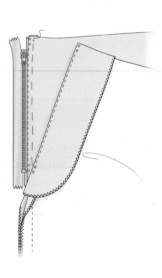

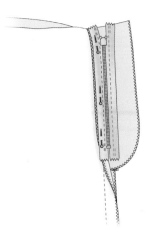 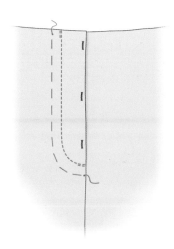 

4 Working from the right side, with the zipper teeth closed, lay the seamed edge of the right faced opening ¼ in (6mm) beyond the zipper teeth and pin in place. Turn over to the wrong side and baste the loose zipper tape to the zipper facing only. Machine stitch the tape to the facing. Remove the basting stitches but leave the pins in place.

5 Working from the wrong side again and keeping everything flat, baste the zipper facing to the right front leg or skirt. Turn the garment over to the right side and carefully topstitch the facing in place, using the topstitching marker as a guide, if your pattern has one, and reverse stitching at each end to secure. (If your pattern doesn't have a guide, see Topstitching Guide, below.)

6 Press the zipper placket in half lengthwise, with wrong sides together, and finish the long and short unnotched edges together. Baste and then stitch the long finished edges of the placket to the left front opening seam allowances. Working from the wrong side, with the zipper closed and the placket covering the wrong side of the zipper, stitch the base of the placket to the zipper facing only. Remove the basting stitches.

Topstitching guide

One of the most visible parts of the fly front is the curved topstitching, which can be done in a contrasting color, such as on jeans, to make it really stand out. It is essential to make sure that this stitching is nice and straight and runs parallel to the center front seam, with a smooth curve at the base. A topstitching guide is a simple but useful tool to help you achieve this. For an example of a zipper topstitching guide, please see the one included with the jeans-style skirt pattern at the back of this book.

Making a topstitching guide

1 On your pattern, measure the length of the zipper opening from the waist edge to the zipper base. Draw a line on a piece of paper and mark this measurement along the line. Measure 1in (2.5cm) to the left of this line and draw a second line parallel to the first. Using a small curved object, draw a smooth curve from the second line around to the base of the zipper on the first line. Draw a line at right angles at the top of the zipper to join the two lines. Cut out the template.

2 When you are ready to do your topstitching, use double-sided tape to stick the marker onto the right front opening, with the straight side up to the edge of the opening and the lower curved edge at the base of the opening. Baste along the outer curved edge following the template. Remove the template and then carefully work the topstitching row just outside the basting stitches, reverse stitching at each end to secure. Remove the basting stitches.

Applying an invisible zipper

An invisible zipper is a popular choice for dresses, skirts, and pillow (cushion) covers, and can be substituted for either a lapped or a centered zipper application. Many people shy away from putting in an invisible zipper, thinking it will be difficult, but it is one of the easiest to apply. It is applied to an open seam, on the seam allowances only, so no stitching shows on the right side, and is done with the help of a special grooved zipper foot (see Zipper Machine Feet, page 53).

Invisible application

1 Finish the edges of the two garment pieces into which the zipper is to be installed. Place the open zipper, face down, on the right side of the garment, with the zipper teeth running along the seamline and the top stop ³/₈ in (1cm) down from the neck or waist seamlines. Pin in place. Roll the zipper teeth so that they stand away from the tape and fit the right-hand groove of the foot over the teeth. Stitch from the top of the zipper down to the slider, reverse stitching at the ends to secure.

2 Pin the other zipper tape to the right side of the remaining garment piece, with the zipper teeth running along the seamline and the top stop ³/₈ in (1cm) down from the neck or waist seamlines. Fit the zipper teeth into the left-hand groove and stitch in place, as before.

3 Close the zipper and attach a conventional-zipper foot to your machine. Pin and baste the garment seam below the zipper, right sides together. Lower the needle down into the fabric at the end of the zipper stitching line, slightly above and to the left, and stitch the seam to the lower edge of the garment. Tie the thread ends to secure.

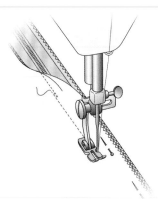

4 To hold the lower zipper ends down, stitch each tape end to the seam allowances only, not the garment.

5 Open the zipper and stitch across the top of each tape, keeping the zipper teeth in the rolled-back position for easy sliding.

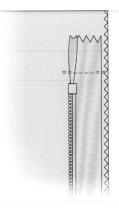

Applying an exposed zipper

Exposed zippers have the zipper teeth left exposed as a decorative feature of the garment. They are normally set into an opening where there is no seam, but open-ended zippers are also often left exposed down jacket fronts. Before the zipper is applied, a facing needs to be attached to the opening, which strengthens and finishes the edges and prevents the opening from stretching.

Exposed application

1 Cut a facing 3¼ in (8cm) wide and 2in (5cm) longer than the zipper. Mark the opening down the center of the garment on the wrong side of the fabric, to the same length as the zipper teeth, plus ⅝ in (1.5cm). With right sides together, baste the facing to the garment, keeping the top raw edges level. Working from the garment side so that you can see your drawn line, stitch ⅛ in (3mm) from the center line on each side and across the bottom. Remove the basting stitches and carefully cut down the center line to within ⅜ in (1cm) of the bottom, then cut diagonally into the corners.

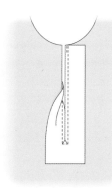

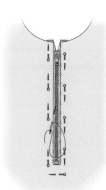

2 Turn the facing to the inside and press flat, making sure that none of the facing shows on the right side. Center the zipper under the opening with the bottom stop at the base of the opening. Pin and then slip-baste (see page 33) the zipper to the garment along both folds at each side and across the bottom.

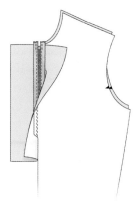

3 Lift the bottom part of your garment up to expose the end of the facing and small triangle of fabric. Using a zipper foot on your machine, stitch across the base of the triangle to secure it to the zipper tapes and the facing, reverse stitching at each end to secure.

4 Fold back one side of the garment until the facing stitching line is visible. Working from the top to the bottom, stitch the garment to the zipper tape along the facing stitching line. Repeat for the other side. Remove the slip-basting.

5 Trim the facing down to within ¼ in (6mm) of the zipper tapes down both sides and across the bottom. Finish the trimmed edges.

Brilliant bean bags

They're bold, fun, versatile, and the ultimate in relaxation. Make them in a trendy cotton print for a teenager's bedroom, or a coated cotton fabric for outdoor living. A simple liner containing the beads is hidden inside thanks to an invisible zipper, allowing the outer cover to be easily laundered.

You will need

Bean bag templates traced off from the pattern sheets at the back of the book (see page 192)

2⅓ yd (2.20m) of 45in- (112cm-) wide cotton print fabric

1yd (90cm) of 45in- (112cm-) wide contrasting cotton fabric

3¼ yd (2.90m) of 45in- (112cm-) wide lining fabric

22in (56cm) invisible zipper to match contrasting fabric

Matching thread

5 cubic feet (0.14 cubic meters) of fire-retardant polystyrene bean bag filling beads

Note

⅝ in (1.5cm) seam allowances are included unless otherwise stated.

Stitch seams with right sides together and notches matching, unless otherwise stated.

Cutting out your fabric

From the print fabric cut out two side panels. From the contrasting fabric cut out two base pieces, one top, and one handle. From the lining fabric cut out two side panels, two base pieces, and one top, making sure that the grainlines are parallel to the selvages on every piece that you cut out (see page 27).

Making the inner bag

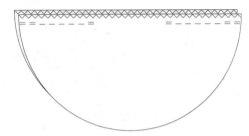

1 Finish the straight edges of the lining base pieces and stitch them together, leaving a large central opening to allow for the filling to be added. Press the seam open and the opening edges ⅝ in (1.5cm) to the wrong side.

2 Fold a lining side panel in half along one of the "V" sections, matching top notches and raw edges. Pin and baste the raw edges together and then stitch from the matched notches on the top edge down to the dot, taking a ⅝ in (1.5cm) seam allowance and reverse stitching at each end to secure. Finish the seam allowances together and press to one side. Repeat with the remaining "V" sections on both side panels.

3 Pin, baste, and stitch the side panels together at the side seams. Finish the seam allowances together and press to one side.

4 Matching notches to side seams, stitch the top piece to the top edges of the side panels, snipping into the seam allowances of the side panels to help you to stitch around the circle. Finish the seam allowances together and press toward the side panels. Repeat to attach the base to the side panels, matching up the seams. Turn the inner bag right side out through the opening in the base, and fill with the beads. Slipstitch the opening edges closed (see page 34).

Making the cover

5 Finish the straight edges of the two base pieces. Positioning the zipper centrally along these straight edges, install the invisible zipper, following steps 1, 2, and 3 of Applying an Invisible Zipper on page 58. Repeat step 3 to close the seam above the zipper.

6 Stitch the "V" sections and join the side panels, as shown in steps 2 and 3 of Making the Inner Bag. Fold the handle piece in half lengthwise and stitch the long edges together, reverse stitching at each end to secure. Press the seam open. Turn the handle right side out and press flat with the seam running down the center back. Topstitch the folded edges ¹/₄ in (6mm) from the edge (see page 42).

7 Matching notches, pin and baste the handle to the right side of the top piece. Attach the top and base to the side panels following step 4 of Making the Inner Bag, ensuring that the zipper is open before you begin, so that you will be able to turn the cover right side out.

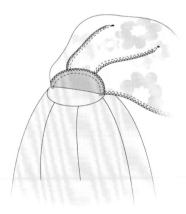

8 With the wrong side of the cover to the right side of the inner bag, catch the two tops together at the side seams with a few hand stitches in the seam allowances. Turn the cover right side out, carefully working the inner bag down through the zipper opening. Holding the handle, give the bean bag a shake to straighten out the inner bag. Make sure that it is sitting correctly inside, then close the zipper.

Making a doorstop

A scaled-down version of the bean bag makes a fabulous doorstop. Trace off the doorstop templates from the pattern sheet at the back of the book, and cut out from ¹/₃ yd (30cm) of 45in- (112cm-) wide cotton fabric. Using ³/₈ in (1cm) seams, make up the cover following steps 1, 2, and 3 of Making the Inner Bag, then follow step 7 of Making the Cover to make and attach the handle. Now follow step 4 of Making the Inner Bag, filling it with rice or lentils and adding dried lavender if desired, before stitching the opening closed.

Workshop 3

Hems

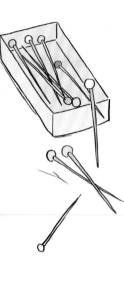

The hem is a sewing basic that gives a neat finish to a raw fabric edge. In this workshop we will show you some different kinds of hems and the basic techniques for doing them by hand and by machine. At the end of the workshop there is a project for a luxurious contemporary throw, which is reversible and which puts into practice some of the hemming techniques covered here.

Turned-up hems

The choice of hem will depend on what effect you want for your project and the type of fabric you are using, but the most common way of finishing an edge is the turned-up hem. Unless it is meant to be decorative, the finished hem is usually invisible on the right side of the garment.

On a turned-up hem, the hem allowance consists of extra fabric added to the bottom edge of your garment, and this is then folded to the inside and secured in place by hand, machine, or fusing. The hem allowance will be already included in the pattern and will be indicated by a line or words. The hem's shape—whether it's straight or gently curved—will dictate how much hem should be turned up. As a general rule, on straight hems such as curtains a deeper hem works best, but the more a hemline curves, the shallower the hem allowance should be.

Double hems

This is one of the simplest and most durable methods of finishing an edge. A double hem is folded over twice, as the name implies, before being machine stitched in place, enclosing the raw edge within the hem. You can make the hem as narrow or deep as you like and the depth of the fabric enclosed within the hem can vary to suit the thickness of the fabric you are using and the size of the hem.

Narrow double hem
This is a neat, inconspicuous finish that is often used on blouses, table linen, and sheer curtains.

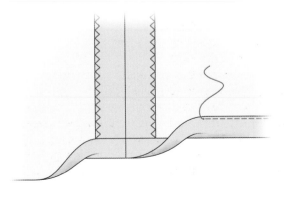

If the hem allowance on your project is for a deeper hem and you want only a narrow one, then trim the fabric down to ³/₄ in (2cm). Fold the raw hem edge over to the wrong side by ³/₈ in (1cm) and pin it in place. Press along the folded edge, taking care not to press on the pins, and removing them as you go. Fold again along the hemline. Pin and baste the pressed edge in place, keeping the grainlines aligned so that the hem doesn't twist. Press the hemline fold, then machine stitch the hem in place close to the first pressed edge. Unpick the basting stitches and give the hem a final press.

Deep double hem

This hem can be used as a more decorative finish, where the stitching becomes a feature. It works best on a straight hem edge. Before you begin to cut out your project, you will need to calculate the hem allowance required. Decide how far in from the finished hemline you want your stitching line to be and add ½ in (1.2cm) to this. Adjust the hem allowance to the calculated depth and cut out your project.

1 Before you begin to fold up your hem it is best to reduce the bulk of seams you've already stitched by trimming any seam allowances to half their original width, within the hem allowance. This is particularly important on thicker fabrics to make sure that the hem lies smoothly at the seams.

2 Fold the raw hem edge over to the wrong side by ⅜ in (1cm) and pin it in place. Press along the folded edge, taking care not to press on the pins, and removing them as you go. Fold again along the hemline. Pin and baste the pressed edge in place. Press the hemline fold, then machine stitch the hem in place close to the first pressed edge. Unpick the basting stitches and give the hem a final press.

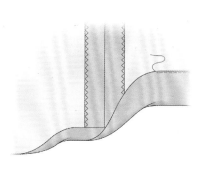

TIP
An ironing board is a great place to work when measuring and folding up a hem, as it enables you to deal with a small section at a time.

Inconspicuous hems

While topstitched hems look great on many items, a discreet finish is often preferable for others. There are many hemming techniques, but blind hemming by machine or by hand, slip hemming by hand, and securing a hem with iron-on hemming tape are all methods that will be barely visible on the right side.

Blind hemming by machine

This type of hem is stitched using a blind-hem foot, which usually comes with your machine, so check your manual to find out whether your machine can do this process. Blind hemming is a strong, fast way of achieving an unnoticeable finish. It uses straight stitches on the hem allowance with a zigzag stitch every sixth stitch or so to catch in the main fabric layer. However, it is a little trickier to master than it looks, so practice a few times on scraps of your fabric before you attempt to stitch any real hems in place.

1 Finish your hem edge (see page 39) and press the hem allowance to the inside, taking care not to stretch it. Pin and baste the hem in place close to the folded hem edge. Attach the blind-hem foot to your machine and set your stitch selector to the blind-hem setting (refer to your manual for the exact details).

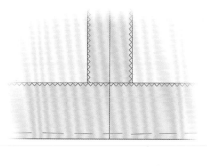

2 Lay the hem allowance face down and fold the garment back to reveal the finished hem edge, so that it extends roughly ¼ in (6mm) beyond the fold. Keeping the extension even, pin and baste it in place all around the hem. With the hem allowance still face down, position the fabric under the machine foot, with the folded edge up against the foot guide. Check the stitch width to make sure that the needle just pierces the fold when it swings over to the left side; if the needle moves over too far, the stitches will show on the right side of the fabric, so adjust the stitch width. When you are satisfied, stitch the hem in place, keeping the guide tightly up against the folded edge. Remove all basting stitches and smooth the hem back down.

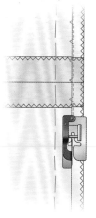

Using fusible hem tape

Avoid stretching the tape during application or letting the iron touch the tape, or you will have a sticky iron that will be difficult to clean.

Fusible hemming tape is very difficult to remove once it has been applied, so make sure your hem is correct and level before you apply it.

Do a pressing test on a scrap of your fabric before you begin, to make sure that the tape bonds securely and that the hem looks all right from the right side.

On heavy fabrics, use the widest tape so that more of the hem is bonded to support the weight. Also allow extra pressing time, especially at the seams.

Blind hemming by hand

These hand stitches are taken inside the hem—that is to say, between the hem and the actual garment—so that on the finished hem no stitches are visible. Also known as blindstitch, this is a quick and easy stitch that can be used on any flat hem with a finished edge.

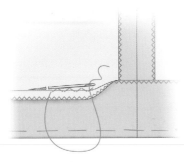

Finish your hem edge (see page 39) and press the hem allowance to the inside, taking care not to stretch it. Pin and baste the hem in place close to the folded hem edge. With the hem allowance on top, work from right to left with the needle pointing to the left (reverse this if you are left-handed). Fold back the top edge of the hem allowance and fasten the thread just inside it. About 1/4 in (6mm) to the left take a very small stitch in the garment (no more than two or three threads), then take the next stitch 1/4in (6mm) to the left in the hem allowance. Continue in this manner, keeping the stitches even and alternating them between the garment and the hem, until your hem is secured in place. Remove the basting stitches.

Slip hemming by hand

Slip hemming by hand is used to secure a folded hem edge in place, and is most commonly used for hemming curtains. This small, neat stitch is also known as uneven slipstitch and is almost invisible on the right side of your work.

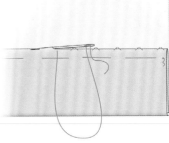

Press the hem allowances to the wrong side, then pin and baste them in place. Working from the right to the left (reverse this if you are left-handed), secure the thread on the inside of the hem fabric, then bring the needle out through the hem fold. Opposite, in the garment, take a very small stitch (no more than two or three threads). Take the needle back into the folded edge and run the needle inside the fold for approximately 3/8 in (1cm). Bring the needle out and draw the thread through. Continue in this way alternating the stitches between the fabric and the fold. Make sure the stitches are not pulled too tightly or the fabric will pucker on the right side.

Hemming tape

This is a strip of nonwoven, fusible bonding web that is inserted between the finished hem allowance and the fabric. When the hem is pressed with a steam iron, it "melts," bonding the two surfaces together. This is the quickest and easiest way to secure a hem, but you need to do it properly for a satisfactory result. Fusible hemming tape can be used on any fabric that can be steam ironed, but ironing times vary depending on the fabric's fiber content and thickness. Fusible hemming tape is available in 3/4in (2cm) and 1 1/4 in (3cm) widths, but it can be applied to hems that are deeper than these measurements.

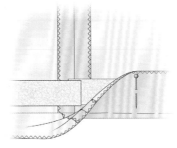

1 Finish the hem edge (see page 39) and press the hem allowance to the wrong side; baste the hem in place close to the hem fold. Starting at a seam, slip the hemming tape between the hem allowance and the garment, with the top edge of the tape just below the finished edge, pinning it in place as you work around the hem. Overlap the tape ends by 3/8 in (1cm).

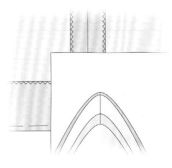

2 With your iron set at the appropriate steam setting for your fabric, bond the hem lightly in place by pressing between the pins with the tip of the iron. Remove the pins. Finally, use a damp pressing cloth on top of the hem to press a section at a time, holding the iron on the cloth until it is dry. Continue all around the hem in this way, allowing the fabric to cool before handling it. Remove the basting stitches.

Faced hems

A facing is necessary when the hem is an unusual shape, such as a curved opening edge of a wrapped skirt or jacket. With a faced hem, the hem allowance is eliminated and replaced with a seam allowance. A facing (a separate band of fabric) is stitched to this and turned to the inside so that it doesn't show from the right side. A separate facing is also recommended for widely flaring skirts—especially ones cut on the bias (see page 27), for which bias binding (see page 98) can be used as a facing.

Applying a shaped hem facing

1 Join the facing sections and press the seams open. Grade the seam allowances to reduce bulk (see page 38) and finish the smaller curved edge (see page 39).

2 With right sides together, pin and baste the facing to the garment hem edge, matching seams and keeping raw edges even. Stitch the facing to the garment taking the appropriate seam allowance, then grade and notch the curved seam allowances (see page 38). Remove the basting.

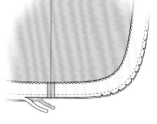

3 Press the seam open and then toward the facing. Now understitch the seam allowances to the facing (see page 43).

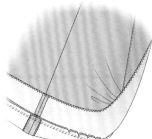

4 Turn the facing to the inside of the garment and blind hem the loose edge of the facing to the garment (see opposite).

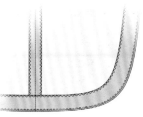

Applying a bias hem facing

1 Either use ¹⁄₂ in- (1.2cm-) wide readymade bias binding or make your own (see Making Bias Binding, steps 1, 2, and 3 on page 98) to use as a facing. If making your own, cut the strips 1in (2.5cm) wide and press over ¹⁄₄ in (6mm) to the wrong side along each long edge.

2 Open out one pressed edge of the binding and fold back ¹⁄₄ in (6mm) at one end. Beginning at a garment seam, pin the bias binding to the hem edge with right sides together and raw edges even, stretching the opened-out edge of the binding slightly to fit if you are applying it to a curved hem. Stitch in place along the press line, finishing about 2in (5cm) from the starting point, taking care not to stretch the hem as you sew.

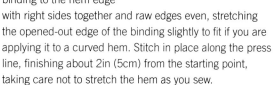

3 Trim away excess binding and lap the finishing end over the starting end. Pin and stitch the remaining binding in place along the press line.

4 Press the bias binding to the inside of the garment, ensuring that it does not show on the right side. Pin, baste, and secure the loose edge of the binding in place, either slip hemming it by hand or topstitching it by machine.

TIPS

If you want to lengthen a garment but there is not enough fabric left for a hem, you can apply a bias-faced hem using a bias binding that is 1–2in (2.5–5cm) wide to form the new hem.

The bias-faced hem method can also be used on a hem where the fabric is very thick and would cause an unsightly lump if folded over twice. Simply fold up the correct hem allowance once and then apply the bias binding over the raw edge, slipstitching it in place (see page 34).

Finishing hem corners

We have now discussed a few methods of securing hems in place, but what happens when your hem ends at a corner, such as on the front of a jacket or the side edge of a curtain? Here are three simple methods for finishing off corners: hemming a faced opening, mitering corners, and slipstitching corners on a double hem.

Hemming a faced opening

You read about faced hems on page 65, but you will also come across faced openings when you make blouses, jackets, or coats. The facing can be either a separate strip of fabric stitched to the front edge, or an extension of the front edge which is folded back to the wrong side. It is usually interfaced to add shape and support for buttons and buttonholes. The method shown below is for a separate facing, but this method can be used for a folded-back one, too.

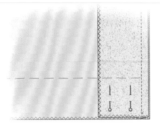 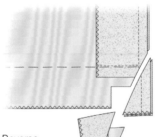 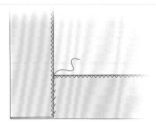

1 Finish the hem edge (see page 39) and mark the hemline position with a row of uneven basting stitches (see page 33). Fold the facing back onto the right side of the garment along the seamline (or foldline), keeping the hem edges even. Pin and baste in place.

2 Reverse stitching at each end to secure, machine stitch the facing to the main garment along the basted hemline, from the inner edge of the facing to the seam or fold at the garment edge. Grade the hem allowances as shown and clip the corners to reduce bulk (see page 38).

3 Turn the facing back to the inside of the garment and press the hem allowance to the wrong side along the basted line. Secure the hem in place using your chosen method, then slipstitch (see page 34) the inner edge of the facing to the hem allowance.

Mitering corners

The need to miter a hem occurs most often in curtain making, but this method can also be used on garments and is particularly useful for bulky fabrics. The definition of a miter is a joint in which each piece is cut at a 45-degree angle to its sides to form a neat, flat, right-angled corner. The hem edges should always be finished (neatened) appropriately before starting work; the miter can then be joined by either machine or hand stitching.

Hand-sewn miter
This is the most popular way to secure a miter and gives a more "bespoke" finish.

1 Pin and press the required lower hem allowance to the wrong side. Pin and press the required side hem allowance (on a curtain) or the facing (on a garment) to the wrong side. Working from the wrong side, open out both hems (or hem and facing). Taking hold of the corner point, fold over a triangle of fabric, up to where the two

hem foldlines cross. Making sure that all the foldlines are matched up, press along the new, diagonal fold, as shown. (These diagrams show hems that are the same depth at both the base and side, which produces what is known as an even miter. If the side hem or facing is not the same depth as the base hem, the procedure is still the same, though it is called an uneven miter.)

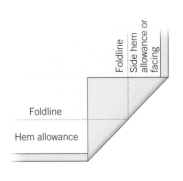

Foldline

Side hem allowance or facing

Foldline

Hem allowance

TIP
These instructions are for a hand-sewn miter on single-fold hems. To miter double hems, leave the first fold on both edges folded, then open out the second fold on each edge and proceed with the miter as for a single-fold hem.

2 Trim away the excess fabric from the folded corner to leave a ⁵⁄₈ in (1.5cm) seam allowance.

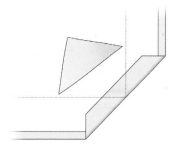

3 Refold the hems (or hem and facing) to form the miter, and slipstitch (see page 34) the pressed diagonal edges together. You can now secure the remainder of your hem in place by either hand or machine (see pages 63–4).

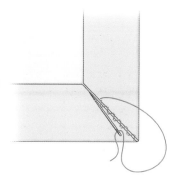

Machine-stitched miter
In this method, the diagonal pressed edges are stitched together first and then trimmed to form the miter.

1 Follow step 1 of Hand-Sewn Miter (see opposite). Open out the diagonal pressed corner and then, with right sides together, refold the corner diagonally in the opposite direction, so that the hem edges are even and the hem press lines lie on top of each other. Do not press, but pin the fabric layers together and stitch across the corner following the first diagonal press line, reverse stitching at each end to secure.

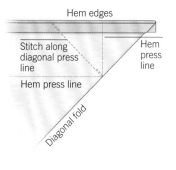

Hem edges

Stitch along diagonal press line

Hem press line

Hem press line

Diagonal fold

2 Trim away the excess fabric from the point to leave a ¹⁄₄ in (6mm) seam allowance and trim the seam allowance at the corner to reduce bulk (see page 38). Press the seam allowances open, then turn the corner right side out, easing out the corner carefully with the help of a small pair of scissors. Press the corner flat and secure the remainder of your hem in place by either hand or machine (see pages 63–4)

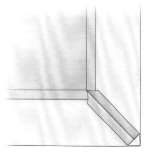

Slipstitching the corners of a double hem
If you are using a sheer fabric for your project, then the above methods are not suitable, as you would be able to see the seam allowances through the fabric. In this case you will need to allow twice the finished hem depth, so that you can double the hems entirely.

Make a narrow double hem (see page 62) down each side edge, as in the diagram showing a curtain. At the lower edge, fold over the required hem depth to the wrong side. Pin in place along the entire length, including the side hems. Press along the folded edge, removing the pins as you go. Fold the hem again so that the raw edge is enclosed and sits along the fold you've just pressed. Pin and baste the hem in place. Press the hemline fold, then either machine stitch or slip hem by hand (see page 64). Remove the basting and finish the hem corners by slipstitching (see page 34) the open edges of the base hem together.

Reversible throw

Nothing brings a "look" together more than a few well-chosen scatter pillows and a throw. We showed you how to make basic pillows in Workshop 1, so now you can create this elegant reversible throw using your newly acquired hemming and mitering skills. It's the perfect accessory for your bedroom or living room.

You will need

3¹/₂ yd (3.10m) of 45in- (112cm-) wide cotton print or embroidered fabric (you may need to purchase a little more of this fabric depending on the pattern repeat of your chosen fabric—see Cutting Out Your Fabric, below)

2yd (1.8m) of 60in- (150cm-) wide polar fleece fabric

Thread to match the cotton print fabric

Note

⁵/₈ in (1.5cm) seam allowances are included unless otherwise stated.

Stitch seams with right sides together, unless otherwise stated.

Cutting out your fabric

Cut out two 38 x 55in (96.5 x 140cm) rectangles from the cotton fabric. Important: These two pieces will be seamed together down the long edges to form one piece, so make sure that the pattern will match across the seam before you start to cut out (see page 174 for more information on allowing for pattern repeats).

Cut out one 47³/₄ x 67¹/₂ in (122 x 172cm) rectangle from the fleece fabric.

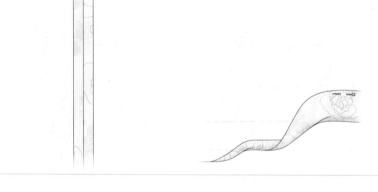

1 Pin and slip baste the two print fabric pieces together down one long edge, taking care to match up the pattern as you go (see page 33). Machine stitch the pieces together, reverse stitching at each end to secure. Remove the basting and press the seam open.

2 Press a double hem (see page 63) to the wrong side, around all edges of the print fabric piece—first pressing over ⁵/₈ in (1.5cm) and then 3in (7.5cm).

3 Lay the print fabric out on a flat surface, wrong side up, and open out the deeper part of the hems. Lay the fleece fabric in the center of the print fabric with its edges up to the deeper hem press line. Smooth out the layers to remove any wrinkles. With the hems still opened out, pin the two layers of fabric together at the corners and mid-points on each side, then baste the layers together, around the whole piece, working close to the edge of the fleece fabric.

4 Refold the deeper hems over the fleece fabric and form a hand-sewn miter at each corner, as shown on pages 66–7. Pin, baste, and then topstitch the remainder of the hems in place through all layers of fabric, working close to the edge of the hem. Finally, remove all basting stitches.

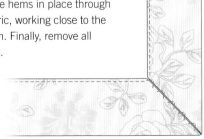

Workshop 4

Fancy stitches and pockets

In this workshop you will learn the basics of simple hand embroidery. Fancy stitches are decorative stitches worked over a traced design, which can be used to embellish all sorts of home-sewn projects. This is a craft that needs no special apparatus, and any person with a little patience can produce astonishing results. The other technique covered in this workshop is making pockets. Read on to find out more, then you will be able to make the charming 1950s-inspired apron.

Starting to embroider

There are two main types of embroidery stitches: freestyle (worked over a traced design or hot-iron transfer) and counted-thread embroidery (worked by counting the threads in the fabric, as in cross-stitch designs). In this workshop, we will be looking at a few freestyle embroidery stitches, which will enable you to embellish many projects.

Transferring and tracing designs

Transfers can be either single-impression or multiuse. As the name implies, the single-impression transfer can be used only once. The multiuse type can be used up to eight times.

Single-impression transfer

Cut out the design from the transfer paper. Heat the iron to a wool setting. Place the transfer face down on the right side of the fabric and secure with pins. Apply the iron for a few seconds and then remove it. Carefully lift the corner of the transfer paper to check that the design has come off satisfactorily; if not, reapply the iron. If the transfer paper sticks slightly to the fabric, gently rub the iron over the paper and peel it off, removing the pins one by one. Take care not to move the transfer or the fabric while you are working, otherwise you may smudge the design.

Multiuse transfer

Follow the instructions for the single-impression transfer, but heat the iron to a high temperature and protect the fabric by placing a sheet of tissue paper over the top before you iron the transfer in place. Check that the design has transferred to the fabric properly. If it hasn't, let the fabric cool slightly and then reapply the iron. Take care not to move the transfer or fabric while working or you may end up with a double impression.

Tracing method

Quite often a design has to be traced from a large sheet, or you will want to make a tracing from an actual reproduction or a design of your own. The simplest method involves using dressmaker's carbon paper (see page 10). This comes in a variety of colors, but yellow or light blue work best on dark-colored fabrics, and dark blue or black on light-colored fabrics. Place the carbon paper face down on the right side of the fabric, then place the drawing or tracing on top. Draw over all the lines of the design with a sharp pencil. Take care to press only on the lines of the design, especially on light-colored fabrics, otherwise the carbon may smudge.

Embroidery tools and materials

The effective combination of fabric, thread, design, and stitching, all carefully chosen for their suitability in relation to each other, can produce a beautiful piece of work. Always try to suit the thread to the fabric, the fabric to the design, and all of them to the purpose for which the article is being produced.

Threads

Embroidery can be done in cotton, wool, or silk thread, but the most commonly used thread is stranded cotton floss (see page 20). This consists of six loosely twisted strands, which you can separate according to the thickness you require. Three to four strands are most commonly used.

Needles

Always use crewel needles for embroidery—these come in sizes 4 to 7; the higher the number, the finer the needle. Avoid using too fine a needle, as the thread must be able to run loosely through the eye.

Thimbles

Thimbles are advisable for hand embroidery, to protect the middle finger when pushing the needle through the fabric. Buy a good-quality one in metal or plastic and make sure it fits well. Ensure that the thimble has no rough edges, otherwise it will catch and pull on your embroidery threads. Also see page 9.

Fabrics

Linen is perhaps the best background on which to embroider, but heavyweight cottons, silks, and brocades are also good. Never work embroidery on a poor-quality fabric, as all your effort will be wasted.

Embroidery hints

■ Clean hands mean clean work—smooth nails prevent snagged threads.
■ Never use too long a length of thread in your needle, as it will start to fray straightaway and it will easily get twisted.
■ Always embroider to the outside edge of a transfer line, so that the embroidery stitches completely cover the transfer lines.
■ Pad your ironing board with a thick blanket before pressing embroidery face down under a damp cloth. This will prevent the stitches from being flattened.

Embroidery hoops and other frames

Opinions vary as to whether to use a hoop or other type of frame when embroidering. For smaller work and certain stitches it is not necessary, but with areas of closely worked stitches the fabric is apt to pucker unless it is held taut in some kind of frame. There are several types, but the most common is the embroidery hoop, used for smaller pieces of work. This usually consists of two wooden or metal rings that fit closely one within the other, so that the fabric can be sandwiched tautly between the two. These rings come in various sizes, the most helpful having a small screw on the larger ring for loosening and tightening it, which allows for any thickness of fabric to be used.

How to use a hoop

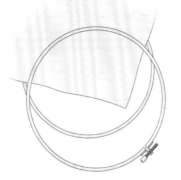

1 Separate the two rings and place the section of the fabric where the embroidery is to be worked over the smaller ring.

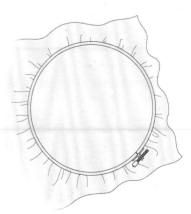

2 Place the larger ring over the top and push it down over the first ring, sandwiching the fabric in between to hold it taut. If a screw is attached, this should be tightened. The warp and weft threads of the fabric (see page 15) must be straight in the ring and not distorted.

Freestyle embroidery stitches

The main families of stitches used in freestyle embroidery are outline, flat, looped, chained, knotted, couched, filling, and composite. In this book we will be covering a selection of simple but useful stitches from most of these groups to get you on the road to discovering the joy of hand embroidery. Note: These instructions are for a right-handed person; reverse the instructions if you are left-handed.

 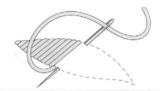  

Stem stitch

Working from left to right, with the needle pointing to the left, take regular-sized stitches, slanting slightly along the line of the design. This stitch is often used for flower stems and outlines, and the thickness can be varied by slanting the needle slightly more or less.
(*Outline stitch family*)

Satin stitch

The stitch is usually worked from left to right. Work straight stitches close together to fill in the shape. If you want to create a raised effect, running stitch (see page 34) or chain stitch (see below) can be worked over the shape first to form padding. The most important thing is to try to keep a good shape to your edge, and don't make the stitches too long, as they are liable to catch on things and be pulled out of position.
(*Flat stitch family*)

Herringbone stitch

Working from left to right, with the needle pointing to the left, bring the needle out on the lower line and insert it in the upper line a little to the right, taking a small stitch to the left. Pull the needle and thread through. Next, insert the needle back down on the lower line a little to the right and take another small stitch to the left, making sure your thread is above the needle. Continue working stitches in the same manner. For the best effect, try to make the stitches and spaces of equal size.
(*Flat stitch family*)

Blanket stitch

Working from left to right, with the point of the needle and the working edge toward you, bring the needle out by the edge. For the first stitch, insert the needle down through the fabric approximately 1/8 in (3mm) up from the edge and to the right (this gives a small stitch—for larger stitches, increase the distance). Take a straight downward stitch, bringing the needle back out at the edge and keeping the thread under the needle point. Draw the needle and thread through to form a looped stitch at the edge. Continue in the same way, spacing your stitches evenly.
(*Looped stitch family*)

Long and short stitch

1 A variation of satin stitch, this gets its name from the fact that the stitches are of varying lengths. It is often used to fill areas that are too large to fill with satin stitch. It can also be used to achieve a shaded effect, by subtly changing the colors of each row. The first row is worked alternately long and short and closely follows the outline of the shape.

2 The stitches of the second row come up through those of the first row, piercing the thread near the bottom of each stitch, and they vary in length. Shade one row at a time, filling the shape with stitches down to its base.
(*Flat stitch family*)

Chain stitch

Bring the thread through from the back of the fabric to the front and hold down the thread with your thumb. Insert the needle back through the fabric where it emerged and make a small stitch, bringing the point of the needle through to the right side. Pull the needle through, keeping the working thread under the point of the needle, to form a looped stitch on the right side. Repeat, taking the point of the needle down into the loop of the previous stitch. Continue in this way along the line of the design.
(*Chained stitch family*)

Feather stitch

1 Working from top to bottom, bring the needle out to the right side of the fabric and draw the thread through. Hold the thread down with your left thumb and insert the needle a little to the right on the same level. Bring the point of the needle back out a little down and toward the center, keeping the thread under the point of the needle. Draw the needle and thread through.

2 Insert the needle a little to the left on the same level and take a stitch down to the center, keeping the thread under the point. Repeat these two steps alternately. For best results, try to make the stitches even in size. (*Looped stitch family*)

Fly stitch

1 Bring the needle and thread through to the right side of the fabric, holding the thread down with your left thumb, and insert the needle a little to the right on the same level. Bring the point of the needle out, halfway between where it first emerged and where it was inserted, but a little lower, keeping the thread under the point of the needle; draw the needle and thread through.

2 Insert the needle back down again, forming a small stitch at the center to anchor the loop of the last stitch and bring the needle and thread back out in the position for the next stitch to start. (*Looped stitch family*)

Daisy stitch

1 This is also known as lazy daisy stitch or detached chain stitch. Bring the needle and thread through to the right side of your fabric at the point where you want the stitch to be, and hold the thread down with your thumb. Insert the needle back into the fabric next to where the thread emerged, and pull most of the thread through to the wrong side, leaving a small loop of thread on the right side. Pass the needle point back up through the fabric, along the length of the first stitch and inside the thread loop. Pull the needle and thread through.

2 Pass the working end of the thread over the loop and insert the needle back down through the fabric, bringing it up close to where the thread emerged originally. Pull the thread through. Repeat working stitches in a circle to make a daisy of four to five petals. (*Chained stitch family*)

French knots

1 Bring the needle and thread through to the right side of your fabric at the point where you want the knot to be. Hold the thread with your other hand and wind it around the needle once or twice, depending on the desired size of the knot.

2 Still holding the thread firmly, insert the needle back down into the fabric, close to where the thread emerged; pull the thread through to the back. Secure the thread if you are doing a single French knot, or pass it on to a second position if it's close by. (*Knotted stitch family*)

Couching

This can be used to outline a design; a thicker thread (the "laid thread") is laid on the surface and held in place by small stitches of a thinner thread (the "couching thread"). Lay a length of thicker thread against the right side of the fabric along the line of the design (or if it isn't too thick, you can bring it up through the fabric). Hold it with your left hand. With a needle and finer thread, work tiny stitches over it. (*Couched stitch family*)

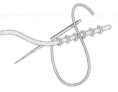

Seeding

This simple filling stitch is composed of small straight stitches of equal length worked at random over the surface of the fabric. (*Filling stitch family*)

Pockets

Although there seems to be an endless variety of pocket styles, there are, in fact, only two basic types: patch pockets, which are shaped pieces of fabric that appear on the outside of a garment, adding decoration and styling detail; and inside pockets, which are placed in seams or slashes, or are attached to seams, and generally tend to be functional.

Making patch pockets

Patch pockets can be square, rectangular, curved, or even gathered. They are one of the most noticeable signs of a garment's quality, so take care to position them correctly and make sure they are level. Pockets used in pairs must be the same size and shape.

Patch pocket with square corners

This type of patch pocket is basically a piece of fabric with the top portion (the pocket facing) and seam allowances turned to the wrong side—but to make it neat, precise, and square, the two lower corners should be mitered.

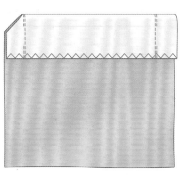 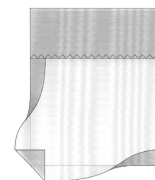 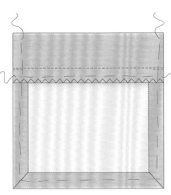

1 Finish the top edge of the pocket facing (see page 39). Turn the pocket facing to the right side along the foldline. Pin, baste, and machine stitch the top facing in place from the fold to the finished edge on each side, along the seamline, which is often ⁵⁄₈ in (1.5cm) in from the raw edge. Reverse stitch at each end of each seam to secure (see page 36). Trim across the top corners to reduce bulk (see page 38).

2 Turn the facing to the wrong side of the pocket, and gently push out the corners with the help of a small pair of scissors; press flat. Press the seam allowances to the wrong side of the pocket down the sides and across the lower edge. To miter the lower corners, open out the seam allowances at these corners and then fold them diagonally across the corners, so that the pressed foldlines match. Press the diagonal folds, then trim off the points, leaving a ¹⁄₄ in (6mm) seam allowance.

3 Baste the top facing and seam allowances in place. If desired, machine stitch the top facing about ³⁄₈ in (1cm) above the finished edge.

Patch pocket with rounded corners

If the lower edges of a patch pocket are rounded, then you will find that there is extra fullness in the seam allowance when it is pressed to the wrong side. This fullness must be removed, so that there is no overlapping of fabric to cause bulk.

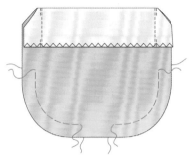

1 Follow step 1 of Patch Pocket with Square Corners (see opposite). Then, on the right side of the fabric, make a row of ease stitching (see page 43) by setting your machine to the longest stitch length possible and stitching around each lower corner, just inside the seam allowance. Trim all the pocket seam allowances down to ³/₈ in (1cm).

2 Turn the facing to the wrong side of the pocket, carefully push out the corners with a small pair of scissors, and press flat. Gently pull up the ease stitching at each lower corner to gather the pocket into a curved shape.

3 Press the pocket's ³/₈ in (1cm) seam allowances to the wrong side, snipping notches into the seam allowances around the curves to reduce bulk (see page 38), but taking care not to snip through the ease stitching. Baste the top facing and seam allowances in place. If desired, machine stitch the top facing about ³/₈ in (1cm) above the finished edge.

Applying patch pockets

Patch pockets can be applied by hand or machine, but the preferred method is by machine. Not only is machining a pocket in place quicker, but it also makes it stronger and more secure. However, you must ensure that your stitching is neat and precise.

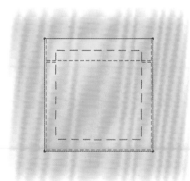

After transferring the pocket position onto the right side of your garment (see right), place the pocket on top; pin and baste it in place. Set your sewing machine to a medium-length stitch, and sew the pocket in place along the side and bottom edges, edge stitching (see page 42) close to the pocket edge. Tie the thread ends on the wrong side to secure (see page 36). Remove all basting stitches.

Marking pocket positions

Pocket positions are normally printed on the pattern pieces. For a patch pocket with square corners, you can simply mark the four corners and then line your pocket up with the marks. The quickest way to do this is to use a chalk pencil (see page 10) and make a dot on the right side of your fabric at each corner.

For patch pockets with rounded corners, you can mark the top corners as for straight corners, but then trace the lower curved edge onto the right side of your fabric, using a tracing wheel and dressmaker's carbon paper (see page 10).

TIP
To give pockets a smoother shape and make them last longer, interface them with a very lightweight interfacing (see page 18). If you are using a woven interfacing, cut it on the bias (see page 27) to avoid making the pocket look too stiff.

Reinforcing pocket corners

Pockets normally get a lot of strain as you push your hands in and out. It is therefore advisable to reinforce the corners to give them more strength.

Stitched triangles

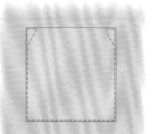

Zigzag stitching

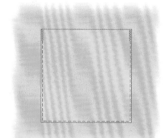

Reverse stitching

At each top corner, topstitch close to the edge for about ¼ in (6mm) along the top edge and then diagonally down to the side edge, forming a small triangle at each corner. Tie the thread ends (see page 36). You will often see this method used on shirts.

Using a closely spaced zigzag stitch (see page 39) ⅛ in (3mm) wide, stitch down each side from the top edge of the pocket for about ⅜ in (1cm), stitching over the straight stitches you used to apply the pocket. Tie the thread ends (see page 36).

Reverse stitch down each side from the top edge of the pocket for about ⅜ in (1cm), and tie the thread ends (see page 36). You will see this method used on blouses.

Making gathered pockets

Patch pockets can be decorated in various ways, from simple topstitching (see page 42) to pleats, tucks, or gathers. Gathered pockets give a very pretty, feminine look and are often found on little girls' clothing. They normally have rounded bottoms and the top either is elasticized or has fixed gathers sewn to a separate band.

Pocket gathered using elastic

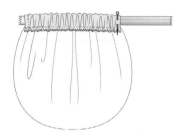

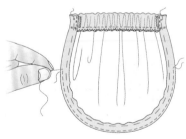

1 Finish the top edge of the pocket facing, which may be either straight or slightly curved depending on your pattern. If the top edge is straight, turn the pocket facing to the wrong side of the pocket along the foldline and press. However, if the top edge is curved, you will first need to make a row of ease stitches (see page 43) along the top edge and gently gather the edge to fit, before pressing the facing to the wrong side, as shown.

2 Baste and then machine stitch the top facing in place ¼ in (6mm) above the finished edge; remove the basting stitches. Using a bodkin (see page 9) or safety pin, thread a length of elastic through the channel formed along the pocket top. Pin and machine stitch one end of the elastic to one open end of the channel. Trim the opposite end of the elastic to the desired length and pin it to the opposite end of the channel; machine stitch the elastic in place.

3 Work a row of ease stitches around the curved lower edge of the pocket and gently pull the bobbin thread to gather it into a smooth curve. Press the pocket seam allowances to the wrong side, snipping into the seam allowances around the curves to reduce bulk (see page 38), but taking care not to snip through the easing row of stitches. Baste the seam allowances in place. The pocket is now ready to apply to your garment (see page 75).

Pocket gathered into separate band

1 Work two rows of gathering stitches (see pages 104–6) across the pocket top edge, and pull up the gathers to fit the pocket band.

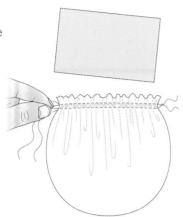

2 Iron fusible interfacing to the wrong side of the pocket band (see page 19). With right sides together and raw edges even, pin and baste the gathered top edge of the pocket to one long edge of the pocket band. Machine stitch in place along the seamline, which is usually ³/₈ in (1cm) in from the raw edge. Press the seam allowances toward the band.

3 Finish the remaining raw edge of the pocket band and fold the band along the top foldline, with right sides together. Pin, baste, and machine stitch the band down each side, along the ³/₈ in (1cm) seamline, reverse stitching at each end to secure. Carefully trim across the top corners to reduce bulk (see page 38).

4 Turn the band right side out, gently push out the corners using a small pair of scissors, and press flat. Baste the loose edge of the band in place. Working from the right side of the pocket, invisibly sink stitch the band to the pocket along the seamline (see page 43). Follow step 3 of Pocket Gathered Using Elastic (see opposite) to complete the pocket.

Inside pockets

Inside pockets are functional pockets hidden inside the garment. Unlike patch pockets, which can be positioned more freely to flatter the wearer or the design of the garment, they must be positioned for easy access.

Inside pockets are either hip pockets that are anchored to the garment at the waist and side seam edges (see overleaf) or in-seam pockets, which are placed in the seams. (In-seam pockets are covered in the previous book, *Sewing Machine Basics*.) There are a few other, decorative types of inside pockets, such as bound pockets and welt pockets, where the pocket is set into a slit, but these are quite tricky to construct, and best left until you are more experienced.

Hip pockets

Front hip pockets feature predominantly in pants (trousers) and skirts. The shape of the opening edge may be curved, straight, or angled, and the pocket is usually topstitched for decoration. All hip pockets consist of a pocket back, which forms part of the garment, and a pocket facing. The pocket back is cut from fabric, and the pocket facing is usually cut from lining; however, if your fabric is light to medium-weight, it may also be cut from fabric. The pocket opening edge is usually interfaced (see page 18) to prevent it from stretching.

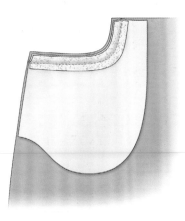

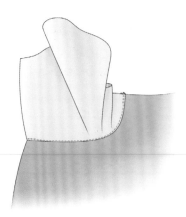

1 Cut a 1in- (2.5cm-) wide strip of fusible interfacing, shaped to fit the pocket facing opening edge. Iron the interfacing to the wrong side of the pocket facing (see page 19). With right sides together, pin and baste the pocket facing to the corresponding garment front at the opening edge, matching the waist and side seam edges. Machine stitch them together, reverse stitching at the start and finish to secure. Your garment will probably have two of these pockets, but the instructions here are for one pocket.

2 Trim and grade the seam allowances, notching them at any curves (see page 38), then press the seam allowances toward the facing. Understitch (see page 43) the seam allowances to the facing and press the facing to the wrong side of the front. Topstitch along the pocket opening edge if desired (see page 42).

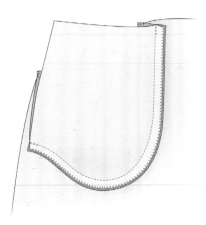

3 With right sides together, pin and baste the pocket back to the pocket facing around the long curved edges. Stitch them together, reverse stitching at the start and finish to secure. Finish the seam allowances together.

4 Baste the pocket to the garment front at the waist and side seam edges. Reinforce each end of the pocket opening with a short row of close zigzag stitches (see page 76), placed parallel to and just outside the waist and side seam stitching lines. Remove the basting.

1950s-style embroidered apron

This gorgeous apron, inspired by genuine 1950s feather-stitch aprons, is the perfect way to practice your newfound hand-embroidery skills. Use the photographs as a guide to choosing which color to use for each part of the stitching, which incorporates chain stitch, blanket stitch, and French knots. If you feel a little more adventurous, then choose some different stitches to work over the lines of the design, to create your own unique style.

Cutting out your fabric

Use pattern pieces 1, 2A & 2B, 3, 4, and 5. (See pages 29–30 for advice on cutting out and page 23 for how to understand pattern markings.) Overlap and stick together the shaded areas on the waistband/tie pattern pieces 2A and 2B to make one complete piece.

Lay the contrast fabric out flat and cut out two waistband/tie pieces. For the bottom band, cut out one 7¹/₂ x 32¹/₂ in (19 x 82.5cm) rectangle with the short ends parallel to the selvages. Also from the contrast fabric cut one 13in (33cm) square for the embroidery, making sure that the sides are parallel to the straight grain.

From the check fabric cut one apron piece and one pocket.

Finally from the interfacing, cut one center front waistband, one pocket band, and two waistband/tie pieces, shaded area only.

You will need

Apron pattern pieces and two embroidery templates traced off from the pattern sheets at the back of this book (see page 192)

²/₃ yd (60cm) of 45in- (112cm-) wide cotton check fabric

1yd (90cm) of 45in- (112cm-) wide plain contrast fabric

¹/₄ yd (20cm) of 36in- (90cm-) wide lightweight iron-on interfacing

Matching thread

Six shades of stranded embroidery floss

1¹/₈ yd (1m) of three shades of rickrack to match the embroidery floss

Dressmaker's carbon paper

10in (25.5cm) embroidery hoop

Note

³/₈ in (1cm) seam allowances are included unless otherwise stated.

Stitch seams with right sides together and notches matching, unless otherwise stated.

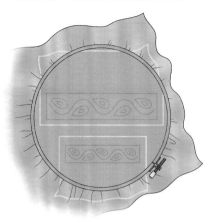

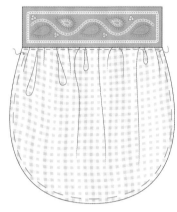

1 Lay out the square of contrast fabric, right side up. Using chalk, draw around the outer edges of the pattern pieces for the center front waistband and the pocket band, keeping the grainlines parallel to the sides of the square. Trace the embroidery designs onto both pieces using dressmaker's carbon paper (see page 70). Using the hoop and three strands of embroidery floss at a time, embroider the designs onto each piece in chain stitch, blanket stitch, and French knots (see pages 72 and 73).

2 Carefully cut out the embroidered center front waistband and pocket band pieces. Make the entire pocket following the instructions for a Pocket Gathered into Separate Band (see page 77). Press the remaining interfacing pieces to the wrong side of the center front waistband and waistband/tie pieces, where indicated.

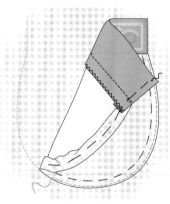

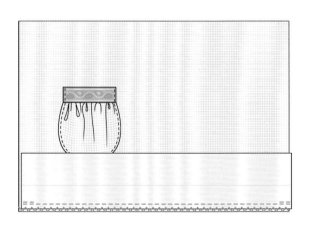

3 Mark the pocket position on the apron as shown in the Marking Pocket Positions box on page 75, following the instructions for patch pockets with rounded corners. Stitch the pocket in place (see Applying Patch Pockets, page 75), reinforcing the top corners with reverse stitching (see Reinforcing Pocket Corners: Reverse Stitching, page 76).

4 With right sides together and raw edges even, pin, baste, and machine stitch the bottom band to the lower edge of the apron with a $^5/_8$ in (1.5cm) seam. Finish the seam allowances together and press toward the apron.

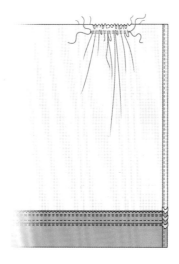

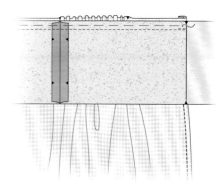

5 Make a 2³/₈ in (6cm) deep double hem (see page 63) along the lower edge of the bottom band, turning under first ³/₈ in (1cm) and then 2in (5cm). After stitching the hem, pin the three pieces of rickrack along the bottom, with the upper piece covering the band seamline, the lower one covering the hem stitching line, and the other one halfway between. Baste and then machine stitch in place with matching thread along the center of each piece of rickrack. Remove basting stitches.

6 Make a narrow ³/₈ in (1cm) double hem down each side of the apron (see page 62). Make two rows of gathering stitches (see pages 104–6) along the top edge of the apron between the notches marked on the pattern. Pull up gathers so that the gathered area measures 3³/₄ in (9.5cm)—see page 105.

7 With right sides together pin, baste, and stitch a waistband/tie piece to each end of the embroidered center front band, matching notches. Press the seams open. With right sides together, pin and baste one long edge of this joined waistband to the top edge of the apron, matching the side edges of the apron to the ends of the interfaced sections, matching each waistband seam to the start of the gathers, and matching all other notches. Machine stitch the pieces together, reverse stitching at each end to secure (see page 36). Press the seams toward the waistband.

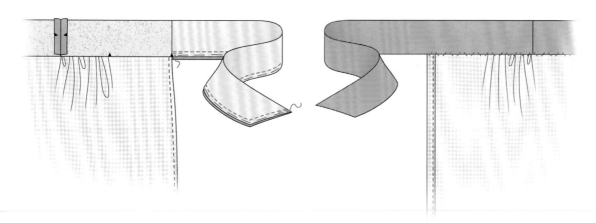

8 With right sides together, fold each waistband tie in half lengthwise. Keeping the raw edges even, pin and baste the tie sections together from the end of the waistband stitching line (at the side edge of the apron) to the point of the tie. Machine stitch the pieces together, reverse stitching at each end to secure.

9 Remove the basting and trim across the tie corners to reduce bulk (see page 38). Now turn each tie right side out, gently pushing out the corners with the help of a pointed object such as a knitting needle. Press each tie flat, making sure that the seamline lies right on the edge. On the remaining loose edge of the waistband, press ³/₈ in (1cm) to the wrong side and pin to the top of the apron, lining up the pressed edge with the waistband stitching line. Slipstitch the loose edge of the waistband in place (see page 34).

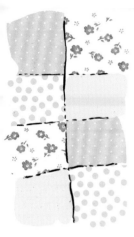

Workshop 5

Quilting and appliqué

To complement the embroidery stitches you learned in Workshop 4, this workshop looks at two more ways in which you can embellish your projects: quilting and appliqué. Quilting can be used on bedspreads, clothing, and a variety of other projects, such as the beautiful pillow project at the end of this workshop. The pillow also features some machine appliqué, a word borrowed from the French language meaning "to apply."

Quilting

Quilting can refer either to the process of creating a quilt or to the sewing together of two or more layers of material to make a thicker, padded material. This workshop covers the latter. Quilting is typically done with three layers: the top fabric, or quilt top; the batting (wadding), or insulating material; and the backing material. The three layers are stitched together in a pattern or design, by hand or machine. The stitching causes the material between the stitches to puff up, creating a pleasing effect of light and shade.

How to make a quilt sandwich

The layers of a quilted item are called the quilt sandwich, simply because you are sandwiching a layer of batting—the soft padding—between two layers of fabric.

Choosing a batting

Several types of battings (also known as wadding) are available, depending on your budget and project requirements. It is available by the yard (meter) in a wide range of widths, from 34in (86cm) up to a massive 124in (315cm) wide for bed quilts. Batting purchased off the roll is ideal, as it has no folds, but it can also be purchased in smaller, pre-cut sizes, which may be folded.

Polyester: This is the cheapest form and comes in a variety of thicknesses. Medium-weight fusible batting is also available, with a diamond-shaped pattern of adhesive to aid cutting and stitching. Polyester battings are fully machine washable.

Cotton: Cotton or a cotton mix is a good type of batting for the beginner, as it doesn't move around when stitching; this is especially helpful when quilting larger projects. This type of batting can also be machined washed.

Wool: Wool batting is the most expensive and needs to be hand washed. However, it does make a very nice quilt.

Preparing the quilt sandwich

1 Press the backing fabric flat and cut it to at least 3in (7.5cm) larger all around than your quilt top. On smaller projects, such as pillows and baby quilts, you won't need to allow quite as much fabric around the edges. For larger projects you may need to join fabric widths to obtain the correct size; use plain seams to do this (see page 36). Trim away the selvages (see page 15) from the fabric before you begin, otherwise they could cause the seams to puckers up, especially when the item is laundered.

2 Cut the batting to the same size as your backing fabric. Again, on larger projects you may need to join pieces to obtain the correct size, although, as already mentioned, wider-width battings are available in some qualities. If you do need to join widths, use lapped seams to do so (see page 41).

3 On a bare floor or large work surface, lay out the backing, wrong side up. Use weights along the edges to keep it taut. Lay the batting on top of the backing and smooth it out gently. Next lay the quilt top, right side up, on the batting, again smoothing it out until there are no wrinkles. Pin the layers together at the corners and at the midpoints of each side, close to the edge.

Basting the layers together
Beginning at the center, baste diagonal lines outward to the corners, making your stitches about 3in (7.5cm) long. Again starting at the center, baste horizontal and vertical lines out to the edges. Continue basting until you have basted a grid of lines about 4in (10cm) apart over the entire quilt sandwich.

TIP
For speed, instead of basting you can use rustproof safety pins, spaced at 4in (10cm) intervals.

For smaller projects you can also use a temporary fabric spray adhesive, from quilting stores and online.

Transferring quilting motifs and designs

The tools used to mark a quilting design on fabric must be carefully chosen. A single marker is not suitable for all colors, textures, and types of fabrics, so it is advisable to test the various types on scrap pieces of your fabric. This will let you see how clearly the marks show up and whether any lines that still show after stitching can be brushed, sponged, or washed away.

Chalk-based markers
These include dressmaker's chalk pencils and tailor's chalk (see page 10). Available in a variety of colors, they leave a clear line, which often disappears after stitching or can easily be removed by a brush. Chalk pencils must be kept sharpened to avoid thick lines.

Pencils
Silver and soapstone pencils, available from specialist quilting suppliers, produce a clear line that is almost invisible after quilting. Colored pencils can also be used on darker fabrics, and lines from water-soluble pencils can be sponged away after you have completed the stitching. Pale fabrics, however, present difficulties for marking with pencils. If you choose a lead pencil, make sure it's an "H" type, which will leave only a fine line.

Tracing wheel
Designs can be transferred from a paper template onto fabric by running a spiked tracing wheel (see page 10) over the lines of the pattern. With many fabrics the indentations or perforated line will last long enough for the work, or a portion of it, to be completed.

Dressmaker's carbon paper
This comes in sheets of various colors (see page 10). It can be used with a pencil, leaving a solid line, or a tracing wheel (see above), which will produce a dotted line on your fabric when you trace around the design lines.

Quilter's tape
This is a narrow, reusable, adhesive tape, which can be placed on the fabric surface, to provide a firm guideline for quilting straight-line patterns.

Tracing paper
Some fabrics are difficult to mark for machine quilting. In these instances the design can be transferred onto tracing paper, which can then be pinned to the surface of the quilt sandwich. The quilting is done by stitching through the paper, which is torn away after quilting with the help of a blunt seam ripper (see page 9).

Freezer paper
Freezer paper has one side that is shiny. When ironed onto fabric, the shiny side will stick. It can be removed and re-ironed several times before it becomes too fuzzy to stick anymore. Freezer paper is a useful weight as you can see through it enough to trace designs. Individual quilting motifs can be cut out of the paper and ironed onto your quilt top, so that you can stitch around the edges. You can also trace more intricate designs onto the matte side of the paper, then iron the whole tracing onto the quilt top and stitch over the design lines through the paper. When the stitching is complete, carefully tear away the paper, with the aid of a blunt seam ripper, to reveal the stitched design.

Styles of quilting

There are various styles of quilting that can be worked by hand or machine, but straight stitch on your sewing machine (see page 36) and hand running stitch (see page 34) are the most commonly used stitches. Here are some simple methods that employ them.

Evenly spaced lines

Some sewing machines have an arm that slots into the back of the machine foot, which can be set as a guide to quilting parallel lines across your quilt. If you don't have one of these, then use one of the methods already discussed (see page 83), such as quilter's tape.

Stitch-in-the-ditch

If your quilt top has been pieced together, as in patchwork, then an effective method is to stitch in straight lines along the seams between the patchwork pieces, known as stitch-in-the-ditch or sink stitching (see page 43).

Motifs

If you are feeling adventurous, you can quilt motifs freehand by eye or use templates as a guide, transferring them to the quilt top by one of the methods previously discussed.

Free-motion or meandering quilting

Another alternative is wiggly lines meandering across the surface of your quilt. To do this it is best to use a darning foot and drop the feed dogs on the machine (see opposite).

Quilting by machine

Before you start to do decorative quilt stitching, there are a few things you should take into consideration, as they will make your life easier and the quilting process more enjoyable.

- Large quilts can be quite bulky and tricky to work on with a domestic sewing machine. To make handling easier, roll up the excess quilt neatly so that it will fit under the arm of your machine.
- Use a table or chair to support the weight of larger quilts that hang out of the back of your machine, as they are heavy and you don't want them to pull on the machine needle as you are stitching.

- It is best to start stitching at the center of your quilt and work out toward the edges. Do the straight lines of stitching first, followed by any motifs and free-motion quilting.
- Small projects, such as the pillow at the end of this workshop, can be sewn with a standard machine foot. However, for a flatter-looking quilt always use a walking foot for straight lines and a darning foot for free-motion quilting (see Specialist Tools, opposite).

Quilting by hand

This is best done with the quilt mounted in a frame or large embroidery hoop (see page 71), but as long as you have basted the quilt sandwich well, a frame is not always necessary. With the quilt top facing upward, begin at the center of the quilt and make even running stitches (see page 34) following the design. It is more important to make the stitches even on both sides of the quilt than to make the stitches small. Start and finish your stitching with backstitches (see page 33) and bury the ends of your threads in the batting.

Specialist tools

Here is a small selection of tools, available from specialist quilting stores, which are designed to give more professional results in quilting, appliqué, and patchwork (see Workshop 6). If you decide that you really love these techniques and can envisage doing lots, then it is worth investing in them. They are also useful for overcoming problems on lots of other sewing projects, including dressmaking.

Quilting feet

For correct machine stitching, the fabric layers should move evenly under the machine's presser foot. However, on thicker fabrics and multiple layers, feeding the quilt evenly under a standard foot can be difficult, so these special feet are designed to overcome this problem.

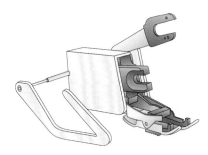

Walking foot: This is a large foot that will stride over your fabric without faltering. It is a wonderful invention, with feed dogs also on the top, so that it pushes the fabric from both the top and bottom to prevent the fabric layers from slipping—an even feed of your fabric will ensure that you get evenly spaced stitching. Although quite expensive, this foot is also brilliant for dressmaking when using thick fabrics such as denim, and also when using velvet or slippery satin—in fact, practically every fabric—plus it is superb for topstitching. It is available with or without a detachable quilting bar.

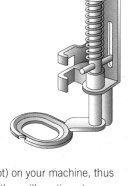

Darning foot: This super "dancing" foot makes darning, free machine embroidery, and free-motion quilting just so easy. Unless the fabric is very thin, an embroidery hoop is not necessary when using this foot. However, to obtain complete free motion of the fabric you must be able to drop the feed dogs (the teeth underneath your machine foot) on your machine, thus disengaging them, otherwise they will continue to move the fabric backward. Check your machine manual to find out whether you can do this on your machine, and how to do it. Practice using this foot on scraps of fabric—it is a totally different method to any that you will have used so far, as you have to physically move the fabric around, rather than the machine moving it for you.

Quilting pins

Quilting pins are long and slim, with either large bead or flat plastic "flower" heads, which are great to handle and which slide easily through multiple layers of fabric.

Mini quilting iron

This miniature iron is lightweight and very portable, making it ideal to sit next to your sewing machine for quick pressing and intricate jobs—handy if you do not have a dedicated sewing room. The small soleplate makes light work of appliqué and patchwork projects, but it can also be used for tiny pieces of any type of stitched work, especially those awkward places to reach like inside collars and cuffs, where a regular iron may not fit and where you risk burning your fingers.

Appliqué

Appliqué is a needlework technique in which pieces of fabric, embroidery, or other materials are sewn onto another piece of fabric to create designs, patterns, or pictures. Appliqué has been practiced all over the world for centuries, using many different styles and methods. Here we show you several simple methods: machine satin stitch appliqué, freezer-paper appliqué (which can be stitched by machine or by hand), and two methods of hand appliqué.

Machine satin stitch appliqué

There are various methods of doing machine appliqué, but this method ensures the appliquéd motifs will be smooth. It stops the motifs from slipping while they are being stitched, because the motifs are first bonded to the base cloth with a fusible web.

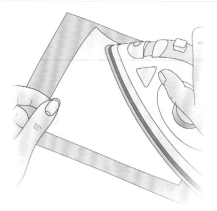

1 Cut a piece of contrast fabric and paper-backed fusible web—available from good notions (haberdashery) stores and departments—large enough to fit the motif that you want to appliqué. Using a hot iron and following the manufacturer's instructions, iron the fusible web to the wrong side of your contrast fabric.

2 Trace your motif onto the paper side of the fusible web and cut out the shape. If you are using a motif cut out of a piece of print fabric, there is no need to draw the shape onto the paper—simply cut around the edges of the design.

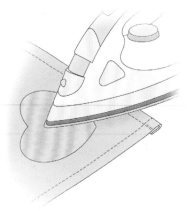

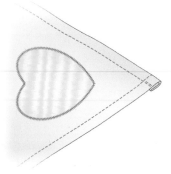

3 Remove the paper backing from your motif and position the motif, glue side down, on the right side of your main fabric. Using a hot iron and following the manufacturer's instructions, fuse the motif in place.

4 Set your sewing machine to a medium-width, short-length zigzag stitch and stitch around the edges of your motif, enclosing all the raw edges. You can use either a matching or a contrasting thread for your stitching.

Freezer-paper appliqué

As described on page 83, freezer paper has one shiny side, which can be ironed onto fabric temporarily, then removed. You can re-iron it several times, making it very handy for doing appliqué either by machine or by hand.

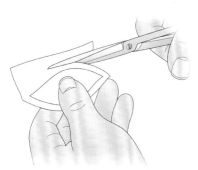
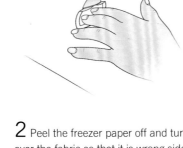

1 Trace your designs onto the matte side of the freezer paper and cut out along the lines. With the waxy side down, iron this template onto the right side of your chosen fabric. Cut around the template leaving an extra $1/8 - 1/4$ in (3-6mm) of fabric all around.

2 Peel the freezer paper off and turn over the fabric so that it is wrong side up. Position the freezer paper on top of your fabric with the waxy side facing up. Using a mini quilting iron (see page 85), carefully press the edges of the fabric over the template. If you get a tuck in the fabric that shows on the right side of your shape, gently peel off the fabric and press that area again.

3 Place small drops of fabric glue on the turned-under edges on the back of your prepared appliqué shape, making sure that the drops are well away from the folded outer edges, where you will be stitching. Carefully place the prepared shape, right side up, in the desired position on the right side of your main fabric, and gently press. Leave to dry for a few minutes.

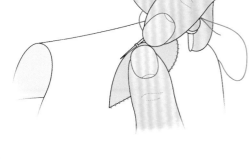
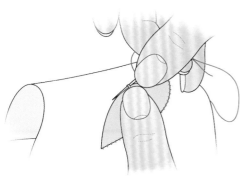

4 You can now do your stitching either by machine or by hand, depending on your preference. For the machine method, choose a small open zigzag stitch or a similar decorative stitch that will show as little as possible, and use a fine, size 10 (70) needle in your machine. For hand application, sew in place around the entire shape using blind-hem stitch (see page 88).

5 After stitching the shape in place, turn the fabric over and either cut a slit on the back of the fabric within the outline of your stitching or cut away the backing all around the shape, inside the stitching. Gently pull out the freezer paper.

Hand appliqué

Good preparation is essential for speedy and accurate hand appliqué. Here are two methods that will make it easier. The card templates method is the best for bold, very simple shapes such as circles, while the needle-turning method works well for simple shapes like leaves and flowers, particularly when used with the finger-pressing technique shown here.

Cardstock templates method

1 From thin cardstock, make a circular template, omitting the seam allowances. Adding a ¼ in (6mm) seam allowance all around by eye, cut out the shape. You will need a separate template for each circle to be appliquéd. Using matching thread, sew a line of running stitches close to the edge of the fabric circle, leaving long ends. Place the template in the center of the circle on the wrong side of the fabric.

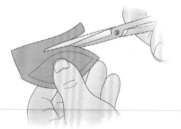

2 Gently pull up the running stitches to gather up the edge of the fabric around the template. Press, using a dry iron, so that no puckers or tucks appear on the right side. Carefully pop out the template without distorting the fabric shape. Pin your shapes to the base cloth and hand sew them in place using blind hem stitch (see below).

Blind-hem stitch

This is a stitch where the motifs appear to be held on invisibly.

Using a matching thread, bring the needle out from the reverse side through the folded edge of the motif, never on the top. Take the needle back down through the base cloth a little to the left and directly under the folded edge. Repeat around the whole shape and fasten your thread off on the reverse side. The stitches must be small, even, and close together to prevent the seam allowances from unfolding and frayed edges appearing. Try to avoid pulling the stitches too tight, or the motifs will pucker.

Note: These instructions are for a right-handed person; reverse the instructions if you are left-handed.

Needle-turning method

1 Transfer the appliqué design onto stiff cardstock, without seam allowances, and cut out. Trace around the outline of your template onto the right side of your fabric using a sharp pencil. Adding a ¼ in (6mm) seam allowance all around by eye, cut out the shape.

2 Hold the shape right side up and fold under the seam allowance along the drawn line. Finger press to create a crease along the line, making sure that the pencil line is just hidden at the back. Continue all around the shape, snipping into any curves to help them turn under. Take care not to stretch the appliqué shape as you work.

3 Pin the first piece, right side up, to the right side of the base cloth. Starting close to one end, stroke the seam allowance under with the tip of your needle as far as the pencil line, and hold securely with your thumb. Hand sew the shape in place using blind-hem stitch (see left), working around the whole shape and carefully stroking under each small section before sewing.

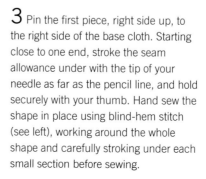

Vintage-style pillow

It's easy to turn a pillow (cushion) cover into a work of art. Using the quilting, appliqué, and embroidery techniques you've just learned, you can create a pretty pillow that is perfect for your bedroom or a cottage-style living room. The appliquéd flowers are cut out from a floral print fabric.

You will need

2/3 yd (60cm) of 45in- (112cm-) wide small floral printed cotton fabric for main cover

2/3 yd (60cm) of 45in- (112cm-) wide cotton lining for quilt backing

2/3 yd (60cm) of 34in- (86cm-) wide lightweight cotton batting

Scraps of two contrasting floral fabrics—a small design for the borders and a larger design for the appliqué cut-outs

Scraps of paper-backed fusible web

Thread to match the main fabric and contrasting fabrics

Selection of stranded embroidery flosses in shades to complement fabric colors

12in (30cm) conventional zipper to match main fabric

16in- (41cm-) square pillow form (cushion pad)

Note

5/8 in (1.5cm) seam allowances are included unless otherwise stated.

Stitch seams with right sides together and notches matching, unless otherwise stated.

Cutting out your fabric

Cut out one 18½ in (47cm) straight-grain square each from the main fabric, batting, and lining, for the cover front. Cut two 17 x 9in (43 x 23cm) rectangles from the main fabric for the cover back. Cut four 10¼ x 1½ in (26 x 4cm) straight-grain strips of contrast fabric for the border.

1 Make a quilt sandwich (see page 82) using the squares of main fabric, batting, and lining and baste the layers together (see page 83). Using a pencil (see page 83), lightly draw two diagonal lines—from corner to corner, crossing in the middle—on the lining side of the cover. Now draw lines parallel to these, 1¼ in (3cm) apart, over the entire surface. Alternatively, use quilter's tape (see page 83). Using a medium-length straight stitch and working from the wrong side, machine stitch over the lines. Complete first one set of parallel lines, then the other set. Remove the basting and trim away the outside edges, to leave a 17in (43cm) square of quilting.

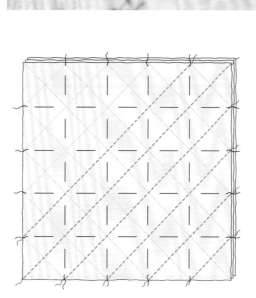

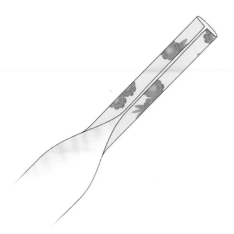

2 Carefully press ⅜ in (1cm) to the wrong side along both long edges of each of the four border strips. A quilting iron (see page 85) is a useful tool for doing this, but you can obtain the same results with a regular iron if you take your time.

3 With the strips right side up on the right side of the cover front, pin and baste the strips 3³/₈ in (8.5cm) in from the cover raw edges to form a square border, overlapping the ends. (It doesn't matter that the ends are raw, as they will be covered by the appliqué.) Machine stitch in place around both the outer and inner edges of the border, with a straight stitch close to the pressed edges. Remove the basting.

4 From the second contrasting fabric, select the flower and leaf shapes that you wish to appliqué onto the cover front. Press paper-backed fusible web to the back of the motifs, as shown in steps 1 and 2 of Machine Satin Stitch Appliqué on page 86. After cutting out the leaves and flowers, peel off the backing paper and place the shapes over the corners of the borders, positioning first the leaves and then the flowers, overlapping the leaves. Following steps 3 and 4 of Machine Satin Stitch Appliqué on page 86, fuse and then stitch the motifs in place, changing the sewing thread color according to the motif being applied.

5 Hand embroider a group of French knots (see page 73) in the center of each appliquéd flower bloom and at random over the front cover to highlight the fabric design. Finish the raw edges of the completed cover front.

6 Finish the raw edges of the two cover back pieces. Join the two pieces with a center back seam and insert the zipper into it, following the Centered Application method shown on page 54. Open the zipper and, with right sides together and raw edges even, stitch the cover back to the cover front. Trim the corners to reduce bulk (see page 38), turn the cover right side out, and carefully push out the corners. Insert the pillow form through the center back zipper opening.

Workshop 6

Patchwork and binding

Patchwork is most often used to make quilts, but it can also be used to make pillow covers, table linen, throws, wall hangings, bags, and items of clothing. In this workshop you will learn the basics of the technique, which will enable you to design your own simple projects and create the stylish recycled bed throw at the end of the workshop, using hand-made binding to finish the edges.

Patchwork

Patchwork, or pieced work, is a form of needlework that involves sewing pieces of fabric together to form a larger design. This can range from joining simple squares to creating complicated pieced blocks, made up of colorful shapes that repeat to create patterns within each block. Whether you are using simple squares or pieced blocks, they are normally sewn together in rows to make the larger composition. Patchwork pieces can be assembled by hand or by machine. Machine stitching is quicker, but hand assembly allows you to carry your patches around with you. The choice is yours—although the method you choose does sometimes also depend on the shape of your pieces. Whatever method you use, precise cutting and joining are necessary for professional-looking results.

Specialist patchwork equipment

As with quilting, special pieces of equipment have been developed to help improve the accuracy of cutting out. These are not essential tools, but they certainly speed up the process of repeat cutting.

Rotary cutter

Used in both patchwork and quilting for cutting fabric, a rotary cutter consists of a handle with a circular blade that rotates. The blades are very sharp and are available in different sizes—smaller blades for small curves, and larger blades for straight lines and big curves. Several layers of fabric can be cut simultaneously, making it easier to cut out patchwork pieces of the same shape and size. The cutter must be used in conjunction with a cutting mat and ruler such as a thick plastic quilter's ruler.

Cutting mat

Designed for use with a rotary cutter, this cutting mat is made from a special "self-healing" material that keeps your cutting blade sharp. Cutting mats come in various sizes and are usually marked with a grid to help you line up the edges of the fabric and cut out larger pieces. Cutting mats are also ideal to use with craft knives and with dressmaker's tracing wheels (see page 10).

Quilter's ruler

Also known as a patchwork ruler, the quilter's ruler is used as a guide when cutting out fabric pieces with a rotary cutter. It is a thick, clear-plastic ruler printed with lines that are exactly 1/4 in apart, the standard seam allowance in patchwork. Metric versions are also available, calibrated to 5mm and 1cm. Sometimes this type of ruler also has diagonal lines, including 45- and 60-degree angles.

Cutting out the patches

In the instructions for a patchwork project, you should find a summary of all the patch shapes required to complete the project. Even if you are making up your own design, you must remember to cut out the patches in the following order to make the most efficient use of your fabric: the border and binding strips first, followed by the largest patch shapes, and finally the smallest ones. The border and binding strips are best cut using a rotary cutter and cutting mat (see opposite).

How to rotary cut

You will need a rotary cutter, quilter's ruler, and cutting mat. Rotary-cut strips are normally cut across the width of your fabric from selvage to selvage, but this is not always the case.

Note: These instructions are for a right-handed person; reverse the instructions if you are left-handed.

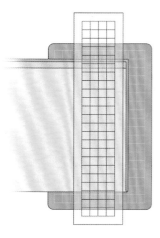

1 Before you begin, press out any folds or creases in the fabric. Fold it in half, bringing the selvages together along the entire length. If you are cutting out a large piece of fabric you may need to fold it several times accordion-style until it fits your cutting mat—a large, sharp rotary cutter can cut several layers of fabric at one time. When there is only a single fold, place the fold facing you, with the bulk of the fabric to your left. To ensure that your cut strips are straight and even, the folds must be placed exactly parallel to the selvages and lined up along a line on the cutting mat.

2 Start by straightening the raw edges of the fabric. To do this, lay the ruler over the fabric, lining up one end of the ruler with the folded edge of the fabric. Hold down the ruler firmly with your left hand, making sure that your fingers are well away from the edge, and press down. Most rotary cutters have a safety guard, so click this out of the way to expose the blade, then smoothly and in one motion push the blade away from you, running it up alongside the edge of the ruler. Never do a sawing motion and never pull the blade toward you. Before moving the ruler, pull away the trimmed piece of fabric and discard it. Open out the fabric and check that the cut edge is straight. Don't worry if it's not perfect—a little wiggle won't show when the patchwork is stitched together.

3 Refold the fabric as in step 1, then lay the fabric down on the mat, with the bulk of the fabric now going off to the right and the trimmed edge on the left. Place the ruler over the trimmed edge by the desired width of the fabric strip, using the marks on the ruler as a guide and making sure that it is perfectly perpendicular to the fabric fold, so that each strip will be nice and straight. Press down on the ruler again and wheel the cutter away from yourself along the ruler. Open out the fabric strip to check the edge. Continue cutting strips in this way until you have the amount that you will need.

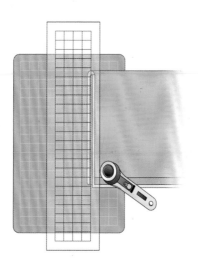

Making templates

Patchwork is rather like doing a jigsaw puzzle, so it is vital that the pieces fit together correctly and each piece replicates the next exactly. The most effective way to do this is to use templates when cutting out your patches. Templates are best made from transparent template plastic, available in sheets from specialist shops and via the Internet. Not only is it durable but it also allows you to see the fabric underneath and therefore to select certain motifs. You can, however, make templates from thin cardboard if template plastic is not available.

1 Trace off the actual template provided either directly onto template plastic or onto tracing paper and then onto thin cardboard. Use a ruler to help you trace off the straight cutting lines, dotted seamlines (if shown), and grainlines.

2 Cut out the traced template using a craft knife, ruler, and cutting mat (see Specialist Patchwork Equipment, page 92).

3 Using an awl (bradawl), punch a hole in each corner of the template, at the points where the seamlines bisect.

Using the templates

The most efficient way to cut out patches using templates is to rotary cut a strip of fabric to the depth of the template, and then mark the width of the template along the strip at the required angle. This method leaves hardly any waste and gives a random effect to your patches. A less efficient way is to "fussy cut," in which you cut out the patches individually by placing the templates on particular motifs or stripes to create special effects. Although this method is more time-consuming and wasteful, it does yield attractive results.

1 Place the template face down on the wrong side of the fabric, with the grainline following the straight grain of the fabric, if indicated—but be sure to check your instructions, as some projects may ask you to cut patches on varying grains. Hold the template firmly in place and draw around it with a sharp pencil, marking the corner dots or seamlines. To save fabric, position the patches close together along the strip, or even touching.

2 Once you have drawn all the pieces needed, you are now ready to cut the fabric into patches, using either a pair of sharp scissors or a rotary cutter with a ruler and cutting mat (see page 13).

Arranging the cut patches

After cutting out the patches, you will have a lot of different fabric pieces and so will need to keep track of what they are and what goes where. Patchwork instructions always give you a layout for how to arrange the patches to form the overall design. Although it is possible just to start stitching the patches together at random, you will generally create a much better effect if you plan the design before you begin.

1 Lay the patches out on the floor, or pin them on a large bulletin board, then stand back to study the effect and swap the patches around until you reach the desired effect.

2 For the first patch in a row or block, write the row or block number on a self-adhesive label to stick to the patch, or on a scrap of paper that you then pin to the patch. It may also be handy to mark on the label whether it is the left- or right-hand side of your patchwork, so that you don't stitch the patches together in the wrong order.

3 Pile up the patches in each row or block in the correct order, with the labeled one on top, then you can take each pile to the sewing machine to work on.

Basic patchwork assembly

The order in which patchworks are pieced together is to assemble the blocks first, then the rows, then the center, and finally the borders. Follow the assembly order that is given in the instructions for your project, or that you have worked out, to piece the individual patches together to form blocks, and then assemble the patchwork blocks together in rows. If your patchwork is made up of simple squares, think of each square as a completed block, when reading these instructions.

Basic machine piecing

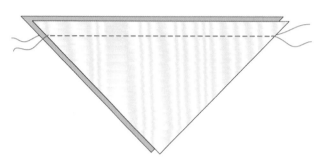

1 Pin two patches with the right sides together and the edges even. Set your sewing machine to 10–11 stitches per inch (2.5mm stitch length) and stitch from edge to edge with a ¼ in (6mm) seam, removing pins as you feed the fabric through the machine. If you wish, you can baste the patches together before stitching. In the diagram shown here, a block consists of just two triangles joined with one seam to form a square, but if a block consists of more patches, join the patches in the same way.

2 Repeat for all the blocks, and press the seams of each block to one side.

3 Now pin the individual blocks together in the correct order of assembly to form rows. Baste if you wish, and then stitch and press as in steps 1 and 2. When pressing the seam allowances to one side, ensure that this will be in the opposite direction to the seam allowances in rows that will be adjacent; this will reduce bulk and make matching easier.

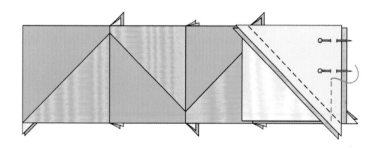

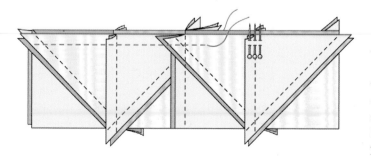

4 You are now ready to join the rows together to form the patchwork top. Pin two rows of blocks together, matching the seamlines, and with the seam allowances pressed in opposite directions. Pin pieces directly through each stitching line and to the right and left of it to hold the seam allowances in place. (Again, you can baste before stitching if you prefer.) Stitch and press as in steps 1–2. Repeat to stitch all the rows together.

Basic hand piecing

Using a pencil, mark the seam allowance corner dots on each patch before you start, then pin two patches with right sides together and edges even. Using a single strand of strong thread, secure the corner of the seamline with a couple of backstitches (see page 33) at one marked corner dot. Sew small running stitches (see page 34) along the marked seamline, making about 8–10 stitches per inch (2.5cm) and ending at the opposite corner dot with a few more backstitches. When hand piecing, never sew over the seam allowances—always start and finish at the corner dots. Sew the other patches together in the same way, following the assembly and pressing instructions in Basic Machine Piecing, page 95.

Foundation piecing by machine

In foundation piecing, the patchwork design is worked onto paper foundations the exact size of your block, including the seam allowances around the outer edges. During the stitching process, the fabric patches are joined together by sewing through the paper foundations to form the block, and then the paper foundations are torn away. Some foundation block projects are worked very precisely and accurately, while others can be worked freehand in a loose manner, creating a noticeably different overall effect.

Precise foundation piecing

For precise blocks you will need to rotary cut your strips of fabric accurately with a quilter's ruler (see page 93) to the widths stated for your project.

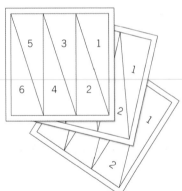

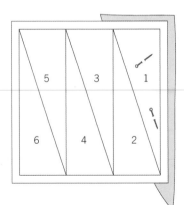

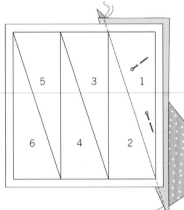

1 To make the paper foundations, trace the correct number of foundation pattern blocks for your project onto newsprint (preferably unprinted) or greaseproof paper, or photocopy them onto lightweight paper. Each block should be the size stated on your project—ie, the finished block size plus 1/4 in (6mm) seam allowance around all four sides. (Seam allowances are not included on the paper for the individual patches within each block.) Number the shapes within each block. The drawn/printed side of the block normally shows the wrong side. Cut out the paper foundation blocks.

2 Roughly cut out the fabric patches that will make up the first block, cutting them wrong side up and adding at least 1/4 in (6mm) seam allowance all around each patch—at this stage the patches can be too large but they mustn't be too small. Place the fabric patch that corresponds to no. 1 under the foundation, with the wrong side of the fabric to the wrong (undrawn/unprinted) side of foundation. Pin the two together, making sure that the fabric patch covers the area and overlaps the seamlines on all sides by at least 1/4 in (6mm).

3 Place fabric patch no. 2 under fabric patch no. 1, with right sides together and raw edges overlapping beyond the outer seamline edge. Pin the patch in position. With the paper side on top, stitch along the marked seamline between patch no. 1 and patch no. 2, starting and finishing at the fabric edges. There is no need to reverse stitch at the end of each stitching line, as the seams will be secured when the next, overlapping seam is stitched.

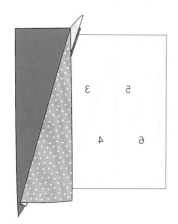 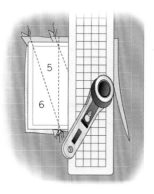 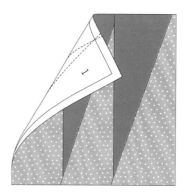

4 Trim the seam allowances to about 1/4 in (6mm). Open out patch no. 2 and press the seam to one side with a hot, dry iron. Do not use steam, as this will make the paper wrinkle.

5 Continue adding the remaining patches to the block, in the same fashion, following the color/fabric sequence for the project. After the last patch has been stitched in place, trim away excess fabric from around the edge of the block with a rotary cutter, ruler, and cutting mat, leaving the designated seam allowance around the outer edge. Do not remove the paper foundation yet.

6 Join the remaining blocks in the same way. Once all the blocks have been joined together, carefully tear away the paper.

Freehand foundation piecing

For freehand foundation piecing, the strips are cut freehand without a ruler, so you don't end up with perfectly straight edges—little wiggles enhance the effect. Make some of your strips wedge-shaped and vary the widths. There will be no definite strip widths stated in the project instructions—the choice is yours, so be as creative as you please.

To assemble the freehand blocks, proceed in the same manner as for the precise blocks (see opposite), laying on the strips and stitching through the paper, but your foundation blocks will not have seamlines printed on them for you to follow, so you should stitch from the fabric side of the block, on order to be able to see what size of seam you are taking.

English paper piecing by hand

This is a very easy way to assemble patchwork by hand, using simple whipstitches (see page 34). It is particularly useful when the patches are hexagonal.

1 Cut out the papers from heavy paper (or lightweight cardstock), to the shape of the patches but excluding the seam allowances. You will need lots of these papers, which need to be cut very accurately before you can start.

2 Cut the fabric patches 1/2 in (1.2cm) bigger all around than the paper pieces. Place a paper piece on the wrong side of a fabric patch, and fold the edges of the fabric over the paper. Using large stitches, baste it to the paper.

3 When you have prepared a lot of patches, attach them to each other by holding two patches with right sides together and making tiny whipstitches along the edge. After all sides of the patch have been sewn to other patches, remove the basting and take out the paper. The papers can be used over and over until they become wrinkled.

Finishing your patchwork

When you have finished piecing together the patchwork and have added any borders, press it carefully. It is now ready to be quilted (see pages 82–5) and finished, according to your project's instructions.

Handmade binding

Binding is a strip of fabric with folded edges, which is used to finish a straight or curved edge in a practical or decorative way. To bind a curved edge, you will need binding that is cut on the bias (see page 27), giving it lots of stretch to enable it to bend around curves. For straight edges, binding can be cut on the straight grain (see page 27), which is more economical on fabric. Readymade binding can be purchased from notions (haberdashery) departments, but the color choice is often limited and the widths restricted, so it is more satisfactory to make your own, which will match your project exactly.

Making bias binding

Bias binding is made from strips of fabric cut on the bias—ie, diagonally across the fabric's width along the bias.

1 To find the bias of the fabric, fold the raw edge (running across the width of the fabric from selvage to selvage) over to form a triangle, so that it lies parallel to one of the selvages; the resulting diagonal fold is the bias.

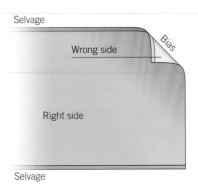

Selvage

Wrong side

Bias

Right side

Selvage

2 Press and cut along the bias fold. Draw pencil lines parallel to the bias, to your required width, which should be twice the finished width of the exposed binding. Cut along these lines until you have enough strips to make the length you need to go all around your garment, plus about 1in (2.5cm).

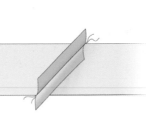

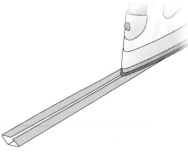

3 To join bias strips together, the ends that are to be joined must each be cut at a 45-degree angle (which will have occurred naturally if the bias strips have been cut all the way to the edges of the fabric in step 2). Place one strip on top of another, right sides together, as shown above, and stitch a ¼in (6mm) seam.

4 Press the seam open as shown above, and trim off the protruding corners of the seam allowances even with the long raw edges of the strip.

5 With wrong sides together, press the strip in half along its length, with the press line slightly off center, so that one part is marginally wider than the other. Open it out flat and press the long raw edges to the wrong side to meet at the off-center press line.

Making straight-grain binding

Straight- grain binding can be used for finishing the edges of quilts and down the edges of curtains—in fact, on any edge that is perfectly straight. Cut the desired number of strips on the straight grain using a rotary cutter (see How to Rotary Cut, page 93). The strips will need to be cut to twice the finished width of the exposed binding. Join the ends of the strips with right sides together, taking ¼ in (6mm) seams and pressing them open.

Binding an edge

You can finish any fabric edge with binding, in either self-fabric or contrasting fabric. There are two basic methods for binding an edge: applying it entirely by machine, and applying it partially by machine and then finishing with slip hemming by hand.

Machine method for applying binding

This is mainly used when both sides of the item will be seen, and it is quicker to do because it does not involve slip hemming, but the machine stitching is visible from the right side.

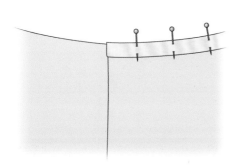

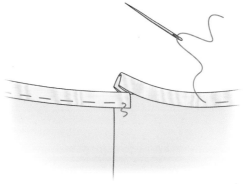

1 Turn under the starting end of the binding by ⅜ in (1cm) and press. Working with the fabric right side up, align the short pressed end of the binding with a garment seam, if there is one, then sandwich the fabric edge between the binding layers, with the wider part of the binding underneath. Pin the binding in place all along the edge.

2 At the finishing end, trim away the excess binding, allowing for ⅜ in (1cm) to underlap the folded starting end. Baste and then machine stitch the binding in place, working from the right side through all the layers of fabric and stitching close to the binding edge. Remove the basting.

Machine and hand stitching method for applying binding

This two-stage method can be used when one side of the binding will not be visible, such as around the neckline of a garment. No stitching is visible on the right side, but it takes longer to do.

1 First the narrower side of the binding is applied to the garment edge with right sides together. Start by opening out the folds on the binding and turn back ⅜ in (1cm) at one end; align this with a garment seam if there is one. With the long raw edge of the binding even with the raw edge of the garment, pin and baste the binding in place. Machine stitch along the top foldline, reverse stitching at the start, and finishing the stitching about 2in (5cm) from the starting point.

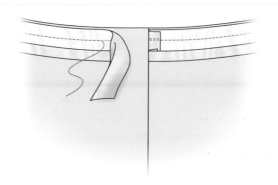

2 Trim away the excess binding, leaving ³/₈ in (1cm) to overlap the turned-back starting end. Still following the top foldline, stitch the remaining binding in place through all layers. Remove the basting and press the seam allowances toward the binding. Now bring the opposite folded long edge of the binding down to meet the seamline on the wrong side of the garment, enclosing the raw edge of the garment. Pin in place and then slip hem (see page 64) the folded edge to the seamline.

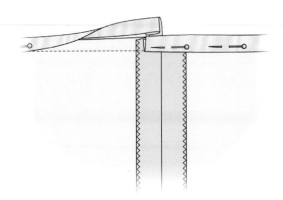

Binding square corners

Sometimes you will have to bind a square or rectangular object like a patchwork quilt, pillow cover, or placemat, in which case you will need to miter the corners for a neat finish.

1 Starting along one long edge, sandwich the fabric edges between the binding layers, with the wider part of the binding underneath. Pin and baste the binding in place up to the first corner only. Now machine stitch the binding in place from the starting end to the first corner, working close to the pressed edge of the binding, and reverse stitching at each end to secure.

2 Fold the loose working end of the binding down in line with the second edge, creating a 45-degree fold in the binding at the corner, on both front and back.

3 Making sure that the 45-degree angles are still correctly in place, fold the binding over to enclose the raw second edge. Pin and baste the binding in place. Starting at the corner, machine stitch the binding to the second side as far as the next corner, reverse stitching at the beginning and end to secure.

4 Repeat steps 2 and 3 to bind the remaining sides and corners. At the finishing end trim away the excess binding, allowing for a ³/₄ in (2cm) overlap of the starting end. Fold under ³/₈ in (1cm) of the overlap and machine stitch in place. Remove the basting. If your binding is wide, you may wish to slipstitch the mitered corner folds (see page 67, step 3) for a neat finish, and to make sure that they don't get caught on anything when the item is in use.

Recycled patchwork bedspread

Take yourself back to grassroots with this project. Just as traditional patchwork quilts were made from reclaimed materials, this fabulous patchwork bedspread is fashioned from men's recycled shirts. The instructions given here are for a twin (single) bed and allow for plenty of overhang, but adding extra patches for larger sizes is very simple.

Cutting out your fabric

Template A (square): From the shirt backs and fronts, "fussy cut" 60 square patches (see Using the Templates, page 94).
Template B (rectangle): From the shirt sleeves, "fussy cut" 30 rectangular patches.
Backing: From the backing/binding fabric, cut one rectangle 44$\frac{1}{2}$ in (113cm) wide x 100in (254cm) long, and two rectangles 17in (43cm) wide x 100in (254cm) long.
Binding: From the remaining backing/binding fabric, rotary cut (see page 93) two straight-grain strips 2in (5cm) wide x the length of the fabric, to form 10yd (9.20m) of binding.

Assembling the patches

Patchwork assembly diagram

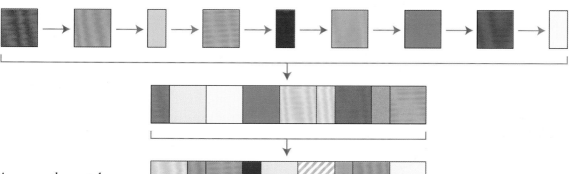

Arrange the patches into 10 rows (see Arranging the Cut Patches, page 94) following this patchwork assembly diagram. Using $\frac{1}{4}$ in (6mm seams), join the patches together into rows and then join the rows together to form the patchwork top (see Basic Machine Piecing, page 95).

You will need

Patch templates A and B traced off from the pattern sheets at the back of this book (see page 192)

Selection of old shirts or blouses salvaged from thrift stores, garage sales, and online auction sites

90 x 108in (229 x 275cm) piece of cotton batting

5$\frac{2}{3}$ yd (5.20m) of 45in- (112cm-) wide fabric in a coordinating color for the backing and binding

Matching thread

Shirt buttons rescued from the shirts

Note

Stitch seams with right sides together, unless otherwise stated.

Size of bedspread

The finished bedspread will measure approximately 74in x 98$\frac{1}{2}$ in (187.5cm x 250cm).

Creating a quilt sandwich

Press the assembled patchwork top. Seam the three backing pieces together with ⅝ in (1.5cm) seams, placing the smaller pieces each side of the larger piece; press the seams open. Layer the patchwork top, batting, and backing together (see Preparing the Quilt Sandwich and Basting the Layers Together on pages 82 and 83).

Finishing the bedspread

Trim the backing and batting edges even with the patchwork top and attach the binding to the edges following the Binding Square Corners method on page 100. To complete the bedspread, stitch the shirt buttons randomly to some of the corners of the patches, using a reinforcement button underneath each one (see page 46). The buttons hold the layers together across the bedspread, so position them with this in mind. Remove all of the basting stitches.

Increasing the size of your patchwork bedspread

The following quantities will help you to purchase the right amount of materials for a larger bedspread. Make up the patchwork top using the same method as for the twin (single) bed and then measure it to find out the sizes to which you should cut out your backing, batting, and binding. Remember to stitch the backing together with a larger piece in the middle.

For a double bedspread
Approximate finished size:
93½ x 98½ in (237.5 x 250cm)
Template A: Cut 80 patches
Template B: Cut 30 patches
Arrange the patches in 10 rows of 8 template A's and 3 template B's, in a similar manner to that shown in the patchwork assembly diagram for the twin (single) bedspread on page 101.

For a US queen- (UK king-) size bedspread
Approximate finished size:
98½ x 98½ in (250 x 250cm).
Template A: Cut 80 patches
Template B: Cut 40 patches
Arrange the patches in 10 rows of 8 template A's and 4 template B's, in a similar manner to that shown in the patchwork assembly diagram for the twin (single) bedspread on page 101.

Also needed for a double or a US queen- (UK king-) size bedspread
8½ yd (7.70m) of 45in- (112cm-) wide fabric in a coordinating color for the backing and binding
120 x 120in (305cm x 305cm) cotton batting

Workshop 7

Gathers, shirring, and smocking

Soft gathers, shirring, and smocking are decorative ways of shaping a flat piece of fabric to fit around the body's contours. This workshop introduces you to these techniques, which can be used in a variety of ways, providing plenty of scope for adding interest to your projects. At the end of the workshop there are a few pointers on making children's clothes, culminating in a pretty shirred sundress for little girls.

Gathers

Gathers are tiny, soft folds formed by drawing up fabric into a smaller area. They are used in a wide range of garments to add fullness, but the most popular application is in ruffles—exuberant trimmings that look good on both garments and home furnishings. It is best to form large areas of gathers by machine, as controlling the fullness evenly across the pieces is easier, but small sections can be gathered by hand if you prefer.

Machine gathering tips

Follow these easy steps to organize your work and use your machine for gathering.

■ Join all the fabric pieces to be gathered, then stitch, press, and finish the seams; for ruffles, hem the free edge as well.

■ Loosen the upper tension on the machine slightly so that the fabric will slide along the bobbin thread more easily.

■ Set your machine to a longer stitch: 12 stitches per inch (2.0mm stitch length) for lightweight fabrics, to 6–7 stitches per inch (4.0mm stitch length) for heavier fabrics. Test the tension and stitch length on a scrap of the fabric first.

■ Stitch from the right side of the fabric, so that the bobbin threads, which are pulled to form the gathers, will be easily accessible when you are working from the wrong side later, adjusting the gathers.

■ Leaving long thread ends, stitch between any seams, keeping the seam allowances out of the way, because gathering does not work well through two layers of fabric.

Calculating the amount of fabric

If you are using a pattern, the calculations are all done for you, but if you are adding a ruffle or making a gathered skirt without a pattern, you have to work out the amount of fabric you'll need for gathering. This will depend on the fullness you want and the type of fabric you are using—thicker, heavier fabrics require less fullness than soft, lightweight fabrics. Try a test piece, gathering up a measured width of fabric to the fullness you require, to find the ratio you need. As a general rule, you will need three times the finished gathered width for very full gathers, twice the width for medium gathers, and one-and-a-half times the width for minimal gathers. Widths of fabric are stitched together where necessary to obtain the correct measurement.

Machine gathering

Machine gathering is done by stitching two rows of long machine stitches along the edge to be gathered, within the seam allowances. The fabric is then gathered up by pulling on the bobbin threads.

Machine gathering the fabric

Before you begin to gather your fabric, refer to the Machine Gathering Tips (see opposite).

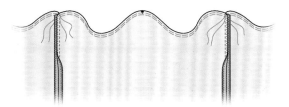

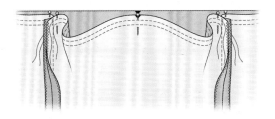

1 Leaving long thread ends, work two parallel rows of gathering stitches 1/4 in (6mm) apart within the seam allowance along your fabric edge, with the outer row of stitching a thread's width from the seamline. Do not stitch over seams—stitch between any seams where necessary.

2 Divide the stitched edge and the edge to which it will be attached into four or more equal sections and mark them with a pin. With right sides together, pin the stitched edge to the other edge, matching marker pins. If you are using a dress pattern, match corresponding pattern markings and seams.

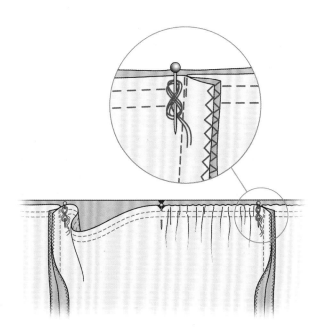

3 At one end, secure the bobbin threads by twisting them around a pin in a figure eight. At the other end, pull both bobbin threads together and gently ease the gathers along the threads. When the gathered edge fits the other piece, secure the thread ends around another pin, as before. On long edges, gather the fabric from each end toward the center, rather than trying to gather across the entire piece all at once.

4 Unwind the thread ends from around each end pin, and knot each pair together to secure them; trim the ends to about 1in (2.5cm). With the gathered side on top, baste the two layers together between the two rows of stitching, using short stitches. Remove the pins.

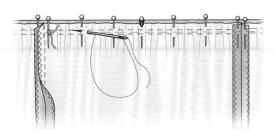

5 Return your machine stitch length and tension to the appropriate setting. With the gathered side on top, machine stitch the gathered edge to the corresponding edge, reverse stitching to start and finish. As you sew, hold the fabric on either side of the machine foot to prevent the gathers from being pushed and stitched into pleats. Remove the basting.

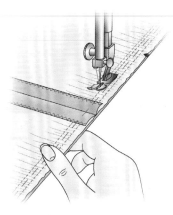

6 Diagonally trim crossed seam allowances as shown to reduce bulk. Using the tip of the iron, press the seam allowances flat as they were stitched, but do not press the gathers. Finish the seam allowances together. Open the sections out and press the seam toward the flat section. Press the gathers by sliding the point of the iron into the gathers toward the seam.

Automatic gathering

Some machines provide an automatic gathering foot, which gathers up the fabric as it stitches; some gathering feet gather one layer of fabric while stitching it to another flat piece of fabric. The thread tension and stitch length are adjusted to increase or decrease the amount of fullness, so a gathering foot is difficult to use in conjunction with a dress pattern or somewhere that you want to achieve a specific fullness. Always refer to your instruction manual if using a gathering foot.

Hand gathering

You can also gather small sections by hand if you prefer; this is done using simple running stitch. Start by making several tiny backstitches (see page 33) to fasten the thread securely at one end of the section to be gathered. Sew a row of small, evenly spaced running stitches just above the seamline, then sew a second row of running stitches parallel to the first, just below the seamline. Pull up the two loose threads and distribute the fabric fullness evenly until the section measures the desired length. Anchor the loose threads around a pin at the finishing end (see Machine Gathering the Fabric, step 3, on page 105) and apply your gathered section as shown in steps 4, 5, and 6 (see page 105 and above).

Shirring

Shirring is a decorative effect formed with multiple rows of gathering stitches. Lightweight fabrics are best for this technique, preferably those that don't require a lot of ironing, as pressing is difficult once the fabric is shirred. Your pattern instructions should indicate the areas to be shirred, and these can range from small areas, such as a pocket top or cuffs, to an entire body section. Rows of shirring must be straight, parallel, and evenly spaced. They may be as close together as 1/4in (6mm) or as far apart as 1in (2.5cm) depending on the look you want. The fabric width to be shirred will be determined by your pattern.

Elasticized shirring

Using elastic thread on the bobbin, with regular thread in the needle, makes the shirred area stretchy and flexible, allowing it to expand and contract with the body's movements.

1 Wind shirring elastic onto your sewing machine bobbin, stretching it slightly until the bobbin is almost full. This can be done by hand or machine. Set your machine stitch length to 9 stitches per inch (3.0mm stitch length) and test the results on a spare piece of fabric to ensure that it gathers up the required amount. Adjust the stitch length and tension if necessary (see your sewing machine manual for more information on how to do this). Sometimes, to achieve the desired fullness, the bobbin (elastic) thread may need to be pulled slightly after stitching, as you do in gathering (see step 3, page 105).

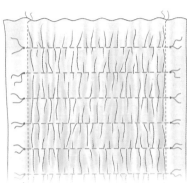

2 Mark the rows of shirring on the right side of the fabric using a chalk marker (see page 10). Or, after marking the first row, if your machine has a quilting guide bar that fits into your regular sewing foot, you can use this to space the other rows of shirring. Stitch along each marked row, holding the fabric taut and flat by stretching the fabric in previous rows to its original size.

3 To secure the ends, pull the threads through to the wrong side of the fabric and knot them together. Run a line of machine stitches within the seam allowance, across all the knots to hold them in place.

Shirring without elastic

Shirring can also be done without elastic, giving a decorative gathered area that will not stretch. This effect can often be found on lingerie and soft blouses.

For this method, use regular sewing thread in the bobbin as well as in the needle. Mark the positions of the shirring rows on the right side as in step 2 of Elasticized Shirring (see above). Stitch repeated gathering rows (see page 105) over the section to be shirred. Now, working from the wrong side, pull up the bobbin threads on each row separately, measuring the first row to make sure that the subsequent rows are the same length, and securing the thread ends around pins (see step 3 of Machine Gathering the Fabric, page 105). To secure the threads permanently, tie the ends together and then run a line of machine stitches within the seam allowance across all the ends of the gathering rows (see step 3 of Elasticized Shirring, above).

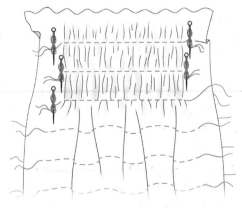

Smocking

Smocking is a traditional English craft of peasant origin that has been used for centuries as decoration, but which originally arose from the need to control fullness of fabric in garments that were cut on very simple, straight lines. Smocking consists of fabric folds, or "tubes," stitched together at regular intervals with a decorative embroidery thread to create a patterned effect. Like shirring and gathering, smocking is done before the garment is constructed. Popular areas to smock are yokes, bodices, and pockets. Smocking is not the quickest technique, as it is worked by hand and a little patience is required, but a handmade garment with classic smocking can soon become a precious family heirloom.

Fabrics for smocking

A variety of fabrics—cottons, linens, fine wools, voiles, and silks—can be used for smocking. However, the important things to bear in mind when selecting a fabric are that it should have good draping qualities, it should be fine in texture, and any pattern should enhance the design rather than taking over—you want to be able to see your lovely stitching!

The amount of fabric you need will depend on the nature of the fabric; it can vary from three times the finished width to four times for very fine fabrics. The fabric should be cut on the straight grain, with the gathering threads stitched along the weft threads (see page 15).

Preparing to smock

Before you start, you will need to prepare your fabric, work out your design, and select the best thread for your project.

Gathering threads

The gathering threads for smocking are sewn by hand. In traditional smocking they used to be worked by the counted-thread method, with even rows of running stitches (see pages 34 and 106) passing over and under the same number of fabric threads. However, there are now quicker methods for marking and working your gathering threads.

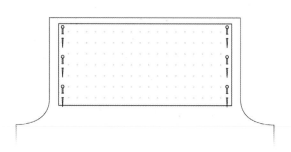

Smocking dots: These are transfers that can be ironed onto the wrong side of the fabric. They are available from good craft stores and notions (haberdashery) departments or online, in a variety of colors. The spacing of the dots varies; for example, on some transfers the dots are positioned approximately 1/4 in (6mm) apart, with 3/8 in (9mm) between the rows. First decide on your design and depth of smocking, and cut out and iron on the required amount of transfer. Peel off the backing to reveal the dots.

Pencil and ruler: If you are unable to obtain a transfer, you can mark the dots yourself using a ruler and transfer pencil, which can be washed out. Alternatively, use a fade-away marker pen, available from good notions departments. Space the dots evenly as discussed in Smocking Dots (see left).

Checked fabrics: If you are using a fabric like gingham, its pattern can serve as a guide in place of a grid. With 1/8 in (3mm) checks, pick up every alternative check. When using 1/4 in (6mm) checks, pick up each side of every check.

TIP
Before you begin using smocking dots, cut off the maker's name, which is usually printed down the side of the transfer, and test the transfer on a scrap of your fabric to ensure that you can see the resulting marks.

Sewing the gathering threads

Always use a standard sewing thread in a color that contrasts with your fabric so that it can be easily seen, making it easier to remove once you have completed your smocking.

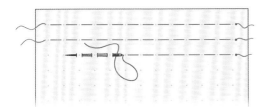

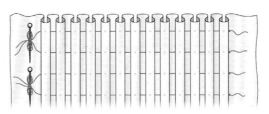

1 Begin the gathering threads on the wrong side of the fabric with a fine knot and a backstitch (see page 33). Taking up each dot on the needle as shown, make a row of running stitches (see page 34) across the entire width of the fabric, leaving the thread hanging free at the final end of each row.

2 After all the rows of gathering stitches have been completed, pull up the threads until all the tubes (fabric folds) are quite tight, then release them a little. There needs to be sufficient room between the tubes for an embroidery needle to be inserted easily. Secure the thread ends around a pin in a figure eight, as shown in step 3 of Gathering the Fabric on page 105.

Working out your smocking design

Always work out your complete smocking design on paper before you begin to do the smocking stitches. Count the tubes on your finished, gathered piece and find the center to ensure that your pattern will fit symmetrically. Start with a simple design to begin with—any of the stitches on pages 110–11 would be suitable. Remember that all points must be symmetrical and spaced attractively. Avoid cramming too many rows of stitching into the pattern—the true beauty of smocking lies in its simplicity. A firm stitch such as stem stitch or cable stitch (see page 110) should be used for the first row of stitching, as this will hold the tubes securely in place and enable the yoke or band to be attached more easily.

Smocking threads

Stranded embroidery floss is a good choice for smocking stitches, although a twisted embroidery thread can be used, too. Normally three strands will give a good effect, but for bold smocking and if the fabric is thicker, four to six strands may be preferable. The color can match the fabric or contrast with it. Always use a crewel needle (see page 71) and make sure that it is not too fine, as the thread must run loosely through the eye of the needle.

Working smocking stitches

The first row of smocking stitches should be worked on the right side of the gathered panel approximately ¾in (2cm) down from the top edge of the fabric. That will leave ½ in (1.2cm) to be set into the yoke or band, plus a space between the first row of stitching and the yoke or band. All smocking stitches are worked on the right side of the fabric.

Note: These instructions are for a right-handed person; reverse the instructions if you are left-handed.

To begin smocking, secure the end of the floss with a knot and a small backstitch at the back (see page 33). Be sure to allow enough thread to complete the whole row of stitching, so that you don't have an unsightly join at the back, which could also create a weak spot. Work from left to right, bringing the needle through from the back on the left-hand side of the first tube. Working carefully with an even tension, sew one of the stitches shown under Smocking Stitches (see pages 110–11). Don't pick up more than a quarter of the depth of the tube with each stitch—approximately ¹⁄₁₆ in (1mm)—and keep the stitches in a straight line parallel to the top edge. Avoid pulling the stitches too tight, to ensure that the finished piece will have elasticity.

TIP
Work a small sample of the fabric first to practice the stitch and get the tension right before you start on the garment itself.

Smocking stitches

Here are a few basic stitches, all of them simple to do and mostly based on backstitch and stem stitch (see pages 34 and 72). By combining stitches, many designs are possible.

Stem or rope stitch

This is a good, firm stitch to work for the first row of your design, as it has little stretch.

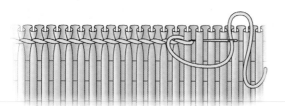

Working from left to right with your needle pointing to the left, make a small backward stitch in each tube, keeping the working thread below the needle. Work in this way until the end of the row.

Cable or basket stitch

A basket-weave pattern makes a firm surface for your smocking. To create a basket-weave effect, work consecutive rows of cable or basket stitch, directly below each other.

Working from left to right with your needle pointing to the left, make a small backward stitch through the second tube, keeping the working thread above the needle. With the thread now placed below the needle, make a small backward stitch through the third tube. Proceed working with one tube at a time, with the thread alternating above and below the needle, until you have completed the row.

Chevron stitch

This is worked from left to right to form a zigzag or half-diamond pattern. Several rows can be stitched close together to form a solid chevron, or if alternative rows are worked in reverse, a full diamond pattern is formed. Care

needs to be taken, however, to ensure that you have the same number of stitches, or steps, up to the top and bottom of the chevron. Also, if working a full diamond shape, make sure that the points are directly above and below each other.

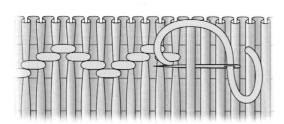

1 Working from left to right with your needle pointing to the left, bring the needle and thread out on the left side of the first tube. With the thread above the needle, work the downward side of the chevron by making a small backward stitch through the second tube, bringing the needle out just below the first stitch. Pass the needle over the third tube and make a backward stitch as before. Continue in this manner across the tubes until you reach the desired depth of your chevron, normally 3–5 stitches.

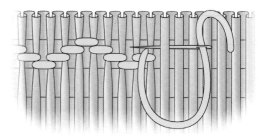

2 Pass the working thread below the needle and then work the upward side of the chevron in the same manner, taking the same number of stitches over the tubes and bringing the needle out just above the previous stitch. Repeat steps 1 and 2 to the end of the tubing panel.

Honeycomb stitch

Using honeycomb stitch for your smocking will create a very stretchy panel, which is valuable when making children's clothes, as it will allow for growth.

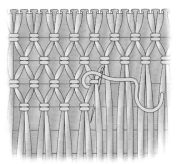

1 Working from left to right with your needle pointing to the left, and using two gathering threads or basting lines as a guide to work between, bring the needle and thread out on the left side of the first tube by the upper gathering thread. With your working thread above the needle, make a small backward stitch over the first and second tubes. Now make a second stitch over the same two tubes, this time slipping the needle down the inside of the second tube to come out in line with the lower gathering thread on the left side of the tube.

2 With your working thread below the needle, make two stitches in the same way over the second and third tubes, taking the needle up in line with the first gathering thread to come out on the left side of the third tube. Continue in the same way to the end of the row. The next row is worked in line with the third and fourth gathering threads.

TIP

If you accidentally prick your finger and get blood on your work, act immediately—don't let it dry. Take a length of white cotton sewing thread and rub it into a ball in the palm of your hand. Wet it thoroughly in your mouth and then rub the stain with the wet thread. (The enzymes in saliva help break down the proteins in blood.) Repeat until the stain is removed.

Mock chain stitch

This is another firm, non-elastic stitch that is suitable for the first row of smocking stitches, as it will hold the tubing in place effectively without stretching.

Work a row of stem or rope stitches (see opposite) across your tubing panel, keeping the working thread above the needle. Now work a second row close to the first row, but this time keep the working thread below the needle. Working the two rows close together will give the appearance of a chain.

Completing the smocking

When all the rows of smocking stitches are finished, carefully remove any basting stitch guide lines and all but the top row of gathering threads. This is left in to keep the tubing in place while you set the panel into the yoke or band. Afterward, this thread can be removed. To ensure even positioning, divide the yoke and the smocking panel into four equal sections and mark them with pins, which can then be matched when the edges are joined.

Never iron smocking or you could squash the tubing. However, if you find that your smocking is too tight, carefully hold it near a boiling kettle or a steamer, and stretch it out to the desired width, taking care not to scald yourself or overstretch the work.

Sewing for children

Making children's garments appeals to the novice seamstress, as the garments are smaller and quicker to make than for adults. However, although constructed in the same way as adults' clothing, children's garments have to be strong enough to survive the children's vigorous activity and the repeated laundering, as well as being easy to put on and take off and offering room for growth.

Selecting patterns

Children's patterns tend to be grouped into types that reflect a child's development, ie, babies, toddlers, children, girls, and boys. However, you should not assume that your child fits neatly into any one category. As for adults' garments, you must measure the child and compare the measurements with the size chart. Try to choose a pattern type and size that will require as few alterations as possible.

Whichever style you choose, make sure that it is going to be comfortable and that it allows for enough ease at the neck, at the armholes, and between the legs. If it has long sleeves, there should be plenty of length. There also needs to be ease across the back—in other words, the style needs to allow for the fact that children grow quickly, particularly in height.

Taking body measurements

Children can be difficult to measure, as they won't stand still for long. If you have problems with this, take measurements from garments that fit them well and then compare the measurements to the garment measurement chart on the pattern envelope. To take body measurements, strip your child down to their underwear. Use a good-quality tape measure (see page 9) and record the measurements in the chart opposite. With infants' patterns (for babies who are not yet walking), you will need only the weight and length of the baby—measured with the foot at a right angle to the leg, as if the baby were standing.

> **TIP**
> Remember to check your child's measurements regularly as they can change rapidly.

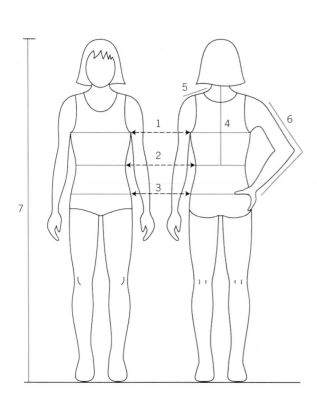

Basic measurements

1 Chest
Measure under the arms, taking the tape over the fullest part of the chest at the front and just under the shoulder blades at the back.

2 Waist
Take this measurement around the natural indentation in the child's trunk. Tying a piece of string around the midriff and letting it settle helps with the measuring process.

3 Hips
Take the tape around the fullest part of the buttocks.

4 Back neck (nape) to waist
Measure from the prominent neck bone at the center back down to the string at the waistline.

5 Shoulder length
Measure from the base of the neck—ask the child to shrug their shoulders to locate this position—to the outer bone on the shoulder.

6 Arm length
Measure from the top of the arm (outer shoulder bone) to the wrist, with the elbow bent.

7 Height
Ask the child to stand barefoot against a wall. Place a ruler on top of their head, parallel to the floor, and mark where the underside touches the wall. Measure down to the floor.

Crotch depth
Measure the outside leg on a pair of trousers that fit well and subtract the inside leg measurement, which gives you the crotch depth.

Special considerations

■ **Elasticizing:** Make pants and skirts easy to pull on and off, by including elasticized waist casings (see pages 119–21). Elasticized shirring (see page 107) allows dresses and tops to be put on and pulled off quickly.

■ **Hook-and-loop tape:** This type of fastener (see page 137) makes it easy for children to dress themselves, especially younger children who haven't yet mastered the art of doing up buttons.

■ **Snaps:** Snaps are another simple fastener that children can manage. They can be applied either individually or on a continuous tape (see pages 135–7).

■ **Pockets:** Always add a pocket (see pages 74–7), even if your pattern doesn't include it, as children like to collect precious little things from their day's adventures, and it also provides somewhere to store hankies and coins.

■ **Durability:** For extra strength, use two rows of stitching to reinforce areas that will be subject to extra strain. To extend the life of the garments, choose fabrics that are washable and have easy-care properties.

■ **Room for growth:** Introduce extra fabric into the length of a skirt by adding circular tucks (see page 132), which can be let down at a later date and any stitching lines disguised by adding a braid or ribbon trim. On any garment, if it doesn't make your hem too bulky, incorporate a deep double hem (see page 63), with the same amount of fabric folded twice, and slip hemmed (see page 64) in place; do not machine stitch the hem. To lengthen a garment with no extra allowance, add a contrasting border around the hem.

Basic measurement chart

Keep a record of your child's measurements in the chart below using a pencil. Note the child's measurements in the first column, the pattern's body measurements in the second, and the difference between the two in the third column. A difference of $1/4$ in (6mm) in length and $3/8$ in (1cm) in width means you will have to adjust the pattern slightly (see pages 24–6).

	Child's measurements	Pattern measurements	Difference
Chest			
Waist			
Hips			
Back neck to waist			
Shoulder length			
Arm length			
Height			
Crotch depth			

Little girl's shirred sundress

The perfect summer dress for a little girl, this is made from a cool cotton border print with lace trim detail at the hem. The shirred bodice stretches to allow plenty of room for growth, and when the dress gets too short, simply team it with cropped leggings for a great sun top.

Fabric suggestions

Soft cotton or poly-cotton prints and plains, cotton border prints, lawn, cheesecloth, soft chambray

You will also need

Dress pattern pieces traced off from the pattern sheets at the back of this book (see page 192)

Matching thread

Shirring elastic

1¾ yd (1.5m) of matching or contrasting lace trim, with two finished edges

Note

⅝ in (1.5cm) seam allowances are included unless otherwise stated.

Stitch seams with right sides together and notches matching, unless otherwise stated.

Size

	Age	5–6 years	7–8 years	9–10 years
	Chest	24in (61cm)	26in (66cm)	28³/₈ in (72cm)
	Waist	22³/₈ in (57cm)	23¼ in (59cm)	24³/₈ in (62cm)
	Height	45⁵/₈ in (116cm)	50³/₈ in (128cm)	55¹/₈ in (140cm)
	Length (back neck to hem, excluding lace trim)	27½ in (70cm)	30½ in (77cm)	33½ in (85cm)

Front view   Back view

Fabric quantities

45in- (112cm-) and 60in- (150cm-) wide fabric			
	1¾ yd (1.70m)	1¾ yd (1.70m)	2yd (1.80m)

Cutting out your fabric

Use pattern pieces 1, 2, 3, and 4A & 4B.

Sundress—all sizes
45–60in- (112–150cm-) wide fabric

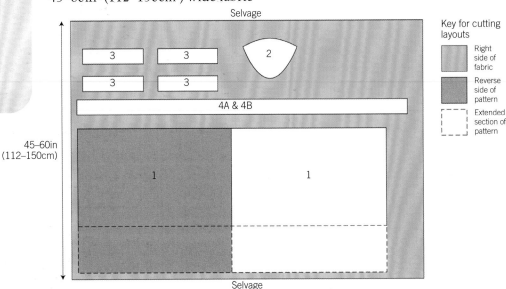

Key for cutting layouts

Right side of fabric

Reverse side of pattern

Extended section of pattern

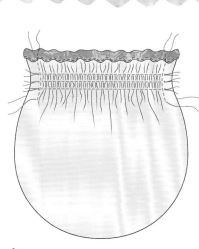

1 Following the cutting layout, cut out all your fabric pieces. (See pages 29–30 for advice on cutting out and page 23 for how to understand pattern markings.) Turn and stitch a 1/4 in (6mm) narrow double hem (see page 62) across the top edge of the pocket. Mark the top row of shirring 5/8 in (1.5cm) below the top edge of the hemmed pocket, then work three rows of Elasticized Shirring (see page 107) a machine-foot width apart—this should be approximately 1/4 in (6mm) apart.

2 Attach the pocket to the dress panel at the position marked, following the method for a Patch Pocket with Rounded Corners on page 75, stitching triangles at the top corners to secure (see page 76).

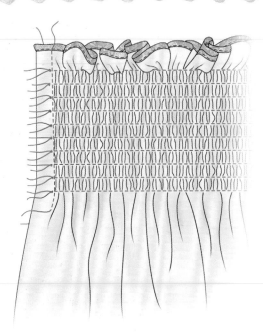

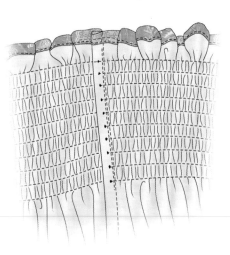

3 Turn and stitch a ¹/₄ in (6mm) narrow double hem across the top edge of the dress piece. Mark the first row of shirring ⁵/₈ in (1.5cm) below the top edge, then work 10 rows of shirring, each a machine-foot width apart, as in step 1.

4 Join the left side seam with a French seam (see page 41), matching the rows of shirring and the top hemmed edge. Press the seam toward the dress back and stitch across the top of the seam allowances to hold them in place, following the top hem stitching line.

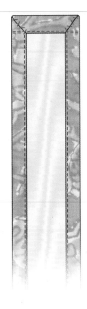

5 Finish the lower hem edge (see page 39) and press ³/₈ in (1cm) to the wrong side along this edge; baste in place. Working from the right side and starting with the first end extending ³/₈ in (1cm) beyond the side seam, lay the lace trim over the hem edge, overlapping it by ¹/₈ in (3mm). Pin in place. At the finishing end of the lace, allow an extra ³/₄ in (2cm) and cut off the excess. Turn under this end by ³/₈ in (1cm) and overlap the first end of the lace, so that the fold on the overlapping end aligns with the side seam. Baste and machine stitch it in place close to the lace edge. Hand sew the loose edges of the lace together down the trim and along the base edge. Remove the basting.

6 Turn and stitch a ¹/₄ in (6mm) narrow double hem down both long edges of the shoulder ties. Press a narrow double hem along one end of each tie, and pin in place. Fold under each of these hems diagonally at the corners and press in place. Hand sew the diagonal corners of the hems in place, and then machine stitch the rest of these hems, reverse stitching at each end to secure.

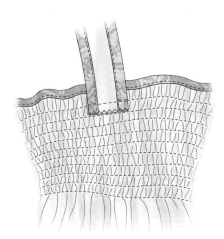

7 Finish the remaining short end of each tie. Pin and baste these ends to the top edge of the dress at the positions marked on the pattern, with the right side of each tie to the wrong side of the dress, and the finished edge of each lined up with the second row of shirring. Try the dress on your child and tie the shoulder ties into knots to fit at the shoulders; adjust the positions of the ties if necessary. Carefully remove the dress and machine stitch the ties in place along the top row of shirring, stretching it out as you stitch and reverse stitching at each end to secure.

8 Turn and stitch a ¼ in (6mm) narrow double hem down both long edges of the tie belt. To finish the short ends, follow the method shown in step 6 for finishing the ends of the shoulder ties. Finally, make a thread belt carrier (see page 124) on the left side seam at the position marked on the pattern. Lay the dress out flat with the left side seam on the fold, and mark the position for a belt loop along the fold at the opposite side of the dress (ie, where a right side seam would be if there were one). Make a thread belt carrier at this point to correspond to the other one. Thread the tie belt through the carriers and tie in a bow at the back.

Workshop 8

Darts and waist finishes

One of the most basic structural elements of dressmaking, a dart is another method of adding shape to a flat piece of fabric to allow it to curve to the body's shape. Darts at waistlines are very common, and in this workshop we will also show you several ways in which to finish a waistline. Once you have learned these techniques, there's a project for a jeans-style skirt to put your newfound skills into practice.

Darts

A dart is a tapered fold in a piece of fabric, which is stitched to give a garment shape. Darts are principally used on women's garments to shape the fabric around the bust, hips, and waist, but they may also be used to shape the back shoulders and elbows on very tailored garments. There are two main types of darts: plain darts and contour darts. You may also come across French darts, which are constructed in a special way, but these are not covered in this book.

Plain darts

Plain darts are folds in the fabric stitched with a tapering seam to form a point. A plain dart is shown on your pattern piece as a triangle with two stitching lines and sometimes a central foldline. There may also be two notches at the edge and a dot at the point (see page 23).

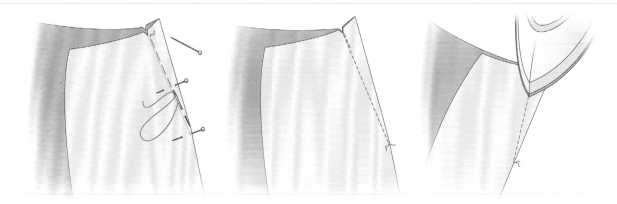

1 Transfer the dart markings to the wrong side of your fabric (see Transferring Pattern Markings, page 31). Working from the wrong side of the fabric, fold the dart in half through the center, matching the stitching lines and other markings. Pin and baste the dart in place.

2 Starting from the wide end of the dart, and reverse stitching at the start to secure, stitch toward the point. To finish, take the last couple of stitches a thread's width from the fold. Cut the thread ends, leaving at least 4in (10cm). Knot the ends together, but do not pull too tightly. Trim the thread ends to 3/8 in (1cm). Remove the basting.

3 To press, lay the dart flat on an ironing board with the fold of the dart to one side, and iron toward the point—but no further, otherwise you will crease the rest of the garment.

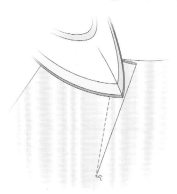

4 Open out the fabric and press the dart in the direction instructed; this is usually toward the center for waist darts and toward the waist for bust darts.

TIP
Practice stitching on a scrap of fabric before you attempt darts on your garment, as it is important to make your stitching straight, without any tucks at the pointed end, and to make pairs of darts the same length.

Contour darts

These are long darts, which have a point at each end; they are often used on fitted and semi-fitted dresses. The widest part of the dart fits into the waistline and then tapers off to fit the bust and the hip, or the shoulder blades and hip. Contour darts are usually shown on patterns as a long, thin diamond, with stitching lines and a series of dots to be matched.

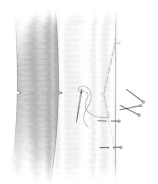

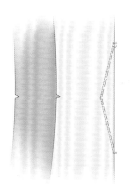

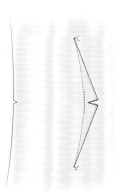

1 Transfer the dart markings to the wrong side of your fabric (see Transferring Pattern Markings, page 31). Working from the wrong side of the fabric, fold along the center of the dart. Match and pin the dots and stitching lines, first at the waist, then at the points, and then at any marks in between. Baste the dart in place just inside the stitching lines and remove the pins.

2 A contour dart is stitched in two halves, always starting at the middle (waistline) and stitching toward the point. Instead of reverse stitching to start, overlap the stitching at the waist and tie the ends of the thread at both points, in the same way as for the single point of a plain dart (see step 2 of Plain Darts, opposite).

3 Remove the basting stitches and clip into the dart at the waistline to within 1/8 in (3mm) of the stitching line; this will allow for the dart to curve smoothly at the waist. Press the dart flat as it was stitched, then press it toward the center of the garment.

Waist casings

The waistline finish acts as an anchor to hold the garment in the correct position on your body. There are two ways to finish a waistline edge: fixed methods such as a waistband or a facing (see pages 122–3), and flexible methods such as an elasticized or drawstring waist casing. A casing is a channel made to enclose elastic or a drawstring to draw in the fabric around the waist. It is simple to construct and also practical, as it can easily be adjusted to fit. There are two main types of casings: "fold-down" (page 120) and "applied" (page 121).

Fold-down casings

A fold-down casing is formed by turning down an extension on the garment waist edge to the inside, rather like a hem, to form a channel, which is stitched in place. This type of casing is best suited to straight edges but can be used on a curved edge if kept very narrow.

Fold-down casing for elastic

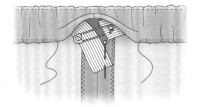

1 Turn under and press the hem allowance of the casing extension, and trim away any excess so that the hem allowance is 1/4 in (6mm) deep. Now turn under the casing extension itself, and pin and baste it in place.

2 Machine stitch the lower edge of the casing in place, leaving a gap through which you will be able to thread your elastic. Make a second row of stitching close to the top folded edge, overlapping the ends of the stitching to secure. Remove the basting.

3 Attach a safety pin or bodkin (see page 9) to one end of the elastic and pin the other end of the elastic to the garment to stop it from disappearing into the casing. Thread the safety pin or bodkin attached to the elastic through the casing, making sure that it does not twist as you work it around. Adjust the elastic to fit, overlap the ends, and pin. Now box stitch the ends of the elastic together as shown under Box Stitching, below. Trim off the surplus elastic and remove the safety pin or bodkin.

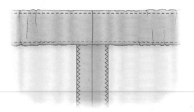

4 Stretching the elastic slightly to keep your work flat, machine stitch along the lower edge of the casing at the opening, overlapping the original stitching at each end to secure and taking care not to catch the elastic as you sew.

Box stitching

Box stitching, as the name suggests, is stitching in a square shape, with a cross in the center. It is done in one operation without removing the work to change direction. Box stitching is used wherever a strong, reinforced join is required, such as when joining the ends of elastic together for a waist casing, or when attaching straps or ties to garments and bags.

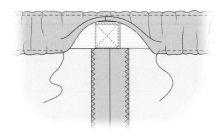

Starting at one edge, machine stitch across the width of your elastic or strap, then continue stitching around to form a square, finishing at the starting point with the needle down. Pivot the work around the needle and stitch diagonally across the square to the opposite corner, then along the side of the square following the first line of stitching, and finally diagonally across the square to the opposite corner. To really reinforce the stitching, stitch around the square one more time. Remove the work from the machine and cut the threads.

Fold-down casing for a drawstring

1 Make two buttonholes (see pages 46–8) at the position marked on your pattern, then follow step 1 of Fold-Down Casing for Elastic (see opposite). Machine stitch the lower edge of the casing in place, overlapping the ends of the stitching to secure. Make a second row of stitching close to the top folded edge, and once again overlap the ends of the stitching to secure.

2 To insert the drawstring, attach a safety pin or a bodkin (see page 9) to one end of the cord. Insert it through one of the buttonholes and work it around the garment until it emerges back out through the other buttonhole. Remove the safety pin or bodkin from the drawstring.

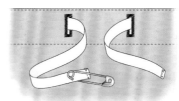

TIP
Use readymade wide bias binding to make a quick applied casing, rather than cutting out your own strip from fabric.

Applied casings

A fold-down casing is not always suitable for a project, especially if your waist edge is shaped or if there are hip pockets that come up to the waist edge, in which case an applied casing may be preferable. It is normally worked on the circle, for a totally pull-on finish, but when a zipper placket is involved it may be applied on the flat—for example, at the bottom of a bomber jacket.

1 Referring to How to Work out the Casing Size (see right), cut out a strip of fabric on the straight grain if the garment waistline is straight, or on the bias grain (see page 27) if the casing will need to curve. Finish one long edge of the strip (see page 39). Press 3/8 in (1cm) to the wrong side at each end, and machine stitch in place.

2 Trim the garment waist seam allowance to 3/8 in (1cm). Starting and finishing at one side seam, and with right sides together, pin, baste, and machine stitch the casing to the waist edge of your garment, taking a 3/8 in (1cm) seam and overlapping the stitching at the ends to secure. Remove the basting, trim the seam allowances down to 1/4 in (6mm), and press the seam open.

3 Fold over and press the casing to the wrong side of the garment. Pin, baste, and machine stitch the lower edge of the strip in place, 3/8 in (1cm) from the long finished edge, overlapping the ends of the stitching to secure. Remove the basting. Topstitch just below the top edge of the casing, again overlapping the ends.

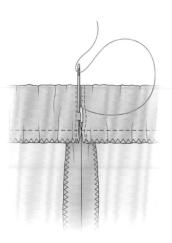

4 Follow step 3 of Fold-Down Casing for Elastic (see opposite). Slipstitch the opening edges together (see page 34), taking care not to catch the elastic in the stitches.

How to work out the casing size

Your casing should be at least 1/4 in (6mm) wider than whatever you are going to be threading through it, plus 3/4 in (2cm) for seam allowances.

The length is determined by the circumference of the garment at the place where it is going to be stitched, plus a total of 3/4 in (2cm) for the hems at the ends.

Fixed waist finishes

Fixed waist finishes are not flexible, but are made to fit the body's waist measurement, with some extra allowance for the wearer's comfort and ease. They include straight waistbands, waist facings, and grosgrain ribbon. The first two of these need to be reinforced with interfacing.

Reinforcing fixed waistbands

For a fixed waistband to hold its shape and retain strength throughout the life of the garment, it must be reinforced with interfacing (see pages 18 and 19). The type of interfacing used will depend on the fabric that the garment is made from. However, it will need to be sturdy, flexible, and crease-resistant and to have the same care properties as the garment fabric. You should use a heavier weight of interfacing for waistbands than for other parts of your garment like collars and cuffs.

Straight waistbands

These give a neat finish to a garment. They can be of varying depths, but preferably no more than 2in (5cm), otherwise they will tend to collapse. They are made to fit the waist edge, with a small extension at one end to allow for the ends to overlap and for you to make a buttonhole and attach a button or hooks and eyes for fastening.

TIP
For straight waistbands, look out for a special triple-slotted iron-on interfacing tape, available in three widths. Simply cut a length to your required waistband length, iron it onto the wrong side of your fabric, and cut out. The slots give an accurate guide for folding and stitching to help create a perfectly straight waistband.

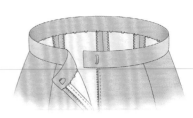

1 Apply interfacing to the wrong side of your waistband piece, then press the waistband in half lengthwise, with wrong sides together. Open the waistband out flat again. With right sides together, pin, baste, and machine stitch the long notched edge of the waistband to the garment waist edge, matching the notches at each end of the waistband to the zipper opening edges, and matching the remaining notches to the side seams.

2 Fold the waistband in half lengthwise (against the press line), with right sides together. Pin, baste, and machine stitch across the short end of the waistband at the left-hand zipper opening, from the folded edge to the waistband stitching line. At the other end of the waistband, pin, baste, and machine stitch around the waistband extension from the folded edge to meet the waistband stitching line. Remove all the basting.

3 Snip the corners of the waistband seam allowances (see page 38), then turn the waistband right side out. Press the loose waistband edge to the wrong side, and slip hem (see page 64) the pressed edge along the machine stitching, enclosing the raw edges. Attach fastenings to close the waist (see page 136).

Shaped waist facings

A waist facing provides a smooth, streamlined finish that does not extend above the waistline edge.

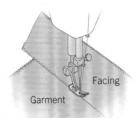

1 Apply interfacing to the wrong side of your facing pieces, then stitch the facing pieces together with a plain seam (see page 36), but leave unstitched the seam corresponding to the zipper placket. Press the seam open and finish the lower edge (see page 39).

2 Pin the facing to the garment, right sides together, matching all seams and notches. Pin 1/4 in- (6mm-) wide cotton tape over the waist seamline, and baste in place. Stitch the seam and then layer the seam allowances, clipping into the curves (see page 38). Remove the basting.

3 Press the facing and the seam allowances away from the garment. Working from the right side, understitch the seam allowances to the facing (see page 43). This will stop the facing from rolling to the outside of the garment during wear.

4 Turn the facing to the inside of the garment and press along the waist edge. Baste the lower edge of the facing to the garment, making sure that it lies flat. Turn under the seam allowances at the facing ends and pin in place, making sure that they do not catch in the zipper. Slipstitch the facing ends to the zipper tape (see page 34). Catch the lower edges of the facing to the side seams and darts with a few hand stitches. Remove the basting and then attach fasteners to close the waist (see page 136).

Grosgrain ribbon finish

Curved grosgrain ribbon about 1in (2.5cm) deep is available from notions (haberdashery) departments, either by the yard (meter) or in pre-packed quantities. It gives a similar appearance to a shaped waist facing but is much quicker to do. No interfacing is required for this type of fixed waist finish, as the ribbon itself is strong and stiff.

1 Staystitch the garment waist along the seamline (see page 43), ensuring that the waist remains the same size as on the pattern. Measure the waist along this line and cut a length of ribbon equal to this length, plus 1 1/4 in (3cm) for hems. Trim the garment waist seam allowance to 1/4 in (6mm).

2 Lap the wrong side of the ribbon over the right side of the garment waistline so that the edge of the "inside curve" on the ribbon is just over the staystitched line and the cut ends extend 5/8 in (1.5cm) beyond the zipper opening edges. Pin, baste, and machine stitch the ribbon in place close to the edge of the ribbon. Remove the basting.

3 Turn the ribbon to the inside of the garment and press along the waist edge. Fold under the ribbon ends and pin in place; check that they do not catch the zipper, then slipstitch the ends to the zipper tape (see page 34). Catch the lower edges of the ribbon to the side seams and darts with a few hand stitches, and attach fasteners to close the waist (see page 136).

Belt carriers

Belt carriers are commonly stitched onto a waistband or waistline to enable a belt to sit in the correct position. They can be made of thread or fabric. Both types of carriers need to be large enough to allow the belt to slide through easily.

Thread belt carriers

Thread carriers are made from a thread chain and are almost invisible. They are mainly used on dresses and coats at the side seams to support a belt. The chain can be worked as long as it is needed. **Note:** These instructions are for a right-handed person; reverse the instructions if you are left-handed.

1 Using pins, mark on the garment where the chain will begin and where it will be fastened off—ie, the depth of the belt plus a little extra. Thread a needle with a long length of thread and secure it on the inside of the garment, at the first pin position; bring the thread through to the right side. Take a small stitch through the fabric and draw the thread through, leaving a 4in (10cm) loop. Hold the loop open with the thumb and first two fingers of your left hand, holding the working end of the thread with your right thumb and index finger.

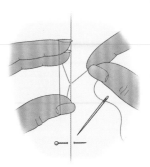

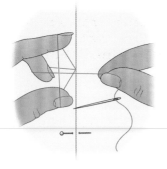

3 As you pull the new loop through, the first loop will start to slide off your other fingers and become smaller as it draws down close to the fabric. Hold the new loop as you did in step 1 and continue making the chain in the same way, until it is the desired length. To secure the end, simply slip the needle through the last loop and pull it up tight. Stitch the end of the chain to the garment at the second pin mark and secure on the reverse side.

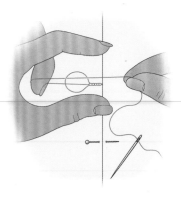

2 Using the second finger on your left hand, reach through and hook the working thread end, and then draw it through the loop to start a new loop.

Fabric belt carriers

Fabric carriers can be wide or narrow, depending on the style of your garment. They can be added during the construction of the waist finish or afterward. They are normally placed around the waistline at strategic points, such as the side seams, center back, and each side of the center back and center front.

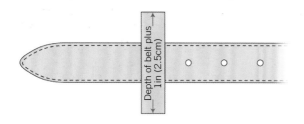

Depth of belt plus 1in (2.5cm)

1 The length of the belt carrier is normally stated on your pattern but, if not, the length of each carrier will need to be the depth of your belt plus 1in (2.5cm). However, if you are working with very thick fabric, you will need to allow a little bit more. Cut a straight-grain strip of fabric three times the finished width of your carriers, by the length required for your total number of carriers.

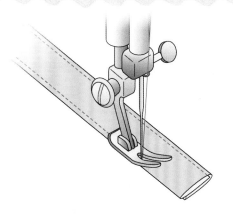

2 Finish one long edge of the strip and then fold the strip to a third of its original width, with the long raw edge inside. Topstitch down both long edges (see page 42). Cut the finished strip into the individual belt carrier lengths calculated in step 1, and apply to your garment using one of the following methods.

TIP
On casual garments create a bar-tack effect by setting your machine to a small, close zigzag stitch instead of a straight stitch to attach the pressed ends of the belt carriers.

Attaching fabric carriers to a straight waistband

1 Before attaching the waistband, position the belt carriers, wrong side up, on the right side of the garment at the positions indicated on your pattern, with one end even with the waist edge. Pin and stitch the carriers in place along the waist seamline.

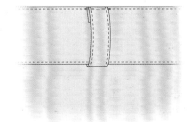

2 Attach your waistband as shown on page 122—the end of each carrier will be caught in the seam that joins the waistband to the garment waistline. Press the carriers up and then turn under the remaining raw end on each carrier. Topstitch each one to the top of the waistband through all layers of fabric, reverse stitching at the start and finish to secure.

Attaching fabric carriers to a faced waistline

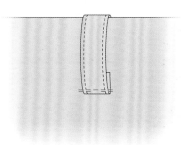

1 Before applying your waist facing, position the belt carriers, right side up, on the right side of the garment at the positions indicated on your pattern, with one end even with the waist edge. Pin and stitch the carriers in place, along the waist seamline. Attach and complete the waist facing as shown on page 123—the end of each carrier will be caught in the seam that joins the facing to the garment waistline.

2 Bring each carrier down on the right side of the garment and turn under 1/4 in (6mm) on the remaining raw end. Topstitch the end of each carrier to the garment through all layers, reverse stitching at the start and finish to secure.

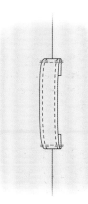

Attaching fabric carriers to a dress
Turn under 1/4 in (6mm) at each end of the carrier and press. Pin the carriers to your garment at the positions indicated on your pattern. Topstitch in place across the pressed ends at the top and bottom of each carrier, reverse stitching at the start and finish to secure.

Jeans-style skirt

This drop-waist, jeans-style mini-skirt is perfect for hot summer days. Made in a soft needlecord with a contrast waist facing and front pockets that form belt carriers, it's a style that you'll want to wear and wear.

Size

Size	US 6 (UK 8)	US 8 (UK 10)	US 10 (UK 12)	US 12 (UK 14)	US 14 (UK 16)	US 16 (UK 18)
Waist	23³/₄ in (60.5cm)	24³/₄ in (63cm)	26³/₄ in (68cm)	28³/₄ in (73cm)	30³/₄ in (78cm)	32³/₄ in (83cm)
Hips	33¹/₂ in (85.5cm)	34¹/₂ in (88cm)	36¹/₂ in (93cm)	38¹/₂ in (98cm)	40¹/₂ in (103cm)	42¹/₂ in (108cm)
Finished length (waist to hem)	16¹/₂ in (42cm)	16¹/₂ in (42cm)	16¹/₂ in (42cm)	16¹/₂ in (42cm)	16¹/₂ in (42cm)	16¹/₂ in (42cm)

Fabric quantities

45in- (112cm-) wide fabric						
Main	1¹/₃ yd (1.20m)	1¹/₃ yd (1.20m)	1¹/₃ yd (1.20m)	1¹/₃ yd (1.20m)	1¹/₃ yd (1.20m)	1¹/₃ yd (1.20m)
Contrast	¹/₃ yd (30cm)	¹/₃ yd (30cm)	¹/₃ yd (30cm)	¹/₃ yd (30cm)	¹/₃ yd (30cm)	¹/₂ yd (40cm)
60in- (150cm-) wide fabric						
Main	1yd (90cm)	1yd (90cm)	1yd (90cm)	1¹/₈ yd (1.00m)	1¹/₈ yd (1.00m)	1¹/₈ yd (1.00m)
Contrast	¹/₃ yd (30cm)	¹/₃ yd (30cm)	¹/₃ yd (30cm)	¹/₃ yd (30cm)	¹/₃ yd (30cm)	¹/₃ yd (30cm)
36in- (90cm-) wide medium-weight fusible interfacing						
	¹/₂ yd (40cm)	¹/₂ yd (40cm)	¹/₂ yd (40cm)	¹/₂ yd (40cm)	¹/₂ yd (40cm)	¹/₂ yd (40cm)

Skirt—all sizes
45in- (112cm-) wide main fabric

Skirt—all sizes
60in- (150cm-) wide main fabric

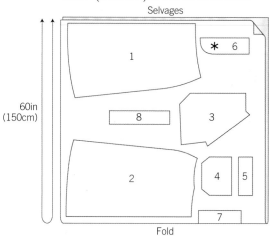

Front view

Back view

Cutting out your fabric

Use pattern pieces 1, 2, 3, 4, 5, 6, 7, 8, 9, 10, 11, and 12.

Note

Fabric quantities and cutting layouts are for one-way fabric only. If using a fabric with a two-way design, you may be able to fit pattern pieces into a smaller amount of fabric, but remember that grainlines must run parallel to selvages.

Key for cutting layouts

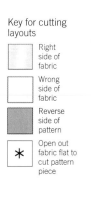

- ☐ Right side of fabric
- ☐ Wrong side of fabric
- ▨ Reverse side of pattern
- ✳ Open out fabric flat to cut pattern piece

Interfacing—all sizes
36in (90cm) wide

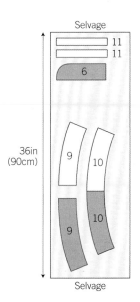

Selvage

11
11
6
9   10
10
9

36in (90cm)

Selvage

Contrast fabric—sizes US 6–14 (UK 8–16)
45–60in (112–150cm) wide

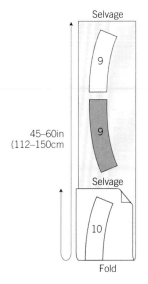

Selvage

9

9

45–60in (112–150cm

Selvage

10

Fold

Contrast fabric—size US 16 (UK 18)
45–60in (112–150cm) wide

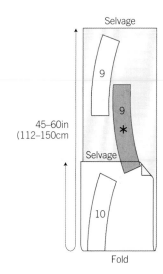

Selvage

9

9
✳

45–60in (112–150cm

Selvage

10

Fold

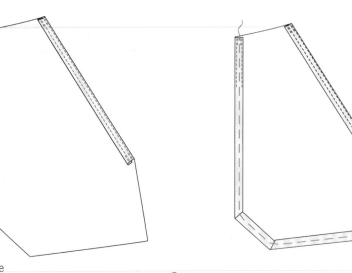

1 Following the appropriate cutting layout, cut out all your fabric and interfacing pieces. (See pages 29–30 for advice on cutting out and page 23 for how to understand pattern markings.) On each front pocket, press the interfacing strips to the wrong side of the fabric along the diagonal pocket edges. Press ¼ in (6mm) to the wrong side on each diagonal pocket edge and then press over a further ⅜ in (1cm) enclosing the raw edge. Stitch the pressed edges in place with two rows of topstitching (see page 42), with the first row close to the pressed edge and the second row ¼ in (6mm) away.

2 Press ⅜ in (1cm) to the wrong side along the other straight edges of the front pockets, apart from the waist edge and the side seam edge; baste in place. Starting at the waist edge, stitch the long pressed edge of each pocket in place with two rows of topstitching, as in step 2, but for 2½ in (6.5cm) only, and reverse stitching at the start to secure.

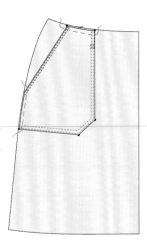

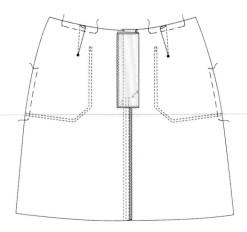

3 Stitch the darts on the skirt front and back pieces (see pages 118–19) and press toward the center front and center back. Place one skirt front right side up on a flat surface and lay the corresponding front pocket right side up on top, lining up the pocket corners with the marked pocket dots, and matching the waist and side seam edges. Pin and baste the pocket in position around all edges. Repeat with the remaining skirt front and pocket. Working from the right side of the fabric and starting at the side seam edge, stitch each pocket in place with two rows of topstitching, finishing 2in (5cm) below the waist edge, and reverse stitching to secure.

4 Finish the center front skirt edges and stitch together from the matched dots to the hem edge. Press interfacing to the wrong side of the zipper facing and finish the curved edge. Insert the zipper following the fly zipper method on pages 56–7, starting at step 2. If you have not already done so, snip into the left center front seam allowance at the base of the zipper, and press the seam allowances toward the right front. Stitch the seam allowances in place with two rows of topstitching from the base of the zipper to the hem edge.

5 Stitch a pocket band to the top edge of each back pocket, matching notches, with a ⅜ in (1cm) seam. Finish the seam allowances together and press them toward the pocket band. Topstitch the seam allowances in place, working one row close to the seamline and the second row ¼ in (6mm) away. Press ¼ in (6mm) and then a further ⅜ in (1cm) to the wrong side on the top edge of the band, enclosing the raw edges. Stitch the pressed edges in place with two rows of topstitching, as before. Press ⅜ in (1cm) to the wrong side on the remaining pocket edges.

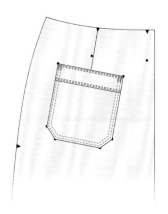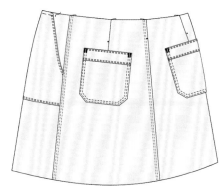

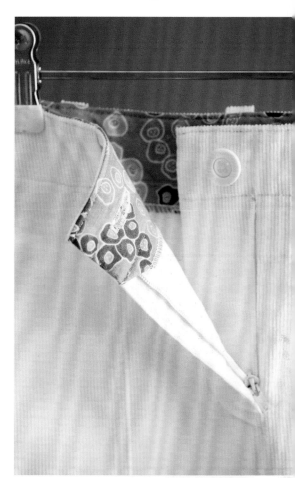

6 Apply the pockets to the skirt backs as shown in Applying Patch Pockets on page 75, making two rows of topstitching around the pressed edges to match the pocket top edges. Reinforce the pocket corners with zigzag stitches, as shown on page 76.

7 Stitch the skirt front to the skirt back pieces at the side seams. Finish the seam allowances together and press toward the backs. Topstitch the seam allowances in place with two rows of topstitching to match the pockets. Stitch the skirt back pieces together at the center back seam. Finish the seam allowances together and press toward the left back; topstitch in place, as before.

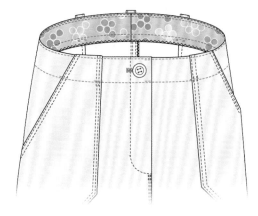

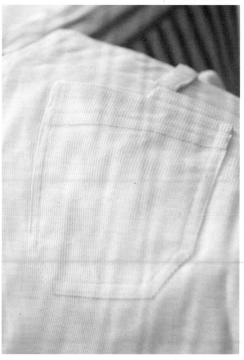

8 Make up the belt carriers as shown in step 2 of Fabric Belt Carriers on page 125, cutting your strip into three equal lengths. Attach the carriers as shown in step 1 of Attaching Fabric Carriers to a Faced Waistline on page 125, but do not attach the fasteners at this point. Keeping the belt carriers out of the way, topstitch the waist facing in place, stitching one row close to the waist edge, and a second row 1³/₈ in (3.5cm) down, reverse stitching over the edges of the pockets to secure at the front. Remove all basting, then stitch the loose ends of the belt carriers in place following step 2 of Attaching Fabric Carriers to a Faced Waistline, page 125. Work a buttonhole on the right waist and attach a button to the left waist to correspond (see pages 44–8). Finally, finish the hem edge (see page 39), press 1¹/₂ in (4cm) to the wrong side, and machine stitch in place.

Workshop 9

Tucks, pleats, and more fastenings

Tucks and pleats are another method of disposing of fabric fullness—or in other words, drawing in a piece of flat fabric to fit the body's shape. This workshop also covers various types of fastenings, from fabric-covered buttons to hooks and eyes, snaps, and hook-and-loop tape. At the end of the workshop you will find a gorgeous evening skirt, which features plenty of pleats and tucks to practice on!

Tucks

A tuck is a fold of material held in position by a line of machine stitches. On your pattern each tuck will be marked with two stitching lines that are brought together to create a fold. The width of a tuck and the spacing between tucks depend on the fabric thickness and the effect you want to achieve. Most tucks are purely for decoration, but they can also be used to control fullness or, in the case of circular tucks, to reduce length (see Sewing for Children, page 113).

Types of tucks
Most tucks are stitched on the straight grain, parallel to the fold, which means that they are uniform in width. There are four main types of tucks: blind, spaced, release, and pin tucks.

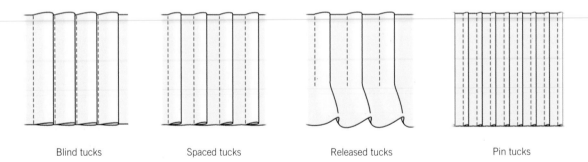

| Blind tucks | Spaced tucks | Released tucks | Pin tucks |

Blind tucks: These tucks meet or overlap.
Spaced tucks: Here the tucks are stitched with spaces between them.
Released tucks: Sometimes known as dart tucks, released tucks are stitched to a certain point and can be used to control fullness over the bust and hips.
Pin tucks: Purely decorative, pin tucks are spaced tucks that are very narrow—around ⅛ in (3mm) wide.

Fabric allowance for tucks
The amount of fabric required per tuck is generally three times the finished width of the tuck—ie, the underside of the tuck plus the upper part of the tuck plus the area that it covers. For example, four 1in- (2.5cm-) wide tucks will require 12in (30cm) of fabric.

Stitching straight tucks

When marking the position of tucks on your fabric, there is no need to transfer all the stitching lines from the pattern pieces for every single tuck. Instead, you can mark the lines for one tuck at the edge of a group, stitch it, and then use a simple cardboard gauge to baste the remaining tucks in place, as shown here.

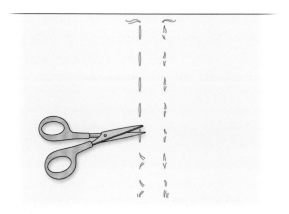

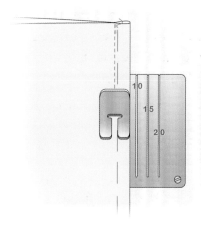

1 To mark the stitching lines of the first tuck, work a row of large uneven basting stitches (see page 33), using a double thread in your needle. Sew through the pattern and the fabric together, then cut the thread at the center of each long stitch. Carefully remove the pattern, without pulling out the marker threads you've just sewn. With wrong sides together, fold the tuck along the center, bringing the stitching lines (indicated by the marker threads) together. Pin the tuck just outside the stitching lines and press flat, taking care not to iron over the pins. Baste the tuck just inside the marker threads, then remove the pins and marker threads.

2 Reverse stitching at the beginning to secure, machine stitch the tuck along the line of removed marker threads, using your machine foot or seam guide (see page 35) as an aid to keeping your stitching straight and even. To finish, tie the ends together on the wrong side (see page 36). Remove the basting and open out the fabric layers. Using a pressing cloth between the fabric and the iron, press the tuck flat in the required direction.

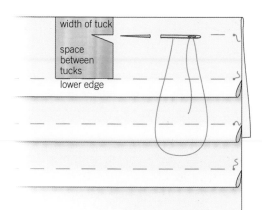

3 To mark and stitch the remaining tucks, measure the width of the tuck and the space between the stitching lines—both should be shown on your pattern piece. Cut a cardboard rectangle as long as the sum of these two widths, and about 1in (2.5cm) wide. Measuring from the top of the gauge, mark the tuck width on it with a notch. Refold your fabric, wrong sides together, and place the gauge on it, so the gauge lower edge is along the previous stitching line and upper edge is along the fold. Pin the tuck along the whole length at the notch position and then baste the layers together just below the pin line. Machine stitch the tuck as in step 2, but along the line of the removed pins; press. Repeat to form the remaining tucks, then stitch across the ends within the seam allowance to keep them in place.

Stitching circular tucks

Circular tucks can be used to shorten a skirt or top, while creating a decorative feature around the lower edge. If you are using an opaque fabric, they can also be used to "secretly" add length by hiding a joining seam on the underside of the tuck. Circular tucks need to be stitched "in the round," so you will need to join the side seams first.

1 For circular tucks it is easier to mark the foldlines than the stitching lines. To do this, follow step 1 of Stitching Straight Tucks, page 131. Then, once you have removed your pattern pieces, stitch and press any side and center back garment seams. Fold the garment in half with wrong sides together along one of your marked foldlines, making sure the marking threads sit right on the edge of the fold. Pin the two layers of fabric together all around your garment and then press the fold.

2 Using a tape measure, or a cardboard gauge indicating the depth of your tuck—see step 3 of Stitching Straight Tucks, page 131—pin and baste around the garment at the tuck stitching line position. Machine stitch the tuck in place just to the side of the basted line, using a seam guide as an aid to keeping your stitching straight (see page 131) and overlapping your stitching ends to secure. Remove all the basting and then open out the fabric layers. Using a pressing cloth between the fabric and the iron, press the tuck toward the hem.

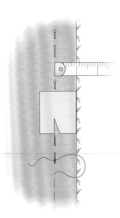

Pleats

Another method of disposing of fullness in a decorative manner, pleats are formed by creating vertical folds in fabric along the straight grain. Unlike tucks, pleats are never stitched all the way down; they usually hang free from a top fixing such as a waistband, though sometimes they are topstitched on the edge partway down, falling free beneath the topstitching. A pleat can appear as a single pleat, in a group of pleats, or as part of an entire pleated section, and can be pressed into sharp creases or left unpressed to fall into soft folds. Pleats can be folded in several ways to give a variety of styles, but the easiest ones to create and use are inverted pleats and box pleats (see opposite).

Choosing fabrics for pleats

The right choice of fabric is important for pleated garments. For soft, unpressed pleats choose a fluid fabric that does not crease easily, such as crepe de chine. Not every fabric will hold a pressed pleat, so for pressed pleats choose smooth, crisp, light- to medium-weight, firmly woven fabrics, such as linen or gabardine. Sharp pressed pleats are easier to maintain if you use a fabric that can be dry cleaned, because the pleats are pressed as part of the process. If you have to wash the fabric yourself, you may need to re-form and press the pleats afterward (although you can baste them in place before washing the garment to make this job easier). Another possibility is to edge stitch the pleats (see page 42) to make life simpler when you come to re-press the garment.

Understanding pleats

Each pleat will have a foldline and a placement line, both of which are marked on the pattern and should be transferred to the fabric (see page 31). Arrows are normally printed on the pattern to show you the direction in which to fold the pleat.

To form a pleat, you fold the fabric so that the foldline is brought to meet the placement line. The fabric between the two is called the underfold and its crease line is called the backfold.

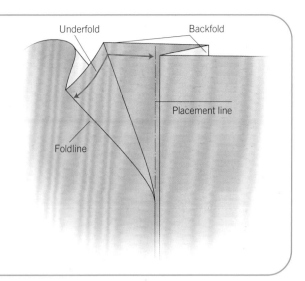

Underfold

Backfold

Placement line

Foldline

TIP

If you are not following a pattern and want to form an inverted or box pleat, fold your fabric on the straight grain, as illustrated in the diagrams on the left, then pin it in place and check the effect. As a rough guide, allow 3–4in (7.5–10cm) for each underfold to allow the pleats to hang well.

Inverted pleats and box pleats

Inverted pleats are more versatile, as you can use them on garments, such as skirts and coats, and also on home furnishings, especially bed skirts, valances at windows, and chair slipcovers. They can be used either in groups or individually, whereas box pleats are normally used in groups.

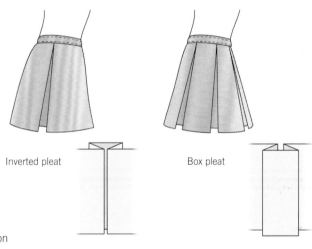

Inverted pleat

Box pleat

Inverted pleats have two foldlines that meet at a common placement line, and the backfolds face away from each other. There is also a version that has a separate back to the pleat, which allows for more economical use of your fabric and gives you the opportunity to bring in a contrast fabric.

Box pleats have two foldlines and two placement lines; the folds face away from each other and the backfolds toward each other.

Forming inverted and box pleats

Both inverted and box pleats are formed on the right side of the fabric using the same process—the only difference is in the direction of the foldlines to the placement line. The following diagrams illustrate a single inverted pleat.

1 To transfer the pleat markings onto the right side of the fabric, sew a row of large uneven basting stitches (see page 33) using a double thread in your needle. Sew the stitches through the pattern and the fabric together, then cut the thread at the center of each long stitch. Carefully remove the pattern, without pulling out the threads that you have just stitched.

Foldline

Foldline

Placement line

2 Working from the right side, fold the fabric along a foldline, and then bring this fold to its placement line. Pin the pleat in place through all layers of fabric. Repeat with the second foldline, bringing it over to meet the first one at the placement line. Remove all the thread markings as you pin. Baste the pleat in position close to each foldline through all layers of fabric, removing the pins as you work.

Bring foldline to placement line

TIP

When sewing the basting stitches, it is helpful to use one color of thread for the foldlines and another for the placement lines.

TIP

If you intend to press your pleats into crisp folds, it is best to finish and turn up the hem edge before you form the pleats.

3 If you want to press the pleats into sharp creases, work with the right side up and press the pleat using a damp pressing cloth between the fabric and the iron. Let the pleat dry before moving it off your ironing board and removing the pressing cloth. Now, with the wrong side up, press the pleats again using a pressing cloth.

4 If the backfolds have left an impression on the right side of your garment, work with the right side up and slide strips of thick paper under the fold of each pleat, then press again. Leave the basting in place for as long as possible during the construction of your garment.

Inverted pleats with separate underlays

This version of an inverted pleat has a separate underlay that forms the underside, or back, of the pleat and is joined at the backfold positions with a seam.

1 Transfer the foldlines to the wrong side of your fabric, as shown in step 1 of Forming Inverted and Box Pleats (see page 133). Place the two sides of the pleat with right sides together and the foldlines matching. Baste along the foldlines. Open out the pleat extensions and press flat.

2 With right sides together, place the pleat underlay on top of the basted pleat extensions, matching any pattern markings. Pin them together along the raw edges and baste the pleat edges together. Now stitch the pleat edges together, starting just over twice the hem depth up from the hem edge, and finishing at the top of the pleat; reverse stitch to secure. Remove the basting stitches and press the seams flat as sewn.

3 Unpick the foldline basting stitches. Finish the hem edge of both the garment and the pleat underlay. Now fold up the hems to the wrong side and sew in place (see page 64). Pin and re-baste the unstitched edges of the pleat extensions and underlay together, then machine stitch each side from the matched hem edges to the previous stitching, overlapping the stitching to secure.

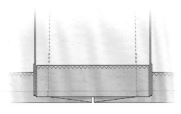

4 Press the seams flat as sewn, then diagonally trim across the corners of the seam allowances at the hem edges. Finish the main seam allowances together and finish the base corners at the hem edges with closely spaced overcast stitch (see page 34).

Topstitching pleats

Topstitching helps pleats to hang correctly and lie flat. Although it is normally just decorative (see page 42), in this instance it is a practical way to hold pleats in place from the waist to the hip. The topstitching is worked through all fabric layers of the pleat.

Topstitching a box pleat

Working from the right side, mark with a pin where the topstitching will begin on the pleat, then stitch through all thicknesses of fabric, along the folded edge, from the pin to the top of the pleat. Do not reverse stitch at the beginning and end of the stitching—instead, tie the thread ends on the wrong side to secure (see page 36). Repeat on the other side of the box pleat.

Topstitching an inverted pleat

Working from the right side, mark with a pin where the topstitching will begin on the pleat. Insert the machine needle down through the pleat foldlines at the pin position, and remove the pin. Take two or three steps across the pleat, pivot the work (see page 37), and stitch up to the top, parallel to the foldline. Beginning again at the position where the pin was, topstitch the remaining side of the pleat as before but in the opposite direction. Tie the thread ends on the wrong side to secure (see page 36).

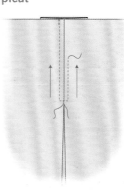

Fastenings

Buttons/buttonholes and zippers, which are common ways of fastening something, were covered in Workshops 1 and 2. Now we are going to take a look at the various other types of closures available, some of which are purely functional and hidden from view, while others are designed to provide an essential decorative element.

Snaps

Snaps can be either sew-on or no-sew (see page 136). Both types have the same method of closure—a ball that fits into a socket. Sew-on snaps, also known as press studs, are purely functional and can be used anywhere that a lightweight fastening is required. They can also be an additional fastener and are often used at the neckline of a garment that has a button fastening. They are readily available in black and silver metal and clear plastic. No-sew snaps, also known as poppers or poppa snaps, are held in place by metal prongs. The holding power of these fasteners is strong, so they are suitable for heavy fabrics. Available in a variety of colors and types and in a number of weights and sizes, they are ideal for children's wear (see page 113), casualwear, sportswear, and home furnishings.

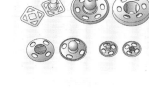

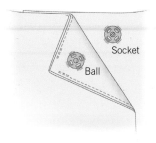

Socket

Ball

Standard hooks and eyes

Standard hooks and eyes are made of metal and come in both black and silver finishes, and in sizes ranging from 1 (the smallest) to 3 (the largest). The eyes can be straight or round. A straight eye, often called a bar, is normally used when the edges of your garment overlap, and a round eye on butted edges.

Standard hook and straight bar

Standard hook and looped eye

Sew-on snaps

Metal sew-on snaps are usually round and are available in sizes ranging from 1/4 in (6mm) to 3/4 in (20mm) in diameter; they are suitable for medium- to heavyweight fabrics. Plastic sew-on snap fasteners, which can be either round or square, are more delicate. They are perfect for lightweight fabrics such as semi-sheers and lingerie, and are available in sizes 1/4 –3/8 in (6–10mm).

To sew on a snap, position the ball half on the underside of the overlap, far enough in from the edge that it will not show on the right side. Sew four hand stitches through each hole, without stitching through to the right side of the garment; finish with backstitches (see page 33) at the snap edge. Position the socket half of the snap on the right side of the underlap to align with the ball. Sew the socket firmly in place in the same way as for the ball.

No-sew snaps

No-sew snaps consist of four parts: two caps, which form the top and base of the snap, plus a pronged ball and a pronged socket, which form the closure and which anchor the caps to the fabric. There is also an open-ring version available for knitted fabric, which allows the fabric to show through the central ring. The position of the prongs varies according to the use, but the application is generally the same. The packs of snaps come with a special tool for attaching them, so follow the manufacturer's instructions for attaching them to your garment.

Hooks and eyes

Hooks and eyes are small, strong metal fasteners, which come in different sizes and strengths. They are great for fastening waistbands and also as an extra fastening at the top of a zipper. When choosing what type of hook and eye you should use, think about where it will be placed, the strain it needs to withstand, and the weight of the fabric—a small, standard one is fine at a neckline, but totally inadequate on a skirt waistband, where a special, heavy-duty waistband hook and bar would be best. There are large thread-covered hooks and eyes with round loops, used on coats, jackets, and garments made from pile fabrics.

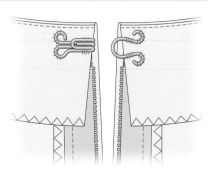

Attaching to overlapping edges: Place the hook on the underside of the garment overlap, about 1/8 in (3 mm) in from the finished edge. Mark the position with a chalk pencil. Secure your working thread and then stitch around each hole without stitching through the right side of the fabric. Pass the needle between the fabric layers to the end of the hook, and stitch around the "neck" to secure it flat to the fabric. Fasten off the thread with a couple of tiny stitches. Overlap the garment edges correctly and then, using the chalk pencil, mark the spot on the underlap where the hook end finishes. Stitch a straight eye in place at that position, stitching through each hole as before.

Attaching to butted edges: Both the hook and the eye are sewn on the inside of the garment. Place the hook a scant 1/8in (2–3mm) in from the inside edge, then mark the position with a chalk pencil and sew it in place as shown under Attaching to Overlapping Edges. Place a round eye on the opposite inside edge, aligning it with the hook and making sure that the loop extends slightly over the finished edge. Mark the position of the eye, secure the thread, and sew in place through the holes. Pass the needle between the fabric layers and take three stitches around each side of the eye loop, near the edge, to hold it flat to the fabric. Secure the thread with a couple of backstitches.

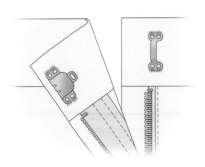

Attaching a waistband hook and bar: Place the hook part centrally on the underside side of the waistband overlap 1/8 in (3mm) in from the edge, making sure the bar will be hidden when the hook is fastened. Sew it in place with several stitches through each hole, following the instructions for the standard hook and eye (see Attaching to Overlapping Edges, opposite), but in this case the front end of the hook does not need to be secured flat to the fabric. Overlap the waistband to close the opening, and position the bar on the right side of the waistband so that it corresponds to the hook. Mark the position of the bar with pins, then sew the bar in place through each hole and all the fabric layers. Secure the thread on the underside with a couple of backstitches.

Tape fasteners

Tape fasteners are available in two types: hook-and-loop tape and snap tape. The hook-and-loop tape is made up of two tape strips—one with a fluffy, looped pile or nap, and the other with a rough, hooked surface. When pressed together, these two surfaces grip and remain locked until you pull them apart. The snap tape has ball snaps on one side of the tape and corresponding socket snaps on the other, which press together to close, and pull apart to open.

Hook-and-loop tape

Hook-and-loop tape comes in widths from 3/8 in (10mm) to 3/4 in (20mm). It is available in white, black, and beige, although other colors can sometimes be purchased from specialist sources. There are various types, from entirely sew-on through sew-and-stick to purely stick-on, plus a wider, heavy-duty stick-on type, all produced for varying uses. Where the backs of the tapes have a sticky surface, they are for sticking hard surfaces together. Sew-and-stick, in which one side can be sewn to fabric and the other can be stuck to a hard surface, is handy for projects such as hanging a fabric shade (blind), or attaching a cornice (pelmet) to a valance shelf over a window. The sew-on variety can be used on garments and home furnishings such as pillow covers and slipcovers.

Snap tape

Sometimes called popper tape or poppa tape, snap tape is much lighter than hook-and-loop tape and is often used on baby garments, children's wear (see page 113), sportswear, and duvet covers. When stitching the tape in place, you will need to attach a zipper foot to your machine so that you can stitch past the snaps. Depending on your garment instructions, the cut ends of the tape are normally enclosed in a seam, so make sure that you cut the snaps well clear of where you need to stitch for the seam.

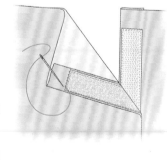

To attach sew-on hook-and-loop tape, cut it to the required length and then pin and baste the hook side to the right side of the opening's underlap; the tape is tough, so use a thimble (see page 9). Machine stitch the tape in place along both long edges and across the ends, overlapping the stitching to secure. Press the second side of the tape onto the first and then fold over the other side of the opening. Pin in place so that the tape is not visible from the right side. Separate the tapes, then baste and machine stitch in place, as before. Remove the basting and then overcast the cut ends (see page 34), sewing through one layer of fabric only.

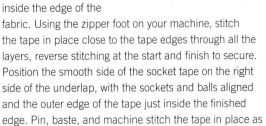

To attach snap tape, cut the tapes to the desired length, then pin and baste the smooth side of the ball tape to the underside of the opening's overlap, with the outer edge of the tape just inside the edge of the fabric. Using the zipper foot on your machine, stitch the tape in place close to the tape edges through all the layers, reverse stitching at the start and finish to secure. Position the smooth side of the socket tape on the right side of the underlap, with the sockets and balls aligned and the outer edge of the tape just inside the finished edge. Pin, baste, and machine stitch the tape in place as for the ball tape.

Covered hook and eye

These large, thread-covered hooks and eyes can be used as fasteners for coats and fur garments. On fabric coats they are attached using the same method as standard hooks and eyes, but on fur coats they are often set into seams.

Waistband hook and bar

These are special metal fasteners created for closing skirt or pants waistbands. Flat and strong, they are designed to prevent the loop from sliding out of the bar easily. It is advisable to use a strong topstitching thread when attaching these fasteners, as they will be put under great stress during wear.

TIP
Look out for a rouleau-loop turner, which is a long, thin metal rod with a latch hook at one end and a ring at the other. You insert it through the stitched tube, hook first, and then at the opposite end you will need to catch some fabric into the hook. To turn the rouleau tube right side out, gently pull on the ring.

Rouleau tubes

Rouleau tubes are thin, self-filled tubes of fabric. They can be used for fine shoulder straps and ties and are also used to make rouleau button loops.

1 To make a rouleau tube, cut a 1in- (2.5cm-) wide bias strip of fabric (see page 98) and fold it in half lengthwise, with right sides together. Stitch down the length of the fabric 1/4 in (6mm) in from the fold, slightly stretching the bias as you stitch. Thread a large needle or bodkin (see page 9) with a length of heavy-duty thread. Fasten the thread into the seam allowance at one end of the tube. Insert the needle, eye first, into the tube.

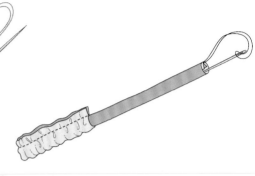

2 Work the needle through to the other end of the tube, gradually turning the tube right side out by pulling on the thread and feeding the seam allowances into the tube.

Rouleau button loops

Rouleau button loops can be substituted for buttonholes, especially on more delicate fabrics. You will often see them on bridal and eveningwear. They work best with fabric-covered or ball-shaped buttons but can also be used with shank buttons. Rouleau button loops can be used on the cuffs of sleeves, as well as on the fronts and backs of dresses, blouses, and waistbands. They are made from a rouleau tube cut into shorter lengths.

Adjusting the opening

If you are substituting loops for another kind of fastening, you will need to adjust your pattern, as the loops are stitched in on the edge of the garment, and not set in from the edge as with standard buttonholes. First cut out from fabric the side of the garment to which the buttons are going to be sewn, according to the pattern. Then, on the pattern, mark the center front or center back line on the side to which the loops are going to be sewn. Add a 5/8 in (1.5cm) seam allowance and draw in a new cutting line. Adjust the corresponding facing in the same way. Cut out your adjusted pattern pieces from fabric.

Using a paper template

A paper template will help to ensure that the loops are spaced evenly and are the same size. Before you begin you will first need to decide whether you would like them to be applied as individual loops or in a continuous row. As a general rule, use single, spaced loops if your buttons are large, and continuous loops if your buttons are small. You will also need to have made a single length of rouleau tubing equal to the sum of the lengths of the loops required.

1 Cut a strip of paper to fit the entire length of your opening and draw in the button position line (along which the buttons will be sewn), 5/8 in (1.5cm) in from the right-hand edge; this amount will be the seam allowance. Draw a second line parallel to the first, within the seam allowance and 1/4 in (6mm) from the previous line; this is where the ends of the loops should finish when they are applied.

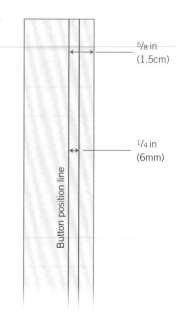

5/8 in (1.5cm)

1/4 in (6mm)

Button position line

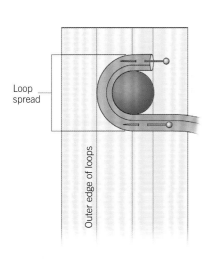

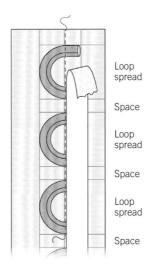

Loop spread

Outer edge of loops

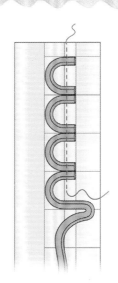

Loop spread

Space

Loop spread

Space

Loop spread

Space

2 Place the center of a button on the button position line at the top of the template where the first button will sit. Wrap a length of the rouleau tube around the button, with the seam side up, and pin the starting end at the ¹/₄ in (6mm) line. Pin the other end of the tube below the button where it meets the ¹/₄ in (6mm) line. Mark the outer edges of the tube on the template above and below the button. The distance between these marks is called the loop spread. Also mark the outer edge of the loops, and draw another parallel line down the whole length of the template at this point.

3 For individual loops, continue with this step and skip step 4; or for continuous loops, skip to step 4 without doing this step. Continue marking the spread of each loop and the spaces in between them down the entire length of the paper template. Using the first pinned loop as a guide, cut up the remaining tube into same-size lengths—you'll need one piece for each loop. Position the loops on the guide, holding them in place with masking tape, then carefully machine baste (see page 35) the loops to the template close to the button position line.

4 For continuous loops, place the tube on the template and pin in place, turning the tube for the next loop at the ¹/₄ in (6mm) line in the seam allowance. Repeat for each loop, trimming or clipping the turns in the tube so that the loops lie flat and close together. Hold the loops in place with masking tape and then carefully machine baste the loops to the template close to the button position line.

Attaching button loops

1 To attach the loops to your garment, pin the paper template to the right side of your garment with the loops on top, matching up the ⁵/₈ in (1.5cm) line with the seamline of your garment. Remove the masking tape and carefully machine baste the template and loops in place following the first line of stitching. Make sure that your machine stitches correctly over the tubing and does not skip stitches. Work a second row of stitching if necessary and then carefully tear away the paper template.

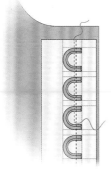

2 With right sides together, pin and baste the garment facing to the main garment, sandwiching the loops in between. Working from the garment side, stitch the facing in place along the row of machine basting. Trim the seam allowances, understitch the facing to the seam allowances (see page 43), and turn the facing to the inside along the seamline. Press flat.

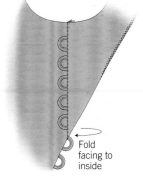

Fold facing to inside

Organdy evening skirt

This beautiful double-layered skirt with pleat and tuck detailing is perfect for the evening, but if you make up the lining section on its own, you will have a flattering A-line skirt for the daytime, too!

Fabric suggestions

Main fabric, for overskirt: Organdy, organza

Contrast fabric, for lining: Shantung or shot silk, acetate, or polyester lining fabric

You will also need

Skirt pattern pieces traced off from the pattern sheets at the back of this book (see page 192)

Matching thread

8in (20cm) zipper

Medium-weight fusible interfacing (see Fabric Quantities)

3/8 in (10mm) self-cover button

Note

5/8 in (1.5cm) seam allowances are included unless otherwise stated.

Stitch seams with right sides together and notches matching, unless otherwise stated.

Size

Size	US 6 (UK 8)	US 8 (UK 10)	US 10 (UK 12)	US 12 (UK 14)	US 14 (UK 16)	US 16 (UK 18)
Waist	23¾ in (60.5cm)	24¾ in (63cm)	26¾ in (68cm)	28¾ in (73cm)	30¾ in (78cm)	32¾ in (83cm)
Hips	33½ in (85.5cm)	34½ in (88cm)	36½ in (93cm)	38½ in (98cm)	40½ in (103cm)	42½ in (108cm)
Finished length (waist to hem)	24in (61cm)	24in (61cm)	24in (61cm)	24in (61cm)	24in (61cm)	24in (61cm)

Fabric quantities

45in- (112cm-) wide fabric						
Main	2½ yd (2.30m)	2½ yd (2.30m)	2¾ yd (2.50m)	2¾ yd (2.60m)	3 yd (2.80m)	3⅛ yd (2.90m)
Contrast	1½ yd (1.40cm)	1½ yd (1.40cm)	1½ yd (1.40cm)	1½ yd (1.40cm)	1½ yd (1.40cm)	1½ yd (1.40cm)
36in- (90cm-) wide medium-weight fusible interfacing						
	⅛ yd (10cm)	⅛ yd (10cm)	⅛ yd (10cm)	⅛ yd (10cm)	⅛ yd (10cm)	1¼ yd (1.10cm)

Skirt—all sizes
45in- (112cm-) wide main fabric

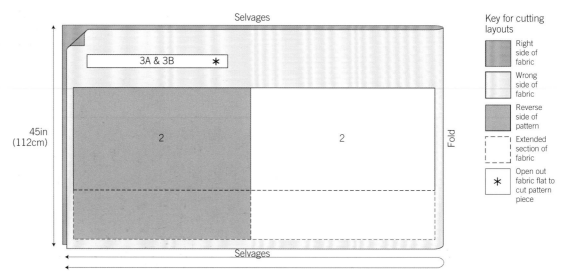

Key for cutting layouts

Right side of fabric

Wrong side of fabric

Reverse side of pattern

Extended section of fabric

* Open out fabric flat to cut pattern piece

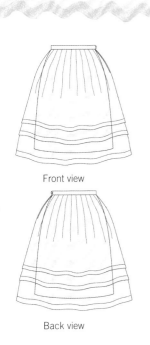

Front view

Back view

Cutting out your fabric

Use pattern pieces 1, 2, 3A & 3B, and 4.

Note

Fabric quantities and cutting layouts are for one-way fabric only. If using a fabric with a two-way design, you may be able to fit pattern pieces into a smaller amount of fabric, but remember that grainlines must run parallel to selvages.

Skirt—all sizes
60in- (150cm-) wide main fabric

Interfacing—size
US 16 (UK 18)
36in (90cm) wide

Interfacing—sizes
US 6–14 (UK 8–16)
36in (90cm) wide

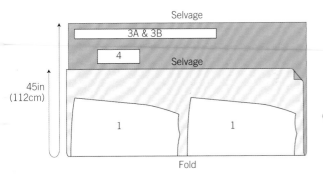

Selvage

3A & 3B

4

Selvage

45in
(112cm)

1   1

Fold

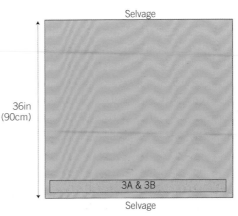

Selvage

36in
(90cm)

3A & 3B

Selvage

Selvage

36in
(90cm)

3A & 3B

Selvage

TIPS

If you would prefer your evening skirt to be a little longer, see Basic Pattern Alterations: Skirts and Pants (page 25).

To make a simple A-line skirt, follow steps 1, 2, 3, and 4, then attach the waistband following the Straight Waistband method on page 122. Attach a skirt hook and bar to fasten the waist (see page 137).

1 Following the appropriate cutting layout, cut out all your fabric and interfacing pieces. (See pages 29–30 for advice on cutting out and page 23 for how to understand pattern markings.) Staystitch the waist edges of the lining pieces (see page 43). Stitch the darts on the lining front and back (see page 118) and press toward the center front and center back.

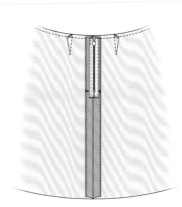

2 With right sides together, pin and baste the lining front to the lining back at the left side seam. Machine stitch the side seam from hem edges to the zipper notches, reverse stitching at each end to secure. Finish the seam allowances separately, including the zipper opening edges, then install a zipper in the lining following Lapped Application method on page 55.

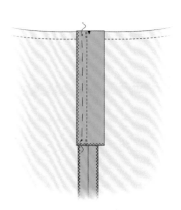

3 Press the zipper placket in half lengthwise, with wrong sides together, and finish the long and short unnotched edges together. Working on the wrong side, place the placket over the zipper, with raw waist edges even and the notch at the top in line with the zipper teeth. Baste and stitch the long finished edges of the placket to the lining back seam allowances.

4 With right sides together, pin, baste, and machine stitch the lining back to the lining front at the right side seam. Press the seam open and finish the seam allowances separately. Make a narrow double 3/8 in (1cm) hem around the lower edge (see page 62).

5 On the overskirt pieces, press a very narrow double 1/8 in (3mm) hem to the wrong side along both edges of the zipper opening in the left side seam, tapering them to nothing just below the zipper notches. Machine stitch the hems in place.

6 Join the left side seam, from the overskirt hem edge to the zipper notches, with a French seam (see page 41). Join the right side seam from waist to hem in the same way. Press both seams toward the overskirt back.

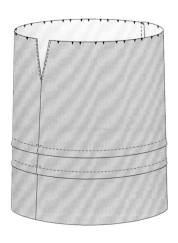

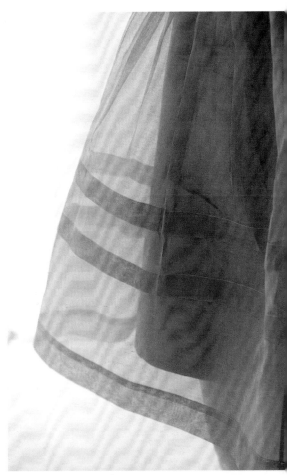

7 Make two 1in- (2.5cm-) deep tucks around the entire overskirt, following the instructions for Stitching Circular Tucks on page 132.

8 Form the pleats around the waist edge of the overskirt by bringing the notches together, in the direction shown on the pattern, and pin in place along the waist seamline. With the wrong side of the overskirt to the right side of the lining, pin the two layers together around the waist edge, matching the side seams and adjusting the pleats to fit if necessary. Baste the layers together just above the waist seamline.

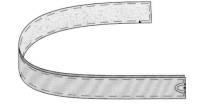

9 Apply interfacing to the wrong side of the lining waistband. Lay the overskirt waistband on top of the lining waistband, with the wrong side of the overskirt waistband to the right side of the lining waistband and the raw edges even. Pin and baste the waistband pieces together around the outer edges. Make up the rouleau button loop from the overskirt fabric (see Rouleau Tubes, page 138). Cut the tube to a length of 2$\frac{1}{8}$ in (5.5cm). Fold it in half and place it on the right side of the overskirt waistband at the position marked on the pattern, with raw edges even; stitch in place. Attach the waistband to the skirt waist using the Straight Waistbands method on page 122, taking care not to catch the loose end of the rouleau button loop into the seams as you stitch.

10 Make a 1$\frac{5}{8}$ in- (4cm-) deep double hem along the lower edge of the overskirt (see page 63). To finish, cover the button with lining fabric following the manufacturer's instructions, and sew it to the waistband to correspond with the rouleau button loop. Remove any remaining basting.

Workshop 10

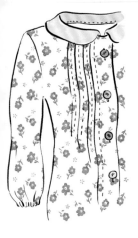

Necklines and collars

This workshop introduces a few simple collar styles and shows you how to finish off a neckline professionally. All tops and dresses have a neckline of some description, which is finished off with or without a collar. If there is no collar, then the neckline edge is finished with either a facing or a binding. At the end of the workshop you will find a fabulous summer dress featuring a Peter Pan collar and circular skirt, plus a bonus project for a pretty detachable collar.

Neck facings

A facing is a piece of fabric that is cut to match the outside shape of the garment exactly; when stitched in place, it sits on the inside of the garment providing a neat finish to the edge. Facings are normally cut from the same fabric as the main garment but can also be cut from contrasting fabric for a special design feature, or in a lighter fabric if the main fabric is particularly heavy or thick. Facings are generally separate pieces of fabric, but on straight edges such as a center front opening, they can be an extension of the main garment, in which case they are called extended facings.

We have already covered hem facings and waistline facings in Workshops 3 and 8, and in this workshop you will learn to apply neck facings, which can be used to finish a neckline edge. Whether the actual neckline shape is round, square, V-shaped, or sweetheart, the construction is much the same. On a garment with a button and buttonhole fastening down either the front or the back, the neck and opening facings are usually joined together. The facings used for the opening can either be separate pieces of fabric or extended sections of the main garment.

The three most common types of neck facings are the shaped neck facing (used where there is a center back opening, usually with a zipper), the shaped neck facing with separate front facings (often found on jacket fronts that close with buttons), and the shaped neck facing with extended front facings (commonly found on blouses that button up the front). Another type, the combination facing, is often used on sleeveless garments.

Shaped neck facing

This type of facing is formed by stitching together a front facing and two back facings. Before you begin, insert your zipper into the garment center back seam (see page 54) and join the garment shoulder seams.

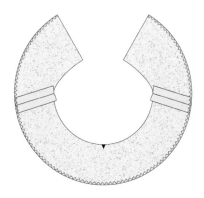

1 Iron interfacing to the wrong side of the facing pieces. With right sides together, stitch the front facing to the back facings at the shoulder seams, taking the appropriate seam allowance. Press the seams open and finish the outer edge of the facing (see page 39).

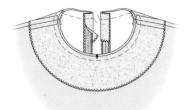

2 With right sides together and with shoulder seams and any notches matching, pin the facing to the neckline edge. Open up the zipper and wrap the short center back ends of the facing over each side of the zipper to the inside of the garment; baste the facing in place around the neckline.

3 Working with the facing on top, stitch the facing to the garment, taking the appropriate seam allowance and reverse stitching at each end to secure. Check that the neck seams line up at center back when the zipper is closed, and re-stitch if necessary, then remove the basting. Trim and grade the seam allowances, and clip into the curved seam allowances (see page 38). If your neckline is V-shaped or square, as shown in this diagram, stitch again over the first stitching at the corners to reinforce, then clip into the corners.

What is a tailor's ham?
This stuffed ironing aid, which is usually covered with plaid fabric on one side and solid-color fabric on the other, enables you to achieve a professional finish when pressing darts, sleeve caps, princess seams, and other similarly curved areas.

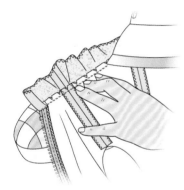

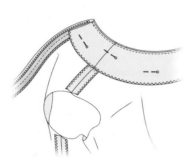

4 Using the corner of your ironing board (or a tailor's ham if you have one—see box, above right), carefully press the seam allowances toward the facing, taking care not to crease the facing or the garment. To keep the facing from rolling to the outside, understitch (see page 43) it to the seam allowances.

5 Fold the facing to the inside of the garment, allowing the seamline to roll just to the inside; pin and press in place. With the shoulder seams even, catch the edge of the facing to the seam allowances with a few whipstitches (see page 34).

6 Fold under the ends of the facing at the center back zipper opening. Making sure that they won't catch in the zipper, pin them in place. Open up the zipper and slipstitch (see page 34) the ends of the facing to the zipper tapes. Close the zipper and then attach a hook and eye at the top to secure (see page 136).

Shaped neck facing with separate front facings

This is formed by stitching a back facing to two separate front facings that extend to form facings for the front opening. Iron interfacing to the wrong side of the facing pieces. With right sides together, stitch the back facing to the front facings at the shoulder seams, taking the required seam allowance. Press the seams open and finish the outer edge of the facing. With right sides together and shoulder seams matching, pin and baste the facing to the front and neckline edges. Working from the facing side, machine stitch the facing in place, taking the appropriate seam allowance and reverse stitching at each end to secure. Remove the basting stitches, then grade and clip into the curved seam allowances. Complete the facing as for steps 4 and 5 of Shaped Neck Facing (see above).

Shaped neck facing with extended front facings

This is formed by stitching a back facing to two front facings that are extensions of the garment itself, rather than separate pieces. Iron interfacing to the wrong side of the back facing and of the front extensions, and join the pieces at the shoulder seams with right sides together. Press the seams open and finish the outer edge of the facing. With right sides together, and matching shoulder seams and any notches, fold the extended front facing back onto the garment, producing a fold down the center front edge. Pin, and then baste around the neckline edge. Working from the facing side, machine stitch the facing in place around the neckline taking the appropriate seam allowance and reverse stitching at each end to secure. Remove the basting, then grade and clip into the curved seam allowances (see page 38). Complete the facing as for steps 4 and 5 of Shaped Neck Facing, page 145.

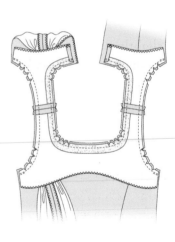

Combination facing

On a sleeveless top or a dress bodice, the neck facing and armhole facings are often joined together as one unit. This makes the inside look neater and gives a more professional finish, but a different method of construction is required. It is suitable for medium- to wide-width garment shoulders, or narrower shoulders on garments made from lightweight fabrics.

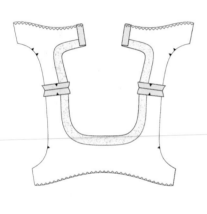
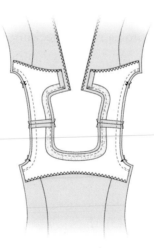

1 Join your garment shoulder seams and assemble, finish, and press all seams that intersect the neckline and armholes, but do not insert the zipper yet. Press the interfacing to the wrong side of the facing neckline edges as indicated on your pattern. With right sides together, stitch the front facing to the back facings at the shoulder seams. Finish the lower edges of the facing at front and back; press the seams open. Press 5/8 in (1.5cm) to the wrong side on the center back seam allowances.

2 With right sides together, pin and baste the facing to your garment neck and armhole edges, matching shoulder seams and any notches, and placing the pressed center back facing edges 5/8 in (1.5cm) in from the garment center back edges. Working from the facing side, machine stitch the facing in place around the armholes and neckline, taking the appropriate seam allowance and making sure that the neck seamlines match at the center back edges.

3 Trim, grade, and clip (see page 38) the neck and armhole seam allowances, then push each back section through its corresponding shoulder "tunnel" to turn the garment right side out. Using the corner of your ironing board (or a tailor's ham if you have one—see page 145), carefully press the seam allowances toward the facing, working as far up to the shoulders as you can, on both the armhole and neckline edges.

4 Around the unpressed shoulder areas on the neck and armhole edges, roll the seams between your fingers and thumbs to work them out to sit on the edge. Press flat, then press the remaining edges of the facing flat. To keep the facing from rolling to the right side, understitch it to the seam allowances (see page 43), stitching as far up to the shoulders as you can and reverse stitching at each end to secure. To do this, you will need to work on each front and back armhole, and front and back neck, individually.

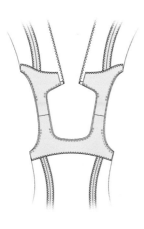

5 Finish the garment side seam edges and open out the facing at the side seam edges. With right sides together, and matching the underarm seams and the finished facing edges, join each garment side seam and armhole facing with one continuous line of stitching. Press the seams flat and trim the matched seams (see page 38) to reduce bulk. Fold the facing to the inside and press flat. With seams aligned, make a few whipstitches (see page 34) to catch the edge of the facing to the seam allowances. Insert your zipper and complete the facing following step 6 of Shaped Neck Facing on page 145.

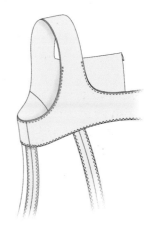

Bound and bias-faced necklines

A slightly daintier method of finishing a round neckline is to use bias binding, which will curve to fit the neckline edge. It can be applied either as a binding for the neckline or as a bias facing. A bound neckline is better for more casual styles as the binding is pressed in half and attached over the raw neckline edge, making it visible on both sides of the garment. For a more formal garment a bias facing works better, as the binding doesn't show on the right side.

Bound neckline

If your pattern is not designed to have a bound neckline, you will have to trim away the neckline seam allowance, as the binding sits right on the neck edge. Staystitch the neckline, working close to the raw edge (see page 43), then join the garment shoulder seams and insert the zipper. Either use a readymade bias binding ¾–1in (20–25mm) wide or make your own, as shown in Making Bias Binding, steps 1–4, on page 98. Apply the binding to the neck edge following the Machine and Hand Stitching Method for Applying Binding on page 99.

Bias-faced neckline

Either use a ⅜ in- (10mm-) wide readymade bias binding or make your own, as shown in Making Bias Binding, steps 1–4, on page 98. Staystitch your neckline edges (see page 43), then trim the seam allowances so they are the same depth as your bias binding's pressed edges. Join the garment shoulder seams, then follow steps 1 and 2 of Applying a Bias Hem Facing on page 65, but fold over the starting end of the binding vertically, not diagonally, by ⅜ in (1cm), and align this folded edge with the center back edge of the garment. At the finishing end, fold the binding back to align it with the opposite center back edge and trim away the excess to leave ⅜ in (1cm). To complete the neckline follow step 4 of Applying a Bias Hem Facing on page 65.

Simple collars

A collar is the part of a dress, shirt, blouse, jacket, or coat that fastens around, or frames, the neck. A collar may be permanently attached to the main garment or it can be detachable. Collars add a decorative touch to a neckline edge and come in many shapes and sizes. Some collars are made from just two pieces—a top collar and a bottom collar—but others can be made up of more pieces; a shirt collar, for example, can have a separate band.

Flat collars

Often referred to as a Peter Pan collar, a flat collar lies flat against the garment, because the inner edge of the collar follows the curve of the neckline. It is easy to make and attach. If the garment has a front opening, it is made in one part; or if it has a center back zipper opening, it is split into two parts.

Making and attaching a flat collar

The following illustrations show how to make a one-piece collar; if you have a two-piece collar, each unit is made in the same way. Before you begin, staystitch the neck edge of the garment (see page 43). Stitch, press, and finish all seams that intersect the neckline. If there is a zipper,

install it (see page 54) before applying the collar. Your pattern will instruct you to cut out two pieces of fabric (along with one piece of interfacing) from the collar pattern—these will be the top collar and the under collar. (For a two-piece collar, you will be instructed to cut out two top collars and two under collars.)

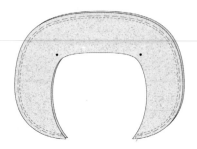

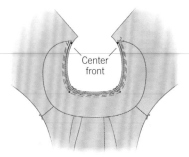

Center front

1 Iron interfacing to the wrong side of the top collar (see page 19). With right sides together and raw edges even, pin and baste the top collar to the under collar, leaving the neck edge open. Machine stitch the pieces together around the outer edge, reverse stitching at the start and finish to secure. Remove the basting, and trim and grade the seam allowances, trimming across any corners and notching or snipping curved seam allowances (see page 38).

2 Turn the collar right side out and tease out any corners. Press the collar, rolling the seam slightly to the underside, then pin and baste the collar neck edges together, matching notches. If you are making a two-piece collar, repeat steps 1 and 2 for the remaining collar pieces.

3 Working from the right side and with raw edges even, pin and baste the collar(s) to the neckline edge, matching notches to shoulder seams and the ends of the collar to the center front (and/or center back) at the neckline seam. (Bear in mind that the center front collar ends may overlap slightly within the seam allowance on a back-opening garment.) To finish off the neckline edge, apply a neck facing, sandwiching the collar between the two layers of fabric—see Neck Facings on pages 144–6. Remove the basting.

Shirt collars

Usually found on men's shirts, a shirt collar is made up of a collar and band. The band allows for the tie to sit under the turned-back section of the collar, but it is also found on women's dresses, shirts, and jackets. This type of collar is used only with a front opening and has pointed fronts. It can be made with a separate collar and band pieces, or as a one-piece collar and band in which the band is an extension of the collar piece. However, whether the stand is cut as one piece or as separate pieces, once it is pieced together it is applied in the same way.

Separate collar (above) and band (below)

One-piece collar and band

Making and attaching a shirt collar

Before you begin, staystitch the neckline edges (see page 43), stitch the front pieces to the back at the shoulder seams, finish the seam allowances, and press the seams open, then construct the front openings. Your pattern will instruct you either to cut out two identical pieces from fabric (along with one piece of interfacing) using each pattern piece.

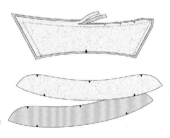

1 Iron interfacing to the wrong side of one collar piece, and to one band (separately if the band is separate, or in one piece with the collar interfacing if the band is an extension of the collar). With right sides together, pin and baste the collar pieces together along the side and upper edges, then machine stitch along these edges, taking the appropriate seam allowance. Remove the basting, grade the seam allowances, and trim the corners (see page 38). Using the corner of your ironing board (or a tailor's ham if you have one—see page 145), press the seam open and then toward the interfaced portion.

2 Turn the collar right side out, carefully pushing the corners out to form neat points. Working from the interfaced side, press the seamed edges flat and topstitch the finished edges if desired (see page 42).

3 Fold up the seam allowance along the neck edge of the non-interfaced band piece (whether or not it is an extension of the collar). Pin and baste in place close to the fold. Remove the pins, press, and trim the seam allowance to ¼ in (6mm).

4 If your band is an extension of the collar, skip both this step and the next one. If your band is separate, pin the lower edge of the collar to the upper edge of the interfaced band piece, with the right side of the interfaced collar piece to the right side of the band piece and with raw edges even, notches matching, and the collar band extending equally beyond the collar at both ends.

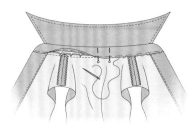

5 Place the other band piece on top, with right sides together, raw edges even, and the collar sandwiched between them. Pin and baste through all fabric layers. Machine stitch the collar and band together, taking the appropriate seam allowance and reverse stitching at each end to secure. Remove the basting, grade the seam allowances, and clip the curves if necessary (see page 38). Turn the band right side out and press the seam flat.

6 Clip into the garment neck seam allowances to enable the neckline to be pulled out flat and straight, making it easier for you to attach the collar. With right sides together and raw edges even, pin the interfaced side of the collar band to the neckline edge, matching the collar notches to the shoulder seams, and with the ends of the collar band in line with the front opening. Baste and then machine stitch in place. Grade the seam allowances, and clip if necessary.

7 Press the neck seam open, then up toward the collar band. Bring the basted edge of the collar band down to meet the neck seamline, pin, and then slipstitch (see page 34) this edge to the garment along the neckline machine stitching. Remove the basting. Topstitch or edgestitch (see page 42) the collar band if desired.

Detachable collar

In recent times, separate collars have been riding high on the fashion radar, as transformative pieces that can add a feminine twist to sweaters, plain tops, and dresses. One of the easiest ways to add to an outfit, they offer endless styling options.

1 Trace the detachable collar and collar band pieces from the pattern sheet at the back of this book (see page 192). Cut two collar pieces and two band pieces from fabric and one collar piece and one band piece from interfacing. Iron the interfacing to the wrong side of one collar piece and one band piece. With right sides together, pin and baste the two collar pieces together along the long, curved outer edge. Machine stitch with a 3/8 in (1cm) seam, then grade the seams, clip the curves, and remove the basting.

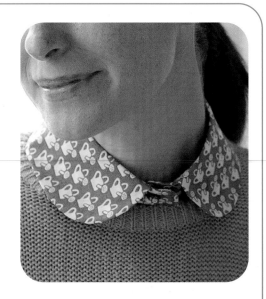

2 Press the seam allowances toward the non-interfaced side of the collar and understitch them in place (see page 43), then follow steps 4 and 5 of Making and Attaching a Shirt Collar, on pages 149–150.

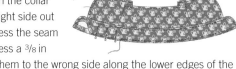

3 Turn the collar band right side out and press the seam flat. Press a 3/8 in (1cm) hem to the wrong side along the lower edges of the collar band, pressing open the seam at the front curved edges of the band to reduce bulk. Pin and baste the pressed edges of the band together, then either slipstitch the pressed edges or machine stitch them close to the folds. Remove the basting. For the closure, use either a button and buttonhole (see pages 44–8) or a snap (see pages 135–6).

TIP
You can decorate your collar in a variety of ways. Try adding a ribbon bow at the front or inserting a lace trim into the curved outer edge seam. Add rhinestones or an embroidered design before you construct the collar.

The perfect summer dress

Feel cool and charmingly feminine in this vintage-inspired cotton print summer dress, with its full circular skirt and Peter Pan collar. The structured bodice with princess seams and shaped midriff creates an elegantly fitted look—simply add a tulle underskirt to create that true 1950s style.

Fabric suggestions

Main fabric, for dress: Cotton prints, cotton poplin, linen, chambray, wool crepe

Contrast fabric, for collar: Plain cotton poplin, poly-cotton, Swiss cottons, fine linens

You will also need

Dress pattern pieces traced off from the pattern sheets at the back of this book (see page 192)

Matching thread

22in (56cm) zipper for sizes US 6/8/10 (UK 8/10/12), or 24in (61cm) zipper for sizes US 12/14/16 (UK 14/16/18)

Lightweight fusible interfacing (see Fabric Quantities)

1 1/3 yd (1.20m) of 1/4 – 3/8 in- (6–10mm-) wide cotton tape

6yd (5.40m) of 3/8 in- (10mm-) wide matching bias binding

Hook and eye

Note

5/8 in (1.5cm) seam allowances are included unless otherwise stated.

Stitch seams with right sides together and notches matching, unless otherwise stated.

Size

Size	US 6 (UK 8)	US 8 (UK 10)	US 10 (UK 12)	US 12 (UK 14)	US 14 (UK 16)	US 16 (UK 18)
Bust	31in (79cm)	32in (81.5cm)	34in (86.5cm)	36in (91.5cm)	38in (96.5cm)	40in (101.5cm)
Waist	23 3/4 in (60.5cm)	24 3/4 in (63cm)	26 3/4 in (68cm)	28 3/4 in (73cm)	30 3/4 in (78cm)	32 3/4 in (83cm)
Hips	33 1/2 in (85.5cm)	34 1/2 in (88cm)	36 1/2 in (93cm)	38 1/2 in (98cm)	40 1/2 in (103cm)	42 1/2 in (108cm)
Finished length (back neck to waist)	16 3/8 in (41.5cm)	16 1/2 in (42cm)	16 3/4 in (42.5cm)	17in (43cm)	17 1/4 in (43.5cm)	17 1/2 in (44cm)
Finished length (waist to hem)	22 1/2 in (57cm)	22 1/2 in (57cm)	22 1/2 in (57cm)	22 1/2 in (57cm)	22 1/2 in (57cm)	22 1/2 in (57cm)

Fabric quantities

45in- (112cm-) wide fabric						
Main	4 1/4 yd (3.80m)	4 1/4 yd (3.80m)	4 1/4 yd (3.90m)	4 1/3 yd (4.00m)	4 1/2 yd (4.10m)	4 2/3 yd (4.20m)
Contrast	1/2 yd (40cm)	1/2 yd (40cm)	1/2 yd (40cm)	1/2 yd (40cm)	1/2 yd (40cm)	1/2 yd (40cm)
60in- (150cm-) wide fabric						
Main	3 3/4 yd (3.40m)	3 3/4 yd (3.50m)	4 yd (3.60m)	4 yd (3.60m)	4 yd (3.70m)	4 yd (3.70m)
Contrast	1/2 yd (40cm)	1/2 yd (40cm)	1/2 yd (40cm)	1/2 yd (40cm)	1/2 yd (40cm)	1/2 yd (40cm)
36in- (90 cm-) wide medium-weight fusible interfacing						
	1/2 yd (40cm)	1/2 yd (40cm)	1/2 yd (40cm)	1/2 yd (40cm)	1/2 yd (40cm)	1/2 yd (40cm)

Dress—all sizes
45in- (112cm-) wide main fabric

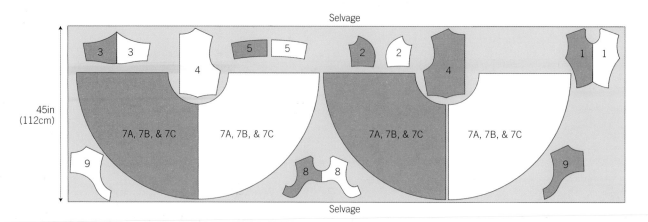

45in (112cm)

Selvage

3 | 3 | 4 | 5 | 5 | 2 | 2 | 4 | 1 | 1

7A, 7B, & 7C | 7A, 7B, & 7C | 7A, 7B, & 7C | 7A, 7B, & 7C

9 | 8 | 8 | 9

Selvage

Dress—all sizes
60in- (150cm-) wide main fabric

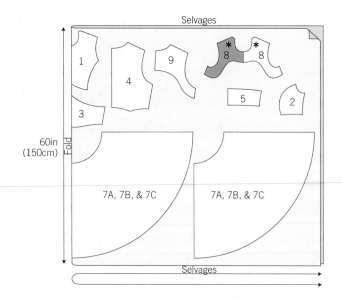

60in (150cm)

Fold

Selvage

1 | 9 | 8 | 8 | 4 | 5 | 2 | 3

7A, 7B, & 7C | 7A, 7B, & 7C

Selvages

Key for cutting layouts

- Right side of fabric
- Wrong side of fabric
- Reverse side of pattern
- * Open out fabric flat to cut pattern piece

Front view

Back view

Dress—all sizes
45–60in- (112–150cm-) wide contrast fabric

Interfacing—all sizes
36in (90cm) wide

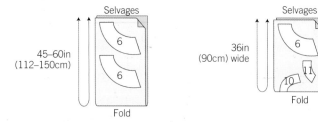

45–60in (112–150cm)

Selvages

6 | 6

Fold

36in (90cm) wide

Selvages

6 | 11 | 10

Fold

Cutting out your fabric
Use pattern pieces 1, 2, 3, 4, 5, 6,
7A, 7B, & 7C, 8, 9, 10, and 11.

Note
Fabric quantities and cutting layouts
are given for a plain fabric or a
multi-directional print. If your fabric
has a large print with a pattern repeat,
such as on our featured dress, then
you will need to allow extra fabric to
match your fabric's design across
the pattern pieces.

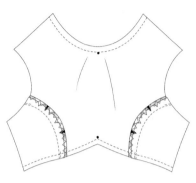

1 Following the appropriate cutting layout, cut out all your fabric and interfacing pieces. (See pages 29–30 for advice on cutting out and page 23 for how to understand pattern markings.) Staystitch the neck edges, top and bottom midriff edges, and the lower edge of the center front panel and side front panels (see page 43).

2 With right sides together and notches matching, pin, baste, and machine stitch the side front panels to the center front panel. Remove the basting, and clip into the seam allowances on the side front panels. Finish the seam allowances together and press toward the center front panel.

3 Stitch the top edge of the front midriff to the joined front panels, matching seams to notches and center front dots, clipping into the seam allowances of the center front panel to within 1/8 in (3mm) of the dot, to help you turn the corner. Double stitch over the center front point for about 1in (2.5cm) each side of the dot to reinforce this area. Finish the seam allowances together and press them toward the midriff.

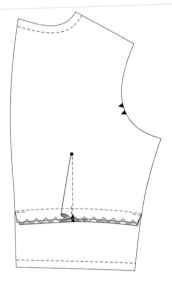

4 Make up the dart in each back (see pages 118–19) and press each dart toward the center back edge. With right sides together, pin, baste, and machine stitch the lower edge of each back to the top edge of each back midriff piece, matching darts to notches. Finish the seam allowances together and press toward the midriffs.

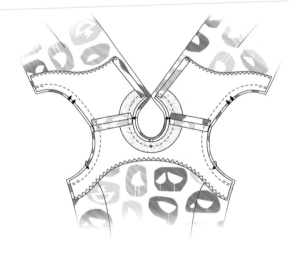

5 Stitch the front to the backs at the shoulder seams and press the seams open. Make and attach the collar as shown for Making and Attaching a Flat Collar on page 148 and apply the facins following steps 1–4 of Combination Facing on pages 146–7.

6 Using the pattern pieces as a guide, cut three lengths of the cotton tape—one length to fit the waist edge of each of the two back midriffs and the front midriff. Gather up the front and back skirt waist edges to fit each tape (see pages 104–6). Pin the tapes to the wrong side of the gathered waist edges and machine stitch in place along the stitching line.

7 With right sides together, and making sure that the underarm and waist seams line up on the front and back bodices, pin, baste, and machine stitch the gathered skirt edges to the midriff waist edges, stitching through both layers of fabric and the tape. Finish the seam allowances together and press toward the midriffs.

8 Apply the zipper following the Lapped Application method on page 55, then finish the garment side seam edges. Matching the midriff and underarm seams, and the hem and facing edges, open out the facings at the underarm and join each garment side seam and facing with one continuous line of stitching. Press the seams flat and trim the matched seams (see page 38) to reduce bulk. Fold the facing to the inside and press flat. With seams aligned, make a few whipstitches (see page 34) to catch the edge of the facing to the seam allowances. Complete the facing following step 6 of Shaped Neck Facing on page 145. Finally, finish the hem edge using the bias binding, as explained under Applying a Bias Hem Facing on page 65.

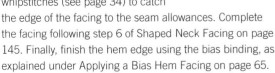

Workshop 11

Sleeves and sleeve finishes

Sleeves range from plain and tailored to gathered and frilly, like the sleeves on our cute baby's outfit at the end of this workshop, while the ever-popular shirt sleeve seems to remain immune to the vagaries of fashion. Here are some guidelines for setting in basic sleeve styles, making cuffs, and finishing the openings. Plus we show you how to make your own piping cord, which can be inserted into the edges of cuffs, as well as collars and soft furnishings.

Sleeves

A sleeve can be made from one piece, or in tailored garments it can be made from two pieces to get a better fit. In this workshop we focus on the type most commonly found in women's blouses, shirts, and dresses—the one-piece sleeve, in the form of either a set-in sleeve or a shirt sleeve—and we also cover raglan sleeves.

Set-in sleeves
You will find set-in sleeves on a variety of garments, but the styles vary enormously. Some may have a slightly rounded head (the top of the sleeve), which falls into a smooth curve from the shoulder down the arm, while others may be full and gathered into the sleeve head. However, the procedure for attaching the sleeve remains the same.

Before you begin, stitch, press, and finish all seams that intersect the armholes of your garment, and make up any pleats or gathers (see pages 132–4 and 104–6) that there may be at the sleeve heads.

1 If the sleeve head is not gathered or pleated, work two parallel rows of ease stitching (see page 43) around the top of the sleeve head, between the outer dots. With the right sides together, pin, baste, and stitch the sleeve underarm seam. Remove the basting, press the seam open, and finish the seam allowances separately. Turn the sleeve right side out.

2 With right sides together, pin the sleeve to the corresponding armhole, matching dots and notches, with the top dot to the shoulder seam and the underarm seam to the side seam. Gently pull up the ease stitching so the sleeve fits the armhole, and pin it in place at ³/₈ in (1cm) intervals.

3 Check that there are no puckers and that the sleeve fits the armhole well, and then remove the pins and the sleeve. With the sleeve right side out, steam press around the wrong side of the sleeve head in order to shrink out any "dimpling" in the easing area.

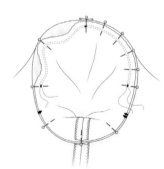

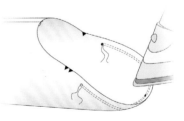

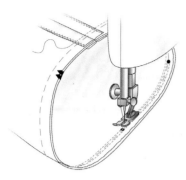

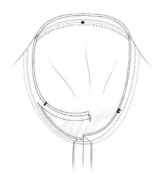

4 With the right sides together, re-pin the sleeve to the armhole as before, and baste it in place using small basting stitches. With the wrong side of the sleeve on top and starting at the underarm seam, stitch the sleeve to the armhole along the seamline, using your fingers to control the easing and overlapping the stitching to secure at the end. Remove the basting.

5 To finish the armhole seam allowances, follow the method for Zigzag without an Overcasting Foot on page 39, and finish the lower edge of the sleeve as desired (see pages 158–62).

TIPS
To create a well-balanced sleeve, make sure that you transfer your markings from the pattern pieces to your fabric correctly, and that you match the top dot on the sleeve exactly to the shoulder.

When choosing a sleeve length, remember that it should be appropriate not only to the garment style but also to the person's proportions.

Shirt sleeves

The shirt sleeve is most commonly found on men's shirts, but it is also used on women's shirts, T-shirts, and leisure tops and in children's wear. With this method the sleeve is set into the armhole before the side seams are joined. This type of sleeve is generally flat at the sleeve head or has slight ease stitching. However, an exception to this can be found on our baby's outfit at the end of this workshop, where the armholes are so tiny that it would be tricky to insert the gathered sleeves using this method.

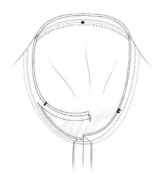

1 Before you begin, stitch and press the garment shoulder seams. With right sides together, pin, baste, and machine stitch the top of each sleeve head to the armhole edge, matching the top dot to the shoulder seam and matching the notches. Remove the basting stitches.

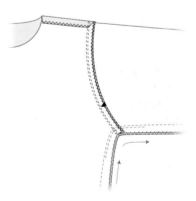

2 Diagonally trim the seam allowances at the shoulders to reduce bulk (see page 38). Make a second row of stitches along each armhole edge, 1/4 in (6mm) inside the first row, to reinforce the seam. Finish the armhole seam allowances together following the method for Zigzag without an Overcasting Foot on page 39; press toward the sleeves.

3 With right sides together, pin the side and underarm sleeve seams together, matching the armhole seams. Baste and machine stitch them together in one continuous row, working from the garment hem edge to the lower edge of the sleeve, reverse stitching at each end to secure. Remove the basting and stitch a second row on top of the first for 2in (5cm) each side of the armhole seams for added strength. Finish the seam allowances together in the same way as for the armholes and press toward the back. Finish the lower edge of the sleeve as desired (see pages 158–62).

Raglan sleeves

Raglan sleeves are distinguished by their diagonal seams, which run from the underarm up to the collarbone. This type of sleeve covers not just the arm but also the entire shoulder. To enable the flat fabric to shape over the shoulder, a dart is required at the neck edge (see page 118), or the sleeve can be made from two pieces that are shaped and seamed together across the shoulder and down the arm.

The method shown here is for a one-piece sleeve. If your sleeve is made up of two parts, the construction is similar, but you will need to stitch the overarm seam rather than form a dart. Before you begin, stitch and press the garment side seams and any seams that intersect the armhole edges.

> **TIP**
> If your armhole seams are likely to take a lot of strain, reinforce them by stitching a length of narrow cotton tape to the seam allowances at the underarms.

1 Stitch each shoulder dart (see page 118) and press them flat on the corner of your ironing board (or a tailor's ham if you have one—see page 145) to create a nice curved shape. With right sides together, pin, baste, and machine stitch the underarm seams. Remove the basting, finish the seam allowances separately, and press the seams flat.

2 With right side together, notches matching, and the underarm seam to the garment side seam, pin and baste the sleeve into the armhole, working with the wrong sides on top.

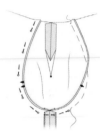

3 Working from the sleeve side, machine stitch the sleeves in place taking the appropriate seam allowance, then remove the basting. To reinforce the seam, stitch a second row between the notches around the underarm, 1/4 in (6mm) from the first row, within the seam allowance. Trim the matched seams to reduce bulk (see page 38) and then finish the seam allowances together (see page 39) and press toward the sleeves. Finish the lower edge of the sleeve as desired (see below).

Sleeve finishes

The hem edge of a sleeve can be finished in various ways depending on the style of your garment, from a simple turned-up hem or a hem facing to a stretchy, elasticized finish or a neat cuff.

Self-hemmed edge

On a straight sleeve a self-hem is common. It can be either invisibly hand sewn or, on more casual styles, machine stitched in place. See pages 62–4 for more information on doing these hems.

Faced hem

If the lower edge of your sleeve is shaped, a hem facing is the best option, or you could use bias binding to create a bias hem facing. See page 65 for details on how to do these.

Elasticized casing

On fuller sleeves an elasticized casing creates a soft, feminine finish to a sleeve. This method is particularly good on children's clothes, as the elastic can be adjusted to fit. It is formed in the same way as a circular fold-down waist casing, so turn to pages 120–1 for more information on how to construct this.

Cuffs and cuff openings

A cuff is a band of fabric that finishes the bottom of a sleeve, with the lower edge of the sleeve either gathered, pleated, or straight-fitted into the cuff. There are two types of cuff: close-fitting, with an opening to allow you to get the garment on and off, and loose-fitting, without an opening. For a close-fitting cuff, a cuff opening is made before the sleeve's underarm seam is stitched and before the sleeve is attached to the cuff, so here are two simple methods for making a cuff opening, both of which can be used with a close-fitting cuff.

Faced cuff opening

1 For each sleeve, cut a rectangular facing from the same fabric as your garment, or if you wish to make a feature of your cuffs, use a contrasting fabric. Cut the facing about 2½ in (6.5cm) wide and as long as the opening slit plus 1in (2.5cm). Finish the top and side edges by pressing ¼ in (6mm) to the wrong side of the fabric and machine stitching in place. Mark the slit on the wrong side of the facing, as shown.

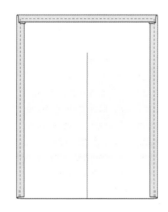

2 With right sides together and raw edges even, place the facing on the lower edge of the sleeve, lining up the marked slits, and pin in place at the corners. Working from the facing side, stitch along the sides of the slit—starting at the unhemmed edge of the facing, ⅛ in (3mm) to one side of the line, reverse stitch to secure and then stitch in a straight line to the top point. Pivot the work (see page 37) and stitch in another straight line back down to the edge, finishing ⅛ in (3mm) to the other side of the marked line, and reverse stitching to secure. Stitch a second row over the first row for about ¾ in (2cm) each side of the point to reinforce it, pivoting the work at the point.

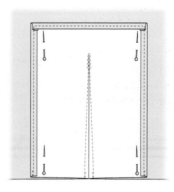

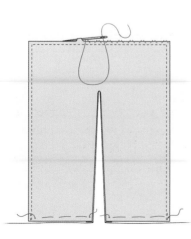

3 Remove the pins and then, with a sharp pair of small scissors, carefully cut along the line through the center of the stitching, taking care not to snip through the stitches at the top. Press the seam allowances toward the facing, then turn the facing to the wrong side of the sleeve, rolling the seams slightly to the inside, and press flat. Baste the lower raw edge of the facing in place, ready for the cuff to be applied, and invisibly slip hem (see page 64) the top edge of the facing to the sleeve; or for a casual style, machine stitch all the edges in place.

TIP
Instead of stitching
a second row at the
top of the slit to
reinforce it, reduce
the size of your
machine stitch
when stitching ³/₄ in
(2cm) each side of
the point.

Continuous lap cuff opening

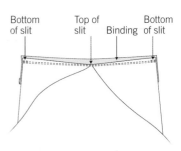

Bottom   Top of   Bottom
of slit   slit   Binding   of slit

1 For each sleeve, cut a rectangle on the straight grain from the same fabric as your garment; it should be 2in (5cm) wide by twice the length of the opening slit. Press ¹/₄ in (6mm) to the wrong side on each long edge.

2 Reinforce the opening edges of the slit with a row of stitches, following the stitching method in step 2 of the Faced Cuff Opening (page 159) but omitting the reference to a facing. Carefully cut up the center of the stitching, taking care not to snip through the stitches at the top.

3 Open up one of the pressed edges of the binding strip. Using both hands, take hold of the two corners of the slit and spread out the stitched edges of the slit into a straight line. Place this against the opened-out edge of the binding strip, with right sides together, and the reinforcing stitching of the slit lined up with the pressed line on the binding. Pin and baste in place. Working from the sleeve side, machine stitch just outside the reinforcing stitching on the slit. Remove the basting.

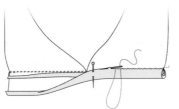

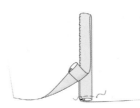

4 Fold the binding back along the press line and press again. Now fold the loose edge of the binding over to the wrong side, aligning the pressed edge with the reinforcing stitching. Pin, baste, and then slip hem this edge in place (see page 64). Remove the basting.

5 Working from the wrong side of the sleeve, let the slit sit back in its original position and align the binding to sit on top of itself, facing toward the front sleeve, with a fold at the top of the slit. Press flat and then baste the binding to the lower edge of the sleeve, ready for the cuff to be applied.

Making and attaching a close-fitting cuff

This method is for a lapped cuff, which means that the cuff has an extension at the back that creates an underlap where you attach your button. If your cuff is a simple straight band, more often than not it will be made of one piece of fabric. However, if you want a contrast backing or if the cuff has a shaped turn-back, then a separate facing, or two-part cuff, is required. Both a one-piece cuff and a two-piece cuff are shown here.

foldline

1 For a one-piece cuff, cut and apply interfacing (see page 19) to half of the cuff depth, or to about ³/₈ in (1cm) beyond the central foldline (as shown here) if you prefer a softer look. For a two-piece cuff, cut and apply interfacing to the wrong side of one of the two cuff pieces.

2 On the non-interfaced side of a one-piece cuff, or on the non-interfaced piece of a two-piece cuff, turn and press the seam allowance to the wrong side along the top edge. Trim down to ³/₈ in (1cm) and baste in place. For a two-piece cuff, skip step 3 and move on to step 4.

3 For a one-piece cuff, fold the cuff in half, with right sides together, along the foldline, aligning the pressed edge with the opposite seamline. Pin, baste, and machine stitch the side edges together, taking the appropriate seam allowance and reverse stitching at both ends to secure. Grade the seams and trim the corners (see page 38). Skip step 4 and continue with step 5.

4 For a two-piece cuff, place an interfaced and a non-interfaced cuff piece on top of each other with right sides together and raw edges even. Pin, baste, and machine stitch the piece together along the side and lower edges, taking the appropriate seam allowance and reverse stitching at both ends to secure. Grade the seams and trim the corners (see page 38).

5 Press the seam allowances open and then press them toward the non-interfaced side of the cuff. Turn the cuff right side out and press it flat, rolling the seams slightly to the wrong side.

TIP
You may find it easier to finish the lower edge of each sleeve before attaching the sleeves to your garment. If you are using the shirt sleeve insertion method (see page 157), stitch up the underarm seam by just 4in (10cm) from the bottom edge, which will allow you to attach the cuff but still enable you to stitch the sleeve head to the armhole on the flat.

6 Work any gathers or tucks along the lower edge of each sleeve (see pages 105–6 or 131), then join the underarm seam. Finish the seam allowances separately and press open. With right sides together, pin the cuff to the lower edge of the sleeve, matching the notch to the sleeve seam—the front edge of the sleeve opening should be flush with the end of the cuff, and the back of the cuff should project beyond the back opening. Baste in place.

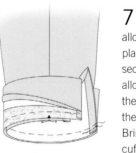

7 Taking the appropriate seam allowance, machine stitch the cuff in place, reverse stitching at each end to secure. Trim and grade the seam allowances so that the widest is next to the cuff. Pull the cuff down and press the seam allowances toward the cuff. Bring the loose, basted edge of the cuff in line with the machine stitching, and pin in place. Slip hem the edge in place (see page 64) along its entire length; press. Remove all basting. Topstitch the cuff if desired (see page 42) and close the cuff with a button on the underlap and a buttonhole on the overlap (see pages 44–8), or with a no-sew snap (see page 136).

Making and attaching a loose-fitting cuff
This type of cuff has no cuff opening—the fabric bands are cut large enough to allow a hand and arm to slip easily through. Before you begin, stitch and press each sleeve underarm seam. If the sleeve has a gathered lower edge, sew the gathering threads (see pages 104–6) and pull up to fit the cuff.

1 Apply interfacing up to the foldline, or to ³/₈ in (1cm) beyond the foldline (as shown) for a softer effect. With right sides together, pin and baste the ends of the cuff together to form a ring. Machine stitch the basted seam, taking the appropriate seam allowance; grade the seams to reduce bulk (see page 38) and press open.

2 On the non-interfaced part of the cuff, turn and press the seam allowance to the wrong side. Trim it down to ³/₈ in (1cm) and baste in place.

3 With right sides together and raw edges even, pin the interfaced edge of the cuff to the sleeve lower edge, with the cuff seam matching the underarm seam. Baste in place, then machine stitch the cuff, taking the appropriate seam allowance and overlapping the ends of the stitching to secure. Diagonally trim the matched seam allowances to reduce bulk (see page 38). Trim and grade the seam you have just stitched.

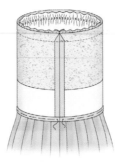

4 Pull the cuff down and press the seam allowances toward the cuff. Bring the loose, basted edge of the cuff in line with the machine stitching and pin in place. Slipstitch (see page 34) the pinned edge to the machine stitches to complete the cuff. Remove the basting and then press.

Handmade piping cord

Made from a cord covered with a bias strip of fabric, piping can be used as a decorative insertion for both garments and soft furnishings. The cord is normally white or natural and comes in a variety of sizes, from 00 (the finest) to 6 (the thickest). It can be either twisted (like rope) or braided. The braided type gives a soft, smooth finish, which is good for dressmaking, while the twisted cord works well with thicker furnishing fabrics. If your finished article is to be washed, check that the piping cord is preshrunk.

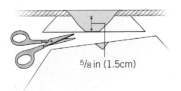

5/8 in (1.5cm)

1 To gauge the width of fabric strip you'll need, measure around the cord and allow an extra 1 1/4 in (3cm) for seam allowances. Alternatively, fold a corner of your fabric over the cord and pin, encasing the cord snugly, then measure 5/8 in (1.5cm) out from the pin and cut, as shown here. Open out the fabric strip to find the correct width.

2 Cut out and join the bias strips following steps 1–3 of Making Bias Binding (page 98). To cover the cord, place the piping cord down the center of the bias strip on the wrong side. Bring the long edges of the bias strip together around the cord and stitch down the length close to the cord, using a zipper foot on your machine.

3 Baste the piping to the right side of one piece of fabric, with the raw edges even and the cord facing inward. If the piping is going around a corner, snip into the piping seam allowances to help it bend. If the piping is going around a curved edge, clip into the piping seam allowances at regular intervals to allow it to curve smoothly (see page 38).

4 If the ends of the cord need to be joined, unpick the machine stitches on the piping for about 2in (5cm) at each end and fold back the bias strip. Trim the cord ends so they butt together, then bind the ends together with thread. Turn under 1/4 in (6mm) of fabric at one end of the bias strip, and slip this over the raw end. Baste in place close to the cord.

5 Lay the second fabric piece over the first, with right sides together and raw edges even. Pin, baste, and machine stitch the pieces together, close to the cord, using a zipper foot on your machine. Remove the basting.

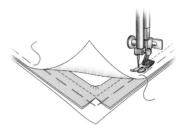

Baby's smocked dress and pants

This gorgeous baby's dress and pants set is the most challenging project in this book, pulling together many of the techniques that you have learned in the previous workshops. The perfect outfit for a special occasion, it will be well worth the effort when the precious little one is admired wearing your handiwork!

Size

Size	6 months	12 months
Weight	13–18lb (6–8kg)	18–21lb (8–9.5kg)
Height	24–26½ in (61–67cm)	26½–31in (67–79cm)
Finished length (base of neck to hem)	17in (43cm)	19in (48cm)

Fabric quantities

45in- (112cm-) wide fabric		
Main	1²/₃ yd (1.50m)	1³/₄ yd (1.70m)
Contrast	¹/₃ yd (30cm)	¹/₃ yd (30cm)
60in- (150cm-) wide fabric		
Main	1¹/₃ yd (1.20m)	1¹/₃ yd (1.20m)
Contrast	¹/₃ yd (30cm)	¹/₃ yd (30cm)
36in- (90cm-) wide lightweight fusible interfacing		
Main	¹/₄ yd (20cm)	¹/₄ yd (20cm)

Fabric suggestions

Main fabric, for dress and pants: Soft cottons, poly-cottons, chambray, gingham, silk dupion

Contrast fabric, for piping on collar: Plain soft cottons, poly-cottons

You will also need

Dress and pants pattern pieces traced off from the pattern sheets at the back of this book (see page 192)

Matching or contrasting thread

²/₃ yd (60cm) of No. 2 soft braided piping cord

Lightweight fusible interfacing (see Fabric Quantities)

One pack of contrasting stranded embroidery floss

One sheet of ³/₈ x ¹/₄ in (9 x 6mm) smocking dots

One packet of ¹/₄ in- (6mm-) wide elastic

Two ³/₈ in (10mm) buttons

Three sew-on snaps

Note

³/₈ in (1cm) seam allowances are included unless otherwise stated.

Stitch seams with right sides together and notches matching, unless otherwise stated.

Dress and pants—all sizes
45in- (112cm-) wide fabric

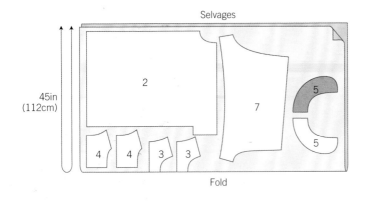
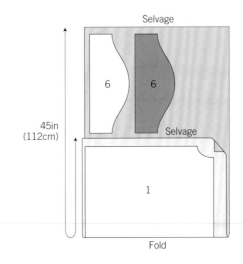

Dress and pants—all sizes
60in- (150cm-) wide fabric

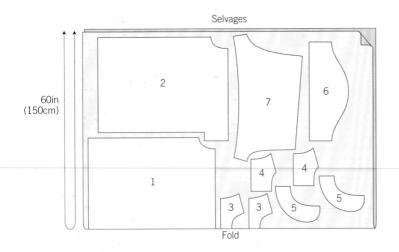

Interfacing—all sizes
36in (90cm) wide

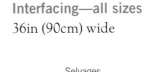

Key for cutting layouts

Right side of fabric

Wrong side of fabric

Reverse side of pattern

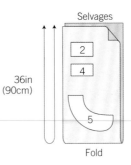

Front view

Back view

Cutting out your fabric

Use pattern pieces 1, 2, 3, 4, 5, 6, and 7.

Note

Fabric quantities and cutting layouts are given for one-way fabric only. If using a fabric with a two-way design, you may be able to fit pattern pieces into a smaller amount of fabric, but remember that grainlines must run parallel to the selvages.

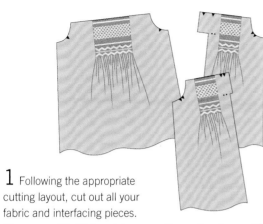

1 Following the appropriate cutting layout, cut out all your fabric and interfacing pieces. (See pages 29–30 for advice on cutting out and page 23 for how to understand pattern markings.) Using the smocking dots, sew 15 rows of gathering stitches on the skirt front and the skirt backs at the positions marked on the pattern, and work your smocking design using three strands of the embroidery floss, as shown on pages 108–11.

2 Iron the interfacing pieces to the wrong side of one collar piece in each pair. Make and apply the piping cord to the outer edges of the collars, sandwiching it between the interfaced and the non-interfaced

piece for each pair, as shown in steps 1, 2, 3, and 5 of Handmade Piping Cord on page 162. Baste the notched neckline edges of each pair together and topstitch close to the piped edges.

3 Iron the interfacing pieces to the wrong side of one left and one right yoke back as indicated on the pattern. Stitch one set of yoke backs to

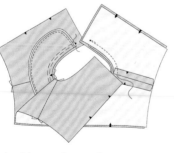

each yoke front at the shoulders and press the seams open. To complete and attach the collar to the neckline edge of the interfaced set of joined yokes, follow steps 2 and 3 of Making and Attaching a Flat Collar on page 148, treating the non-interfaced set of yokes as the facings forming the top layer, so that the collar is sandwiched between the two sets of yokes.

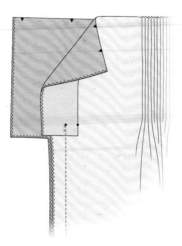

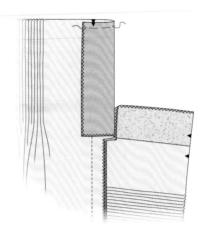

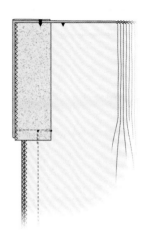

4 Apply the interfacing to the wrong side of each skirt back extension, as indicated on the pattern. With right sides together, seam the skirt backs together from the first set of matched dots to the hem edge, reverse stitching at each end to secure. Finish the seam allowances separately and also the edges of the skirt extensions.

5 To form the skirt placket, fold 1¼ in (3cm) to the wrong side of the right back extension along the edge of the interfacing, matching notches at the top edge. Baste the top edges together.

6 Working with the wrong side of the left skirt back on top, stitch across the bottom of the interfaced section from the inner matched dots to the finished edge, reverse stitching at each end to secure.

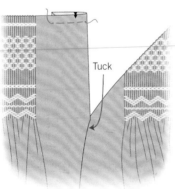

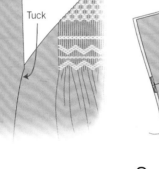

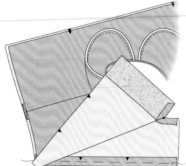

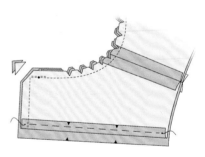

7 To complete the skirt placket, fold the left back over so that the right side of the fabric is on top. Matching the notches at the top edge, press a fold along the opening, above the stitching only, creating a tuck beneath it. Baste the top edges of the left back together.

8 On the lower edge of the non-interfaced yoke backs, turn and press the seam allowance to the wrong side and baste in place. Do the same to the corresponding yoke front.

9 With right sides together, stitch the center back edge of the left back yoke together as shown, from the dot at the collar edge to the pressed lower edge, pivoting your work at the corner and reverse stitching at each end to secure. Repeat for the right yoke back. Trim seams, clip corners, and turn right side out; press flat.

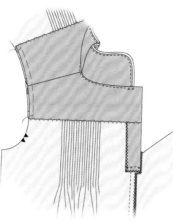

10 Pin the lower edge of an interfaced yoke back to the top edge of the corresponding skirt back, with right sides together, raw edges even, notches matching, and finished ends of the yoke even with the ends of the placket. Machine stitch in place, reverse stitching at the ends to secure, and press the seam allowances toward the yoke. Repeat with the remaining back yoke and the front yoke.

11 Remove the top line of smocking gathering stitches. Then bring the loose, basted lower edges of the yokes down in line with the machine stitches and pin in place. Slip hem (see page 64) the edges in place along the entire length of each yoke. Baste the armhole edges of the yokes together, matching the shoulder seams.

TIP
For a speedier version of the dress, replace the smocked areas with machine shirring (see pages 106–7).

12 Set in the sleeves following the Shirt Sleeves method on page 157, working the gathers across the top of each sleeve head between the notches (see pages 156); finish the lower edge of each sleeve with an elasticized casing (see page 159). To complete the dress, hand sew a deep double hem along the lower edge (see page 63) and make two buttonholes (see pages 46–8) at the positions marked on the pattern. Attach the buttons to correspond and sew on one snap at the top corner of the back opening and the remaining two down the skirt opening (see pages 44–6 and 135–6).

13 To make the pants, stitch the center front and center back crotch seams, with the right sides together. To reinforce the seams, stitch over the first line of stitching and finish the seam allowances separately. Stitch the inside leg seam with right sides together; finish the seam allowances separately, clip the curves, and press open. To complete the pants, make a Fold-Down Casing for Elastic (see pages 120–1) around each leg and the waist edge.

Workshop 12

Simple curtains

This workshop contains your essential guide to creating curtains for your home. It will take you step by step through the stages of measuring, selecting fabrics, choosing the best supports and headings, and making some simple curtains. You'll discover that measuring is not as complicated as it first seems, and once you've got the hang of it, you will soon be making them for any room, plus trying out the fabulous contrast-lined curtains featured on page 179.

Fabrics

When you are drawn to a particular design but you don't know whether the fabric will work for your window, here's how to make sure that it does. As well as thinking about the pattern, you need to consider the texture of the fabric you like: how it handles, drapes, and folds and whether it is likely to crease easily. You will also need to check how it will need to be laundered and how much light it will let through—is it opaque, dense, reflective, or transparent?

Lightweight fabrics
Sheer or open-weave fabrics such as muslin, net, and lace allow plenty of light into a room while at the same time helping to protect furnishings from direct sunlight. They can be used on their own or combined with heavier main curtains, shades, or blinds. If you are going to use them on their own, make sure that you unroll a section and hold it up to the light before you buy—the color density will look completely different when it's not on the roll in the shop.

Heavy fabrics
These make a room warmer, as they exclude light and keep out drafts. Some heavy fabrics such as tapestry can be stiff and bulky and so work best with flatter curtain styles. Velvet, on the other hand, is quite a fluid fabric and looks good in fuller, pleated styles.

Colors and patterns
Once you have decided on a fabric type, you will need to think about the color and pattern. The color is often determined by the room's decor, but do you go for geometrics, stripes, or chintzy florals? The real starting point for choosing a fabric is to make sure that it is right for the job. When you are in the store, imagine the material in its setting and decide whether it is suitable in practical terms for the style of the room.

Take several samples home, and when you have decided on your favorite, either borrow a large sample length from the shop or invest in a yard (meter) length. Remember that the color will seem denser in a large piece and patterns look very different viewed from a distance. Place or hang your sample up near the window, fold it and drape it to see how it reacts, and, finally, view it in both natural and artificial light.

You will also need to bear in mind how the room is used. If you want comfort and warmth, go for rich, warm tones. If you need as much light as possible, choose white or cream shades.

Don't forget that colors can be used to play tricks in a room. For example, the darker the shade, the more it appears to come toward you, and the lighter the shade, the more it seems to recede.

Guide to buying

When purchasing fabric, never skimp on the quantity. Generous full curtains in an inexpensive fabric look much better than skimpy ones made from a more expensive material.

■ Before you part with any money, look at how the fabric hangs. Heavy materials tend to fall into soft, natural folds, whereas some lightweight fabrics can appear starchy and crisp when hung up. Hold up a length of the fabric to see how it reacts—this will help you to decide whether it is right for the room.

■ Think next about the size of the pattern repeat. Small patterns are easier to match and require a lot less fabric.

■ Fabrics printed in different batches may end up as slightly different shades, so make sure that you buy all your fabric at one time, preferably from the same roll.

■ Check whether the fabric has to be dry-cleaned or can be machine-washed. If you are going to be putting up curtains somewhere that they're likely to get grubby quickly, avoid dry-clean-only materials and make the curtains in something that will withstand regular washing. Cotton is a good option.

■ Find out whether the fabric has any special sewing requirements. For example, is it too thick to be sewn with a domestic sewing machine? Do you need any special machine needles? If in doubt, don't be afraid to ask the shop assistant for some advice; they are there to help you!

Curtain linings

There are many practical reasons for lining curtains. It will improve their quality, helping them to drape and hang better, by adding weight and making them look fuller. It also shields the main fabric from the sun, which is especially worth remembering if you are using an expensive material or the window gets a lot of sun. The sun's rays are so powerful that, over time, most fabrics will fade, while some fabrics, such as silk, will actually rot! Lining also helps to reduce the amount of light coming through a window and blocks out drafts. Finally, by enclosing all the hems it makes the curtains look neater from outside.

Types of linings

When we choose curtain fabric, we take a lot of time to ensure that we have the perfect design and color for the room and to match other furnishings, but we often don't give as much thought to the lining. In fact, various types are available, which are suitable for different situations.

Cotton sateen

This is the standard type of curtain lining. It has a slightly shiny finish on one side and it traditionally comes in white, cream, and beige, which are ideal for backing light-colored fabrics. However, it's worth remembering that a range of fade-proof colors is also available, which can create lovely effects when hung at your window.

Blackout

This type of lining is not actually black, but normally white or cream. One side is coated with a rubbery finish that blocks daylight and so is ideal for bedroom curtains. On the other hand, it is quite a heavy lining, so is not really suitable for very lightweight or pale fabrics.

Interlinings

Interlining is a soft padded layer that is sandwiched between the outer fabric and the lining. Curtains can be interlined to make them look and feel more luxurious and to add extra insulation. There are three main types: cotton bump, cotton domette, and synthetic sarille. For the best drape, use cotton interlinings with silk, cotton, and linen curtain fabrics. Both cotton and sarille can be used with natural or synthetic curtain fabrics. Also, sarille is less fibrous than cotton, so may be a better choice for those who are sensitive to dust.

TIP
Always choose a lining that is the same width as the curtain fabric and buy the same amount.

Rods (tracks) and poles

Getting the right support for your curtains is important. The rod (track) or pole needs to be in position before you measure up for your curtains, but how do you choose from the vast selection available? Here are a few pointers to help you decide what would work best for you.

Curtain poles

Traditionally, curtain poles were restricted to brass and wood, but you can now buy them in all types of materials, ranging from Plexiglas (Perspex) to wrought iron, as well as many that combine wood, metal, and paint effects.

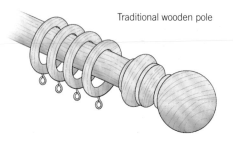
Traditional wooden pole

Wooden poles come in a range of natural, stained, or painted finishes, such as pine, beech, ash, mahogany, chestnut, light and dark oak, and walnut, and in sizes ranging from 1¹⁄₈ in (28mm) to 2¹⁄₈ in (55mm). Some incorporate gilding on the finials.

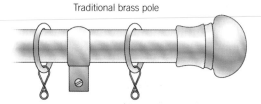
Traditional brass pole

Metal poles, too, are available in a wide choice of finishes. As well as brass and wrought iron, you can get such varied finishes as copper, bronze, chrome, silver, stainless steel, and nickel, in sizes ranging from ⁵⁄₈ in (16mm) to 2in (50mm).

Key facts about poles

■ Poles are generally designed to be visible above the top of the curtains and there are many decorative versions available.

■ You can now also get poles that bend around corners for bay windows, so they are no longer restricted to flat windows.

■ The simplest poles rest on brackets screwed to the wall. Long poles will need a central bracket as well as end brackets.

■ Decorative finials are used on the ends of poles and vary in style.

■ The length of the curtain pole should be the width of the window, plus an allowance for the curtains to stack back at each side when open. The amount will depend on the thickness of the curtains and how much of the window you want uncovered when the curtains are open, but if you wanted a stackback of, say, 10in (25cm) on each side, you'd need to add an allowance of 20in (50cm) to the length of the pole.

■ The curtain is normally supported by rings threaded onto the pole, or the pole is threaded directly through large metal grommets (eyelets) in the curtain heading.

■ Position brackets about 1¹⁄₄ in (3cm) in from the ends of the pole to allow for one curtain ring to sit at each end, beyond the finial. This ensures that the outside edges are secured at the sides of the window and do not get pulled into the center when you close the curtains.

Curtain rods (tracks)

Curtain rods (tracks) are mostly functional rather than decorative, although some premium brands do now manufacture rods with special effects to match your decor, including leather, wood, and paint finishes.

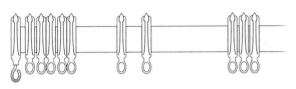

Uncorded plastic rod (track)

Plastic traverse rod (corded track)

Rods (tracks) come in many lengths and are graded for lightweight, medium-weight, and heavy curtains. They can be either metal or plastic.

Traverse rods (corded tracks) are pre-corded, which is great for long curtains or those that are light in color, as handling them can cause the leading edges—the side edges that meet at the center—to get grubby.

Key facts about rods (tracks)

- Though more expensive, metals rods (tracks) last much longer than plastic rods (tracks).
- Metal rods (tracks) can be permanently bent to fit around corners and bays.
- Overlap arms on a rod (track) allow the curtains to overlap when closed, preventing any gaps.
- Some rods (tracks) incorporate a second one, for sheers to be hung behind the main curtains, while others have a second rod (track) for a valance to hang in front.
- To work out the length of your curtain rod (track), see the fifth bullet point under Key Facts about Poles, opposite.

- A rod (track) can be left exposed, but the effect is usually more attractive if it is hidden behind a cornice (pelmet) or valance. Alternatively, the curtain heading can be designed to hide the rod (track) when the curtains are closed but it will, of course, still show when the curtains are open.
- It is possible to find decorative traverse rods (corded "poles") that are designed to be exposed in the same way as real poles. The cord is hidden at the back of the half-round "pole," and the "rings" are half-round ring-slides. From a distance they look like poles, though when you are standing close to the window you can see the workings.

Other options for lightweight curtains

A couple of other types of support—expandable cafe rods and tension wires— are available for hanging lightweight curtains and are relatively unobtrusive.

Expandable cafe rods

These can be used in small window recesses for lightweight curtains such as cafe curtains. The thin plastic or metal rod is slotted through a rod pocket (casing) at the top of the curtain and held in place by an internal spring mechanism.

Tension wires

This fairly new introduction can be shaped to fit any window alcove or even stretched around an entire room. The wire is threaded through a series of brackets screwed to the wall or ceiling and is used in conjunction with a grommet (eyelet) heading, clips, or ties to create a contemporary look.

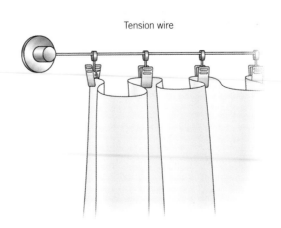

Tension wire

> **TIP**
> Whether you choose a rod (track) or a pole, remember that if your curtains are full-length, they are going to be heavy and will therefore need considerable support. Not only does the rod (track) or pole have to be substantial enough, but it needs to be mounted very securely on the wall.

Curtain headings

Non-tape headings

Informal curtain headings can also be achieved without a heading tape. The following methods are particularly suited to café curtains:

- Pincer clips can be threaded onto a rod and clipped onto the hemmed top edge of a lightweight curtain.
- A rod-pocket (slot) heading, made in a similar way to a fold-down casing (see page 120), can be slipped over a narrow rod or a tension rod, pushing the fabric into soft gathers.
- Ribbon ties or loops can be sandwiched between a facing (see page 120) and the top edge of the curtain, and then threaded onto, or tied around, a pole.

A curtain is attached to a rod (track) or pole by means of a heading, which is the decorative top of a curtain. These days, rather than pleating the headings by hand, people tend to use heading tapes, which can create a variety of effects. In addition, there are some simple headings that can be achieved without the use of tapes (see Non-Tape Headings, left).

Heading tapes

Heading tapes—also known as header tapes, drapery tapes, pleating tapes, or decorator tapes—are strips of fabric, bought by the yard (meter), that contain rows of pockets for inserting hooks and are used to suspend the curtain from a pole or rod (track). Most incorporate integral draw cords that gather the fullness of the fabric in a decorative way.

Many different styles are available, but among the most popular tapes are standard gathering tape, pencil pleat tape, and pinch pleat tape. There is also a heading tape in which the pinch pleats are formed using special four-pronged hooks rather than by pulling up draw cords. Grommet (eyelet) tapes, which do not involve gathering or pleating at all, are becoming increasingly popular in contemporary decor.

Standard gathering tape

Also known as shirring tape, this kind of tape is about 1in (2.5cm) deep and when the cords are pulled up gives a

shallow, random-gathered heading that is suitable for informal and unlined curtains. It has one row of pockets for hooks, and the tape is usually positioned about 1½ in (4cm) below the top of the curtain, to conceal the rod (track) when the curtains are closed, or to hide the rings on a pole. The fabric fullness for this heading should be 1½–2 times the length of your rod (track) or pole.

Pencil pleat tape

Pencil pleat tape is a more formal style. When the cords are pulled up, it gives even, closely packed pleats around 3in (7.5cm) deep. It has

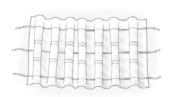

two or three rows of pockets, which allow you to adjust the height of the curtain—hooks in the top row allow the curtains to hang from rings and reveal the pole, while hooks in the middle or lower row will mean that the rod (track) is hidden when the curtains are closed. This tape is attached close to the top edge of the curtain and needs a fabric fullness of 2½–3 times the length of your rod (track) or pole.

Pinch pleat tape with cords

This is used for traditional pinch pleats, also known as French pleats or triple pleats, which suit most decors. When the cords are

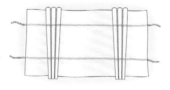

pulled up, it produces evenly spaced triple pleats. It varies in depth from about 1½ in (4cm) to 5½ in (14cm) and needs a fabric fullness of around 2 times the length of your rod (track) or pole, but check the manufacturer's recommendation because its width cannot be adjusted. The two rows of pockets allow you to use it with either a rod (track) or a pole, as for pencil pleat tape. It is attached close to the top edge of the curtain.

Pinch pleat tape used with four-prong hooks

This tape does not have draw cords. Instead, it has deep pockets into which long, four-pronged hooks are inserted into four adjacent pockets, one prong per pocket; the prongs are then

squeezed together to create a triple pleat. The fabric fullness is about 2–2½ times the width of the rod (track) or pole, but you can adjust the spaces between pleats to alter the width of the curtain a little. The tape is attached close to the top edge of the curtain. Short-necked hooks are used if the rod (track) is to be hidden when the curtains are closed or if the rings on a pole are to be hidden, and long-necked hooks are used when the curtains are to hang under the rod (track) or pole.

Measuring for curtains

Follow these simple steps when measuring for curtains and you're certain to get it right; we've even included a chart for you to make a note of your calculations as you go along. Make sure that the rod (track) or pole and any other fittings are in place before you begin to measure—including the carpet if you are making full-length curtains.

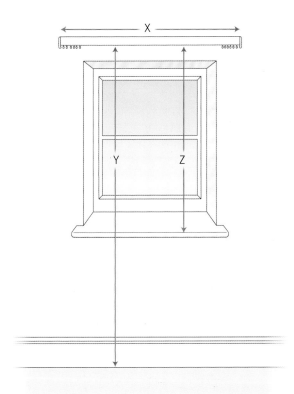

Working out the length

1 First, work out where you want the curtain heading to sit in relation to the rod (track) or pole. To do this, hook a piece of the heading tape onto your rod (track) or pole. If you are using a pencil pleat or pinch pleat heading (see opposite), measure downward starting from the top of the tape. If you are using a standard gathered heading, measure downward from about 1½in (4cm) *above* the top of the tape.

2 Next work out where you want the curtain to end. For full-length curtains that just skim the floor, deduct ³/₈ in (1cm) from measurement Y so that the curtains will not drag on the floor. If you want curtains that "pool," or drape, on the floor, add 4–8in (10–20cm) to measurement Y. For a window with a radiator beneath it, the curtains should hang 2–4in (5–10cm) below the windowsill. For sill-length curtains where the sill sticks out a long way, deduct ¼ in (6mm) from measurement Z to allow the curtains to sit just above the sill.

3 To work out the cut fabric length, add top and base hem allowances to the length you have just calculated.

The two measurements that you require in order to work out how much fabric you will need are:
- The length of your curtain rod (track) or pole (measurement X), plus any overlaps at the center. Bear in mind that the length of a rod (track) or pole should be the width of the window plus an allowance for the curtains to stack back at each side when open (see Key Facts about Poles, page 170).
- The curtain length, from the rod (track) or pole to the floor (measurement Y) or windowsill (measurement Z). For this to be accurate, the rod (track) or pole will need to be in position before you measure up for your curtains.

Example
For a curtain that is 59in (150cm) long, add 6in (15cm) for a base hem, which will allow for a 3in (7.5cm) deep double hem, and 1in (2.5cm) for a top hem. This gives a cut fabric length of 66in (167.5cm).

Note: For a standard gathered heading, you will need to add 3¾ in (9.5cm) instead of 1in (2.5cm) at the top. This extra amount will give 1½ in (4cm) to sit above the pole or rod (track) and 2⅝ in (5.5cm) to fold to the wrong side. The amount folded to the wrong side is made up of 1½ in (4cm) to sit above the heading tape and ⅝ in (1.5cm) seam allowance.

Working out the width

1 The type of heading you are going to use (see page 172) will determine the fabric fullness of your curtains. Multiply your rod (track) or pole length by the fullness required for your heading.

2 To calculate how many widths of fabric you will need to make your curtains, divide the total curtain width by the width of your fabric; this is normally either 48in (122cm) or 54in (137cm). If you are making a pair of curtains and an odd number of fabric widths is needed, cut one width in half lengthwise and join each half width onto the outside edge of each curtain, so that you always have full widths at the center of your window.

Example
A pencil pleat heading needs a fabric fullness of $2^1/_2$–3 times the length of your rod (track) or pole, so a 47in (120cm) rod (track) will need a total curtain width of 118–142in (300–360cm), depending on the fullness you choose.

Example
The required curtain width is 118in (300cm). Divide this by the width of the fabric—48in (122cm)—which equals $2^1/_2$ widths of fabric. So for a pair of curtains, you will need $1^1/_4$ widths of fabric in each curtain.

Note: Obviously you cannot buy half a width of fabric, so you will have to round up to the next full width—in this example three widths—and then trim away the excess fabric to your required width. You can use the fabric you have trimmed off to make matching pillows (cushions). And, of course, if you are making matching curtains for two windows, there's no need to round up, because the two half widths needed for two windows equals one whole width.

Working out fabric and lining quantities

1 For plain fabrics or those with a small printed design, simply multiply the cut length measurement by the number of fabric widths that you have just calculated.

2 If you have chosen a print fabric, see Allowing for Pattern Repeats, right.

3 Calculate the lining quantity in the same way as for plain fabric (see step 1).

Example
For a curtain with a cut length of 66in (167.5cm) x 3 widths of fabric, you need to buy $5^1/_2$ yd (5.1m) of 48in- (122cm-) wide fabric.

Allowing for pattern repeats

If you are using a patterned fabric, you will need to allow extra fabric to match the pattern. Once you have calculated the cut length of your curtain, measure the depth of one complete pattern repeat (this is often noted on the fabric label). Divide the cut length by the pattern repeat and round the result up to the next full repeat. This will give you what you will need to allow for each cut length of patterned fabric.

Example
For a pattern repeat of 10in (25.5cm), divide your cut curtain length—say, 66in (167.5cm)—by 10in (25.5cm), which equals 6.6 repeats. Round up to the next whole number, which is 7. So you will need to allow 7 x 10in (25.5cm) which equals 70in (178.5cm) for each cut curtain length to allow for accurate pattern matching.

Fabric quantities for your own curtains

To work out how much fabric you need, fill in your window measurements on this chart in pencil. Work out the cut length by adding/subtracting the hem allowances and clearance as appropriate, and work out the total curtain width by multiplying the rod (track) or pole width by the fullness, filling in the figures on the chart. Fill in the width of your chosen fabric, and then use this and your calculated cut length and total curtain width to find how much fabric you need.

TIP
Instead of filling your window's measurements directly into this chart in the book, photocopy the page and use the photocopy instead. This way you will be able to reuse the chart many times for different windows.

	Window 1	Window 2	Window 3	Window 4
1 Fill in length from rod (track)/ pole to floor/windowsill (Y or Z)				
Add 1in (2.5cm) top hem allowance*				
Add 6in (15cm) base hem allowance				
For full-length curtains: subtract 3/8 in (1cm) for clearance				
For curtains draping on floor: add 4–8in (10–20cm)				
For sill-length curtains: subtract 1/4 in (6mm)				
For windows above radiators: add 2–4in (5–10cm)				
Resulting total cut length (A)**				
2 Fill in width of your rod (track) or pole (X)				
For standard gathering tape, multiply by 1 1/2 –2 times				
For pencil pleat tape, multiply by 2 1/2 –3 times				
For pinch pleat tape with cords, multiply by 2 times				
For pinch pleat tape using four-prong hooks, multiply by 2–2 1/2 times				
For grommet (eyelet) tape, multiply by 1 1/2 times				
Resulting total curtain width (B)				
3 Fill in width of your fabric (C)				
4 Divide B by C (and round up*) for fabric widths needed (D)**				
5 Multiply A by D for total fabric quantity				

Notes

* If using standard heading tape, add 3 3/4 in (9.5cm) top hem allowance instead.

** For patterned fabrics, divide A by the pattern repeat depth to work out the cut length (see Allowing for Pattern Repeats, opposite).

*** If you are making matching curtains for two windows, there is no need to round up half widths.

Making the curtains

The following instructions are for making simple unlined and lined curtains, suitable for the novice stitcher, with headings made using tapes with draw cords, where good results can be achieved very easily by hand and machine.

Unlined curtains

Unlined curtains provide a soft, translucent finish to your window, allowing daylight to filter through the fabric; they are perfect for summer windows. Standard gathered, pencil pleat, pinch pleat, grommet (eyelet), tie, and rod-pocket (slot) headings are all suitable for unlined curtains. The following example uses a standard gathered heading tape.

1 Cut out the required number of fabric widths to the length you have calculated (see page 175). Matching any pattern (see Matching Patterns, opposite), join the fabric widths together for each curtain using mock French seams (see page 41). If an odd number of widths is needed for the window, cut one width in half lengthwise and join the half width to the outside edge of each curtain. Finish each long side edge of the curtains with a narrow double hem (see page 62) and finish the base hem as shown for Slipstitching the Corners of a Double Hem on page 67.

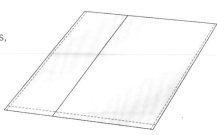

2 Working on one curtain at a time, lay the piece out flat, wrong side up. (The floor is often the best place for this, unless you have a very large table.) Measure the finished curtain length (the length the curtain will be when ready to hang) from the base hem and mark with pins. Fold the top of the curtain to the wrong side along the pinned line, and trim away any excess to leave the appropriate top hem allowance for the heading type (see Curtain Headings, page 172)—in this case $2^{1}/_{8}$ in (5.5cm). Pin and baste in place $^{5}/_{8}$ in (1.5cm) up from the raw edge.

$2^{1}/_{8}$ in (5.5cm)

3 At the end of the heading tape that will be at the leading edge (the edge that will be pulled to close the curtain), pull the tape draw cords through to the back and secure with a knot. Fold under this end by about $^{5}/_{8}$ in (1.5cm) and lay the heading tape on the curtain, wrong sides together, so the upper edge of the tape is against the basted line, and the raw edge of the curtain is covered by the tape. Pin along the basted line. At the opposite edge of the curtain, trim off the excess tape, allowing an extra $^{5}/_{8}$ in (1.5cm) for turning under. Fold under the tape end and pin in place, leaving the cord ends free on the outside. Baste the tape in place around all the edges.

4 Working from the tape side, machine stitch the long and short edges of the tape in place, stitching in the same direction for both long edges so as not to twist the seams; reverse stitch at each end of the stitching lines to secure. Remove the basting, and slipstitch (see page 34) the open side edges of the heading together.

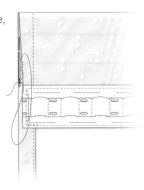

5 Carefully pull up the draw cords on the heading tape to gather your curtain to fit the rod (track). Tie the cord ends together in a double bow at the back. Insert the curtain hooks into the tape pockets to correspond to the slides on the rod (track) or the rings on the pole.

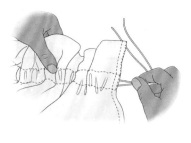

Matching patterns

On a patterned fabric, the pattern needs to be matched first before you attempt to stitch the pieces together. This is the best way of doing it.

To match the pattern, fold and press 1in (2.5cm) to the wrong side along one long edge of one fabric piece. Then, working from the right side, place the pressed edge on top of the second fabric piece, matching the design along the pressed fold. Pin and baste in place using slip basting (see page 33). Open out the pressed edge so that the fabrics are right sides together and machine stitch on the wrong side along the foldline.

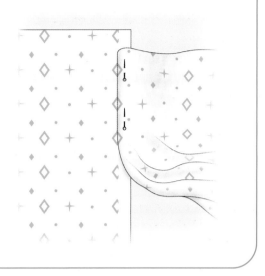

Lined curtains

There are many reasons for lining curtains, as already discussed (see page 169). The following instructions show a simple machine method, using a pencil pleat heading tape, which is an easy way to make basic lined curtains. Bespoke handmade curtains with interlining are best left until you are more experienced.

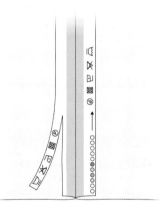

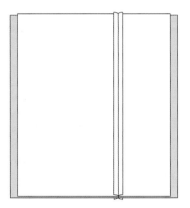

1 Matching any pattern (see Matching Patterns, above), join the fabric widths together for each curtain using plain seams (see page 36), taking a 1in (2.5cm) seam allowance. If an odd number of widths is needed for the window, cut one width in half lengthwise and join the half width to the outside edge of each curtain. Trim away any selvages (see page 15), particularly if they have any lettering printed on them, so that they don't show through to the right side. Repeat with the lining pieces.

2 Working on one curtain at a time, lay the main curtain piece out flat, right side up (the floor is often the best place for this, unless you have a very large table), and lay the lining on top, matching the seams. Carefully trim down the sides of the lining so that they are set back from the edges of the fabric by 2½in (6cm), making the lining 5in (12cm) narrower overall than the main curtain piece.

3 Press under a deep 3in (7.5cm) double hem in the base (see page 63) along the entire width of the main fabric, and slip hem in place (see page 64). Repeat with the lining base, but machine stitch in place.

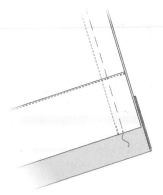

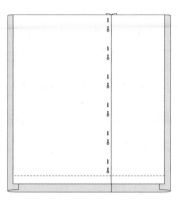

4 With right sides together, lay the lining on top of the main fabric, with the raw edges even at one side, and the lining base hem 1¹/₄ in (3cm) up from the main fabric base hem. Pin, baste, and machine stitch a 1in (2.5cm) seam down the side edge, stopping at the bottom edge of the lining. Repeat at the other side edge.

5 Turn the curtain right side out and carefully press the seamed edges flat. Working on one curtain at a time, lay the curtain out on a flat surface with the lining side up. Line up the lining and main fabric seams, if your curtain has them, and pin along the seams to hold the two layers temporarily together. You should find that the main fabric rolls around onto the lining by 1¹/₄ in (3cm) down each side of the curtain; press these in place.

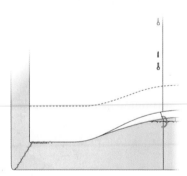

6 At each base corner, fold and press the raw edges of the main fabric hems diagonally to the wrong side to form a mock miter; pin and slip hem (see page 64) the pressed edge in place. Slip hem the lower edge of the lining hem to the main hem for about 1¹/₂ in (4cm) from the corner. To complete the hem, sew a ¹/₂ in- (1.2cm-) long thread chain (see Thread Belt Carriers, page 124) at each matched seam, to hold the lining to the curtain hem, making sure that you sew the chain approximately ³/₈ in (1cm) up from the lower edge of the lining hem, so that it is not visible on the right side.

7 Measure the finished curtain length (the length the curtain will be when ready to hang) from the base hem, and mark with pins along the final top edge. Fold the top of the curtain to the wrong side along the pinned line, and trim away any excess to leave the appropriate top hem allowance for the heading type (see Curtain Headings, page 172)—in this case, 1in (2.5cm). Pin and baste close to the raw edge, trimming away any excess fabric. Pin pencil pleat heading tape in place, in the same way as for standard gathering tape in step 3 of Unlined Curtains (see page 176), but positioning the upper edge of the tape at the top edge of the curtain. Continue following steps 4 and 5 of Unlined Curtains, but ignore the reference to slip stitching the open edges of the heading. Remove all pins and basting.

Contrast-lined curtains

Curtains that have a contrast lining create impact from both inside the room and outside. Lining them with a second curtain fabric, rather than a purpose-made lining fabric, also makes the curtains heavier and warmer, without having to incorporate an interlining. They are made in a similar way to standard lined curtains, but in reverse, so that instead of side hems on the back, you have side borders on the front.

Cutting out your fabric

Cut out the required number of widths from the main fabric to the length you have calculated, adding 1in (2.5cm) for the top hem allowance and 6in (15cm) for the base hem (see pages 173–5). Repeat with the contrast fabric.

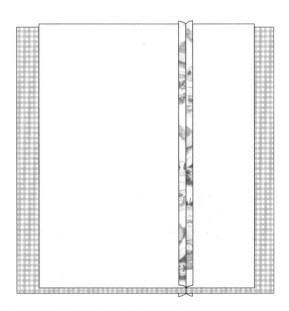

1 Join the fabric widths following step 1 of Lined Curtains on page 177. Working on one curtain at a time, lay the contrast lining piece out flat, right side up, and then lay the main fabric piece on top, right side down, matching any seams. Carefully trim down the sides of the main fabric so that they are set back from the edges of the contrast fabric by 6in (15cm), making the contrast lining 12in (30cm) wider overall than the main curtain piece.

2 To form the base hems on both the main and contrast pieces, follow step 3 of Lined Curtains on page 177, but secure both hems in place with slip hemming (see page 64). With right sides together, lay the main fabric panel on top of the contrast fabric panel, with the raw edges even at one side edge, and the base hems also even. Pin, baste, and machine stitch down the side edge. Repeat for the other side edge. Remove the basting.

3 Turn each curtain right side out, and carefully press the seamed edges flat. Working on one curtain at a time, lay it out on a flat surface with the main fabric side on top. Line up the main and contrast fabric seams (if your curtain has them), and pin along the seams to hold the two layers temporarily together. You should find that the contrast lining rolls around onto the main-fabric side by 3in (7.5cm) down each side of the curtain, creating borders; press them in place.

TIP

Because strong sunlight will damage and fade fabrics, try not to hang contrast-lined curtains at windows which receive a lot of direct sunlight.

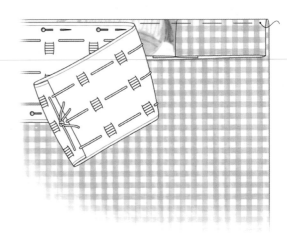

4 At each base corner, invisibly slipstitch the hem edges together for approximately 3in (7cm). To complete the hem, work a 1/2 in- (1.2cm-) long thread chain (see page 124) at each matched seam, to hold the lining to the curtain hem, making sure that they are sewn approximately 3/8 in (1cm) up from the hem edges, so that they are not visible on the right side.

5 Measure the finished curtain length from the base hem, and mark with pins. Fold the top of the curtain to the wrong side along the pinned line, and trim away any excess to leave the top hem allowance of 1in (2.5cm). Pin and baste in place close to the raw edge. Pin the heading tape in place, as shown in step 3 of Unlined Curtains on page 176, but lay the upper edge of the tape against the top edge of the curtain. Continue following steps 4 and 5 of Unlined Curtains, ignoring the reference to slipstitching the open edges of the heading. Remember to remove all pins.

Glossary

Acetate: Man-made fabric widely used for linings (see page 16).

Acrylic: Woven or knitted synthetic fabric (see page 16).

Appliqué: One piece of fabric stitched to another in a decorative manner (see page 86).

Backstitch: Strong hand stitch with double stitching on the wrong side (see page 34).

Basting: Means of temporarily holding two layers of fabric together for stitching; also known as tacking in the UK (see page 33).

Batting: Layer of insulation used in quilting; also known as wadding in the UK (see page 82).

Belt carriers: Sometimes called belt loops; can be made of cloth or constructed with thread to support a belt around the waistline (see page 124).

Bias: Diagonal grain of a fabric, at 45 degrees to the lengthwise and crosswise grain of the fabric (see page 27). Bias-cut fabric drapes well.

Bias binding: Narrow, folded strips of fabric cut on the bias; can be homemade or purchased readymade. Used to finish raw edges (see page 98).

Binding: A method of finishing off a raw edge by wrapping it with a strip of bias binding (see page 99).

Blanket stitch: A stitch worked by hand along a raw or finished edge of fabric to finish (neaten) or decorate it (see page 72).

Blind-hem stitch: Tiny hand stitches used to attach one piece of fabric to another, by hand or machine (see pages 63–64).

Bobbin: The round holder beneath the needle plate on a sewing machine, onto which thread is wound (see page 8).

Bodice: Upper body section of a garment.

Bodkin: Blunt needle with a large eye for drawing tape, ribbon, or elastic through a casing or hem (see page 9).

Bonded fabric: Nonwoven fabric in which the fibers are held together by an adhesive.

Box pleat: Pleat formed by doubling fabric back on itself in opposite directions, thus forming a "box" section, which is secured in place at the top edge (see page 133).

Box stitching: Reinforcing stitching, which is worked in a square pattern, thus forming a box shape (see page 120).

Bump: Thick and lightweight interlining with a brushed surface; inserted between layers of fabric and lining, mainly on curtains, for added insulation and thickness.

Buttonhole: Opening through which a button is inserted to form a fastening (see page 46).

Button shank: Stem between a button and the fabric to which it is attached, which can be part of the button or constructed with thread (see page 44).

Cable stitch: A traditional English smocking stitch, worked in a similar manner to backstitch (see page 110).

Carpenter's square: A flat Plastiglas (Perspex) or wooden triangular tool, with a right-angle and two 45-degree angles; ideal for straightening fabric ends and finding the bias. It is known as a set square in the UK.

Casing: Tunnel of fabric created by parallel lines of stitching, through which elastic, drawstring, or curtain wire is threaded (see page 119). On a curtain it is sometimes called a rod pocket (see page 171).

Center line: Vertical center of a bodice, skirt, or yoke section of a garment; marked on the relevant pattern pieces.

Chain stitch: Versatile hand embroidery stitch that can be used to outline or fill spaces (see page 72).

Chalk pencil: Available in various colors, this is used to mark lines and dots on fabric (see page 10).

Chevron stitch: Used in smocking by hand, this looks a lot like herringbone stitch, but is worked slightly differently (see page 110).

Chintz: Originally a glazed cotton fabric with floral designs; now used to refer to clothing or furnishings that have a floral appearance.

Commercial patterns: Home sewing patterns generally printed on tissue paper and sold in packets containing sewing instructions and suggested fabrics and trimmings (see page 13).

Contour dart: Also known as a double-pointed dart, used to give shape at the waist of a garment (see page 119).

Cornice: A narrow border of flat, stiffened cloth or wood, fitted across the top of a window or door to conceal the curtain fittings. Known as a pelmet in the UK.

Cotton: Made from the fibrous hairs covering the seedpods of the cotton plant (see page 15).

Couching stitch: Embroidery stitch technique for attaching a length of thread to a base fabric by taking tiny stitches over it at regular intervals (see page 73).

Crosswise grain: Direction of the widthwise (weft) threads on the fabric, running from selvage to selvage (see page 27).

Curtain heading: Top of a curtain that attaches to the curtain rod (track) or pole (see page 172).

Cutting layout: Layout diagrams for various widths of fabric, showing the best layout for the pieces in a pattern (see page 29).

Cutting line: Solid or broken lines printed on a pattern piece, used as guide for cutting (see page 23).

Cutting mat: A mat made from a self-healing material; designed for use with a rotary cutter, it not only protects your surfaces, but also prolongs the life of your blades (see page 92).

Daisy stitch: Also known as lazy daisy stitch, this is a detached chain stitch that can be worked alone or in groups (see page 73).

Dart: Tapered, stitched fold of fabric, used to shape fabric around contours of the body (see page 118).

Domette: This cotton interlining from the UK is lighter than bump; used as an insulating layer in curtains (see page 169).

Dressmaker's carbon paper: Paper available in a number of colors, used with a tracing wheel to transfer pattern markings to fabric (see page 10).

Dressmaker's shears: Scissors with an angled lower blade, allowing the fabric to lie flat as it is cut (see page 9).

Ease: Distribution of fullness without the formation of gathers (see page 43).

Edge stitch: Worked on the right side of an item, close to the finished edge, seam, or fold (see page 42).

Elastane: Fiber used to give fabric elasticity (see page 16).

Embroidery hoop: Frame consisting of two rings that clip together; used to keep fabric taut during embroidery (see page 71).

English paper piecing: Patchwork technique of joining fabric-wrapped paper templates by hand to create a mosaic-style pattern (see page 97).

Extended facing: Used at a straight garment edge, this type of facing is cut as one with the garment, and then folded to the inside. Also known as a self-facing.

Facing: Layer of fabric positioned on the inside of a garment and used to finish off raw edges— for example, at a neckline, waist edge, or front/back jacket opening; can be interfaced to add weight (see pages 65 and 144).

Feather stitch: Hand embroidery stitch that creates a vine-like line that is made up of connected open chain stitches (see page 73).

Felt: Cloth made by rolling and pressing wool or similar materials, while applying moisture or heat, causing the fibers to mat together.

Fibers: Natural or man-made filaments from which yarns are spun; the yarns are then made into a variety of fabrics (see page 15).

Finishing edges: Methods of finishing raw edges to improve durability and prevent fraying. Known as neatening edges in the UK. See Flat-fell Seams, French Seams, Mock French Seams, Overcast Stitch, Pinking Shears, and Zigzag Stitch.

Flat-fell seam: Strong, hard-wearing, self-enclosed seam (see page 40).

Fly stitch: Basic embroidery stitch that can be worked singly or in rows; if worked horizontally along a line, it creates a scalloped line of stitches (see page 73).

Foundation piecing: In patchwork, foundation templates are used to stabilize pieces of fabric that are stitched together (see page 96).

Freezer paper: Treated paper used for patchwork and quilting; originally produced for storing frozen foods. One side has a waxy surface, which will stick to fabric when ironed (see page 83).

French knots: Embroidery stitch that forms small raised dots (see page 73).

French seam: Self-enclosed seam that is traditionally used on sheer and silk fabrics (see page 41).

Fusible: Any material that is specified as fusible either has one side treated with an adhesive or is made from a material that is heat-activated by a hot iron; enables one item to be "glued" to another; known as "iron-on" in the UK.

Gathering: Decorative bunches of fabric created by sewing two parallel rows of loose stitches and then pulling them up (see page 104).

Grading: Trimming fabric layers at seam allowances to reduce bulk (see page 38). Also known as layering.

Grain: Lengthwise and crosswise direction of threads in a woven fabric (see page 27).

Grainline: Line that follows the grain of a fabric.

Grosgrain: Stiff, ridged ribbon that can be used as an alternative finish to a waist facing (see page 23); also known as petersham ribbon in the UK.

Heading tape: Fabric tape containing loops for inserting curtain hooks for the purpose of hanging (see page 172).

Hem: Finished lower edge of an item—for example, the bottom of a garment or curtain (see page 62).

Hem allowance: The amount of fabric allowed for turning under to make a hem.

Hemming tape: Heat-activated adhesive tape that can be used to hem skirts and pants quickly (see page 64).

Herringbone stitch: Hand-worked hemming stitch used to join the edges of interfacing or facings inside an item (see page 72).

Honeycomb stitch: This smocking stitch is more elastic than any of the other smocking stitches and is suitable for course and fine work (see page 111).

Hook and eye: Two-piece metal fastener (see page 136).

Hook-and-loop tape: Two-part tape fastening consisting of a "hook" side and a "loop" side; when pressed together, the two pieces grip each other (see page 137). Also known as touch-and-close tape in the UK.

Interfacing: Specially designed fabric placed between the garment and the facing to give support; can be fusible (iron-on) or sew-in (see page 18).

Interlining: Layer of fabric placed between the lining and garment fabric to add warmth and bulk (see page 18).

Inverted pleat: A box pleat in reverse, so the fabric fullness is turned inward (see page 133).

Iron-on: See Fusible.

Knitted fabric: Also called jersey, this is a stretchable fabric made of loosely interlocking threads.

Laminated fabric: A three-layered fabric, where the various layers are bonded (glued) together to create a thicker, stronger fabric.

Lapped seam: Used on non-fraying fabrics, as a flat way to join seams (see page 41).

Layering: See Grading.

Layout: See Cutting Layout.

Lengthwise grain: See Straight Grain.

Linen: A fabric made from the fibers of the flax plant (see page 15).

Lining: An underlying fabric layer used to give a luxurious, neat finish to an item.

Long and short stitch: A hand embroidery technique for fine color-shading. Made up of rows of closely worked satin stitches of two alternating lengths (see page 72).

Machine foot: Also known as a presser foot. The part of a sewing machine that is lowered onto fabric to hold it on the needle plate while stitching (see page 8).

Man-made fibers: Fibers produced chemically from combinations of gas, petroleum, alcohol, and water, such as nylon and polyester; they are hard-wearing and crease-resistant.

Mercerization: Treatment for cotton fabric and thread giving fabric a lustrous appearance.

Metallic: Fiber used in glittery fabrics.

Meter stick: Tool that measures length in meters; see also Yardstick.

Mitered corner: Diagonal seam formed at a corner where two hems meet—for example, at the base of a curtain (see page 66).

Mock chain stitch: In smocking, when two rows of stem or rope stitch are worked with the thread direction reversed in the second row, producing a chain effect (see page 111).

Mock French seam: Used for a French seam, but on curved fabric edges (see page 41).

Monofilament: Single strand of untwisted fiber, such as nylon; used especially for fishing wire, but a finer version can be used for sewing.

Multi-sized pattern: Pattern that has cutting lines for a range of sizes printed on each pattern piece (see page 14).

Nap: Raised pile surface of a fabric, or a printed design pointing in one direction. When cutting out pieces, make sure the nap runs in the same direction (see page 171).

Neatening edges: See Finishing edges.

Needle plate: Polished metal plate that sits under the foot on a sewing machine; its function is to pass the fabric over this area as smoothly as possible.

Needle threader: Gadget that pulls thread through the eye of a needle; useful for needles with small eyes (see page 9).

Netted fabric: Textile in which the yarns are looped or knotted at their intersections, resulting in fabric with open spaces between the yarns.

Notch: An outward- or inward-facing V-shaped mark, indicating alignment with another piece for seaming (see page 23); also V-shaped snip into curved seam allowances (see page 38).

Notions: Items other than fabric needed to complete a project, such as buttons, zippers, or elastic (see page 13). Known in the UK as haberdashery.

Nylon: Very strong fiber often used for linings (see page 16).

Overcast stitch: Hand stitch used to finish raw fabric edges (see page 34).

Paper-backed fusible web: An adhesive web with a paper backing; the glue is activated by a hot iron and is used to bond two layers of fabric together (see page 86).

Patchwork: Needlework in which small pieces of fabric in different designs, colors, or textures are sewn together (see page 92).

Pattern markings: Symbols printed on a pattern to indicate the fabric grain, placement of pattern pieces, and construction details (see page 23).

Pelmet: See Cornice and Valance.

Pelmet board: See Valance shelf.

Pinking shears: Cutting tool with serrated blades used on fray-resistant fabrics to finish a seam allowance with a zigzag finish.

Piping: Trim made out of bias binding and cord, used to edge garments and soft furnishings (see page 162).

Pivoting: Technique used to stitch around sharp corners (see page 37).

Plain weave: Basic flat-finished fabric, where the warp and weft yarns interweave alternately.

Pleat: An even fold of fabric, often partially stitched down, used to take in fullness (see page 132).

Polyester: Strong, crease-resistant, synthetic fabric (see page 16).

Pressing cloth: Clean cloth placed over fabric to prevent marking during ironing. The cloth can be dampened for steam pressing.

Quilter's ruler: Made from clear plastic with printed grids and measurements to facilitate precise cutting in patchwork and quilting (see page 92).

Quilter's tape: A light, adhesive, single-faced tape that will not leave a residue on your fabric. Used to hold appliqué in place temporarily and as a stitching guide when quilting (see page 83).

Quilting: Can refer to the process of making a quilt or to the sewing together of two or more layers of fabric in a decorative manner to make a thicker, padded fabric (see page 82).

Quilt sandwich: The three layers of a quilt. The middle batting is sandwiched between the top fabric and the backing fabric (see page 82).

Raglan sleeve: A sleeve that extends in one piece to the neckline of a dress, sweater, or coat, with seams from the neck to the armhole (see page 158).

Raw edge: Cut edge of fabric, which should be finished to stop fraying (see page 39).

Rayon: Soft, absorbent, man-made fabric, which drapes well but creases easily (see page 16).

Reverse stitch: Straight machine stitching that is stitched backward for a short distance at the beginning and end of a seam to secure the threads (see page 36).

Right side: Outer, or face, side of fabric or the visible side of a garment.

Rotary cutter: Tool generally used by quilters to cut fabric; consists of a handle with a circular blade that rotates (see page 92).

Rouleau button loop: Narrow tubing that can be made in any fabric, sized for your chosen buttons, and spaced to fit the opening of your garment (see page 138).

Running stitch: A hand stitch used for seaming or gathering (see page 34).

Sarille: Inexpensive synthetic alternative to bump and domette interlining (see page 169).

Satin stitch: A long straight embroidery stitch, worked in closely placed parallel stitches, giving the appearance of satin. Also a term used for closely worked machine zigzag stitches (see pages 72 and 86).

Seam: A line where two pieces of fabric are sewn together in a garment or other article (see page 35).

Seam allowance: The amount of fabric allowed for on a pattern where sections of an item are to be joined together with a seam.

Seam guide: Lines marked on the needle plate, or an adjustable attachment used as a guide for sewing straight seams (see page 35).

Seamline: Line designated for stitching the seam, often 5/8 in (1.5cm) from the raw edge.

Seam ripper: Hooked cutting tool used to open or undo seams and slit buttonholes; also known as a quick unpick (see page 9).

Seeding stitch: Also called speckle stitching or isolated backstitch, this is an embroidery stitch used to fill shapes with bits of color (see page 73).

Self-enclosed seam: A seam in which the raw edges are

enclosed to form a neat finish (see page 40).

Self-facing: See Extended Facing.

Selvage: The finished edge on a woven fabric, which runs parallel to the warp (lengthwise) threads (see page 27); spelled selvedge in the UK.

Set square: See Carpenter's Square.

Shirring: Decorative effect formed with multiple rows of gathering stitches (see page 106).

Silk: A natural luxurious fabric, made from silk fiber, which comes from the cocoons of the silkworm (see page 15).

Sink stitching: Also known as stitch-in-the-ditch; a technique used to hold two layers of fabric together, stitching along a seamline (see page 43).

Slipstitch: Hand-worked hemming stitch used to attach a folded fabric edge to another layer (see pages 34 and 64).

Smocking: Decoration on a garment made by gathering a section of fabric into tight pleats, or "tubes," and holding them together with parallel rows of horizontal embroidery stitches (see page 108).

Smocking dots: Iron-on transfer dots for pleating or smocking (see page 108).

Snaps: Known as press studs in the UK, these two-part fasteners are used as lightweight hidden fasteners (see page 135).

Snap tape: Two tapes with a row of corresponding snaps (see page 137).

Staystitching: Straight machine stitching just inside the seamline to strengthen it and prevent it from stretching and breaking (see page 43).

Stem stitch: An embroidery stitch that is a variant of backstitch (see page 72).

Stitch-in-the-ditch: See Sink stitching.

Stitch tension: On a sewing machine, this dial controls the degree of tightness or looseness of the top and bobbin threads when they are interlocking to make a stitch.

Straight grain: The direction of the lengthwise (warp) threads on a woven fabric, which lie parallel to the selvages (see page 27).

Straight stitch: Plain machine stitch, used for most sewing applications.

Synthetic fibers: See Man-made Fibers.

Tacking: See Basting.

Tailor's chalk: Used to mark fabric; easily removed by brushing (see page 10).

Tailor's ham: Tightly stuffed pillow used as a curved mold when pressing curved areas of clothing (see page 145).

Tension wire: Tensioned steel wire used as a simple contemporary method of hanging curtains across a room, window, or doorway (see page 171).

Thimble: Made of metal or plastic, this protective cap fits over a finger during hand stitching (see page 9).

Thread chain: Simple technique for creating a chain from thread, used to form belt carriers and to hold two layers of fabric together (see page 124).

Topstitching: Row of straight stitches worked on the right side of an item for a decorative effect (see page 42).

Tracing wheel: Tool used in conjunction with dressmaker's carbon paper to transfer pattern markings (see page 10).

Tuck: Stitched fold of fabric formed along the straight grain to take in fullness (see page 130).

Underlining: Layer of fabric cut to the same shape as garment fabric, and placed beneath it before seams are joined; used mainly on tailored garments (see page 18).

Understitching: Used to prevent a facing from rolling to the outside of a garment (see page 43).

Valance: Unstiffened strip of fabric that covers the top of a window; sometimes called a pelmet in the UK. An integral valance is attached to the top of the curtain itself. Valance may also refer to a bed skirt.

Valance shelf: Shelf mounted on the wall above curtains, hiding the curtain rod (track) which fits underneath, and with a cornice (pelmet) or valance attached to the outside. Known as a pelmet board in the UK.

Wadding: See Batting.

Waistband: Band of stiffened fabric attached to the waist edge of a garment to give it a neat, stable finish (see page 122).

Waistline: Horizontal line around the waist (see page 11).

Warp: Lengthwise threads or yarns of a woven fabric (see page 15).

Weft: Threads or yarns that run across the width of the fabric, interlacing with the warp yarns (see page 15).

Whipstitching: Method of hand sewing commonly used to join two edges together (see page 34).

Wool: Natural animal fiber, available in a range of fabric weights, weaves, and textures.

Woven fabric: Cloth formed by weaving yarns together (see page 15).

Wrong side: Reverse side of a fabric, which should be on the inside of a finished item.

Yardstick: Measuring tool that measures length in yards (see page 10); see also Meter Stick.

Yoke: Top section of a dress or skirt from which the rest of the garment hangs.

Zigzag stitch: Machine stitch used to finish edges, secure seamed edges, and make buttonholes. The width and length of the stitch can be altered (see page 39).

Zipper: Widely used fastening consisting of two tapes carrying specially shaped teeth that lock together, available in different types, weights, and lengths (see page 52).

Useful addresses

Jane Bolsover
www.janebcreatives.co.uk

UK
Fabrics
The Eternal Maker
www.eternalmaker.com
Online fabric and craft store, south of England.

Fabrics Galore
www.fabricsgalore.co.uk
The name says it all!

The Cloth House
www.clothhouse.com
An excellent selection of fabrics, based over two stores in London.

C & H Fabrics
www.candh.co.uk
A good selection of dressmaking and soft-furnishing fabrics.

Dots n Stripes
www.dotsnstripes.co.uk
Pretty fabrics online, based in Scotland.

John Lewis
www.johnlewis.co.uk
For fabrics and all your sewing supplies.

Liberty
www.liberty.co.uk
Fabulous central London shop and online store for Liberty fabrics and much more.

Notions (haberdashery)
Hobbycraft
www.hobbycraft.co.uk
For tools, fabrics, threads, and more.

MacCulloch & Wallis
www.macculloch-wallis.co.uk
Notions (haberdashery) and fabric shop in central London, plus online store.

Duttons for Buttons
www.duttonsforbuttons.co.uk
Online store and shops in Yorkshire for buttons, trimmings, zippers, and notions (haberdashery).

Sewing and pattern-making equipment
Morplan
www.morplan.co.uk

Needlework museum and resource center
The National Needlework Archive
www.nationalneedleworkarchive.org.uk

US
Britex Fabrics
www.britextfabrics.coim
San Francisco store with a wide range of fabrics and notions.

Fabric Depot
www.fabricdepot.com
Fabric and sewing supplies, with an online store and a retail store in Portland, OR.

Fabdir
www.fabdir.com
Claims to be the world's largest online fabric directory!

Fabricland
www.fabricland.com
Fabric and sewing supplies; they also run sewing classes.

Hobby Lobby
www.hobbylobby.com
Craft and hobby supplies; stores nationwide.

Joann Fabrics and Craft Stores
www.joann.com
Craft and sewing supplies; stores nationwide.

Michaels
www.michaels.com
Craft and sewing supplies; stores nationwide.

A C Moore
www.acmoore.com
Craft and sewing supplies; stores nationwide.

Author's acknowledgments

Many thanks go to all the people that have helped to make this book possible—I really couldn't have done it without you.

Particular thanks go to my dear friend Barbara Christie, who lent a very welcome helping hand, becoming my personal unpaid assistant, when my workload looked set to consume me, as my schedules started to collide; you kept me sane! Thanks also go to Beryl Miller, a brilliant seamstress, who has worked tirelessly for me for many years, always hitting my impossible deadlines—thank you for beautifully making most of the projects for this book.

To Alison Wormleighton, my copy editor, whom I totally respect, and have enjoyed every minute of our working together, plus Stephen Dew for turning my artwork diagrams into beautiful illustrations once again, and Alison Fenton for taking such care with the design. Finally, but not least, to Gillian Haslam, Managing Editor, for her patience and Cindy Richards, Publisher, without whose encouragement this second sewing book would never have seen the light of day!

Acknowledgments also go to everyone who has lent and supplied items for this book: The National Needlework Archive (www.nationalneedleworkarchive.org.uk); IDC Academy (www.inkberrowdesigncentre.co.uk); The Eternal Maker (www.eternalmaker.com) for the 1950s-style Embroidered Apron and The Perfect Summer Dress fabrics; Fabrics Galore (www.fabricsgalore.co.uk) for the Embellished Envelope Pillow and Detachable Collar fabrics; and The Cloth House (www.clothhouse.com) for the Reversible Throw, Little Girl's Shirred Sundress, Jeans-style Skirt, Organdy Evening Skirt, and Baby's Smocked Dress and Pants fabrics.

Index

--- (index) ---

How to use the pattern sheets

1 On the pattern sheets you will find pattern pieces for the following:
Project 1 – Embellished Envelope Pillow: printed in BROWN
Project 2 – Brilliant Bean Bags: printed in ORANGE
Bonus Project 2 – Doorstop: printed in LIME
Project 4 – 1950s-Style Embroidered Apron: printed in PURPLE
Project 6 – Recycled Patchwork Bedspread: printed in GRAY
Project 7 – Little Girl's Shirred Sundress: printed in PINK
Project 8 – Jeans-Style Skirt: printed in RED
Project 9 – Organdy Evening Skirt: printed in GREEN
Project 10 – The Perfect Summer Dress: printed in BLACK
Bonus Project 10 – Detachable Collar: printed in MAGENTA
Project 11 – Baby's Smocked Dress and Pants: printed in BLUE
A numbered list of the pattern pieces you will require is printed with each project.

2 The pattern pieces are printed on both sides of each sheet and overlap, so look carefully. Use the cutting layouts that appear with each project to help identify the shapes of the pieces you need. If it helps, use a light-colored highlighter pen to mark around the shapes required.

3 Lay tracing paper or greaseproof paper over each of the pattern pieces you need, and carefully trace the correct size (see Cutting Line Size Keys, below).

4 Trace all notches, dots, grainlines, and any other markings that relate to your pattern pieces, then cut out each pattern piece from your tracing.

5 Some pattern pieces are printed in two or more parts, so make sure that you have traced each part, and overlapped and stuck together the shaded areas where indicated. The overskirt for the Organdy Evening Skirt, the dress panel for the Little Girl's Shirred Sundress, and the side panel for the Brilliant Bean Bags also require you to add an extra piece of paper to make them the correct length (see details below).

6 Before you start to cut out your fabric, double-check that you have traced off all the pattern pieces correctly by comparing them once again with the shapes on the cutting layouts with the projects.

Cutting line size keys

Jeans-style skirt
····························	US 6 (UK 8)
—·—·—·—·—·—·—	US 8 (UK 10)
— — — — — — —	US 10 (UK 12)
— — — — — — —	US 12 (UK 14)
— — — — — — —	US 14 (UK 16)
—··—··—··—··—	US 16 (UK 18)

Organdy evening skirt
····························	US 6 (UK 8)
—·—·—·—·—·—·—	US 8 (UK 10)
— — — — — — —	US 10 (UK 12)
— — — — — — —	US 12 (UK 14)
— — — — — — —	US 14 (UK 16)
—··—··—··—··—	US 16 (UK 18)

The perfect summer dress
····························	US 6 (UK 8)
—·—·—·—·—·—·—	US 8 (UK 10)
— — — — — — —	US 10 (UK 12)
— — — — — — —	US 12 (UK 14)
— — — — — — —	US 14 (UK 16)
—··—··—··—··—	US 16 (UK 18)

Baby's smocked dress and pants
— — — — — —	AGE 6 months
— — — — — —	AGE 12 months

Little girl's shirred sundress
— — — — — —	AGE 5/6
— — — — — —	AGE 7/8
—·—·—·—·—·—	AGE 9/10

Detachable collar
— — — — — —	S: 12½in (32cm)
— — — — — —	M: 13½in (34.5cm)
—·—·—·—·—·—	L: 14½in (37cm)

1950s-style embroidered apron
Waistband/Tie
— — — — — —	US 6/8/10 (UK 8/10/12)
— — — — — —	US 12/14/16 (UK 14/16/18)

How to extend your pattern pieces

1 Stick spare paper to the extending edge of the Little Girl's Shirred Sundress pattern piece 1 and Organdy Evening Skirt pattern piece 2. Lay a ruler along the crosswise grainline and draw along them, extending them by 7in (18cm) for pattern piece 1 and 10in (25cm) for pattern piece 2.

2 Measure 7in (18cm) or 10in (25cm) down from the extending edge at two further intervals between the center front/center back edge and side-seam edge, and mark these positions in pencil.

3 Draw a line to join all the marks, then lay a ruler along the center front/center back edges and the side seam edges, and draw along them to complete the pattern pieces.

Extend the Bean Bag side panel in the same way, measuring down 19½in (50cm) from the extending edge.

Little girl's shirred sundress
Extending diagram

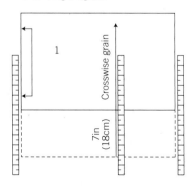

Organdy evening skirt
Extending diagram

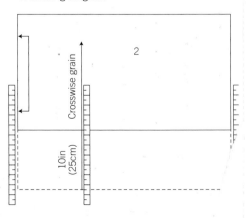